A History of Tourism in Africa

Africa in World History

SERIES EDITORS: TODD CLEVELAND, DAVID ROBINSON, AND ELIZABETH SCHMIDT

James C. McCann
Stirring the Pot: A History of African Cuisine

Peter Alegi
African Soccerscapes: How a Continent Changed the World's Game

Todd Cleveland
Stones of Contention: A History of Africa's Diamonds

Laura Lee P. Huttenbach
The Boy Is Gone: Conversations with a Mau Mau General

John M. Mugane
The Story of Swahili

Colleen E. Kriger
Making Money: Life, Death, and Early Modern Trade on Africa's Guinea Coast

Jared Staller
Converging on Cannibals: Terrors of Slaving in Atlantic Africa, 1509–1670

Todd Cleveland
A History of Tourism in Africa: Exoticization, Exploitation, and Enrichment

A History of Tourism in Africa

Exoticization, Exploitation, and Enrichment

Todd Cleveland

OHIO UNIVERSITY PRESS

Athens

Ohio University Press, Athens, Ohio 45701
ohioswallow.com
© 2021 by Ohio University Press
All rights reserved

Printed in the United States of America
Ohio University Press books are printed on acid-free paper ⊚ ™

31 30 29 28 27 26 25 24 23 22 21   5 4 3 2 1

Library of Congress Cataloging-in-Publication Data
Names: Cleveland, Todd, author.
Title: A history of tourism in Africa : exoticization, exploitation, and enrichment / Todd
    Cleveland.
Other titles: Africa in world history.
Description: Athens : Ohio University Press, 2021. | Series: Africa in world history |
    Includes bibliographical references and index.
Identifiers: LCCN 2020036863 (print) | LCCN 2020036864 (ebook) |
    ISBN 9780821424339 (paperback) | ISBN 9780821447253 (pdf)
Subjects: LCSH: Tourism—Africa—History. | Culture and tourism—Africa—History.
Classification: LCC G155.A26 C54 2021 (print) | LCC G155.A26 (ebook) |
    DDC 338.4791604—dc23
LC record available at https://lccn.loc.gov/2020036863
LC ebook record available at https://lccn.loc.gov/2020036864

To Joe Miller, who guided me on so many
of my travels through Africa's past

CONTENTS

ILLUSTRATIONS

Figures

Maps

ACKNOWLEDGMENTS

Scholarly protocol suggests that I conclude this section with expressions of profound gratitude for my family. In this case, however, it is more appropriate to instead commence with these articulations owing to my family's prodigious contributions to the book. Throughout the protracted conceptualization, research, writing, and revision processes, my wife, Julianna, was incessantly supportive, and she also strengthened the book's content and sharpened its analysis via her expressed insights into external impressions of, and touristic experiences in, Africa. Similarly, although our two boys, Lucas and Byers, inspire my work in a variety of ways, in this instance they also informed my writing, as we've shared a great number of touristic experiences on the continent, endeavors that regularly prompted valuable (and enjoyable) reflection as I generated the text. The extent of my gratitude to Julianna, Lucas, and Byers for their relentless assistance and support will remain incalculable.

Beyond my immediate family, I'd like to thank Joe Miller and Dave Robinson, who, as co-editors of the Africa in World History (AWH) series, responded extremely encouragingly when I initially floated the idea for this book. Tragically, Joe passed away during the writing process, but his imprints are replete throughout the text, and his formidable contributions to the book and, more broadly, to my development as both a scholar and a person, endure; my appreciation and gratitude will unflaggingly persist. Shortly after my initial engagement with Joe and Dave regarding this project, Gill Berchowitz formally brought it into the Ohio University Press (OUP) fold. As with my other books with OUP, this text was significantly enhanced owing to her unwavering support and sage input. Meanwhile, Betsy Schmidt joined the AWH editorial team during the writing process and, in conjunction with Dave, offered astute, constructive comments that have immeasurably improved the book. Upon Gill's retirement from Ohio, Rick Huard seamlessly stewarded the book through the various publication processes, while providing myriad effectual suggestions along the way.

Collectively, the staff at OUP continues to impress; none of these book projects would have reached fruition without their expert guidance.

I'd also like to thank Chase Barney for his contributions during the research process, as well as my sister, Kim Cleveland, for her vital feedback at key points during the writing process. I'd also extend to my gratitude to Joyce Munden, Rowen Schussheim-Anderson, and John Pfautz for their assistance with the images in the book, as well to Maggie Bridges for generating the maps embedded in the text. Finally, I'd like to thank my informants for generously sharing their time and invaluable insights. Thank you, all.

Introduction

Touristic Illusions and Realities

> Africa. There's nowhere like it on the planet for wildlife, wild lands and rich traditions that endure. Prepare to fall in love.
>
> —Lonely Planet *Africa* travel guide, 2017

> I've been able to explore new countries throughout the African continent—from the deserts of Morocco to the pyramids of Egypt, from the Giraffe Manor in Kenya to Victoria Falls in Zimbabwe and Zambia, and especially the bush of South Africa. There's an adventure waiting for you on the continent of Africa!
>
> —Kiersten "Kiki" Rich, a.k.a. "The Blonde Abroad," (https://theblondeabroad.com), 2020

HAVE YOU ever dreamed of visiting Africa as a tourist, as the Lonely Planet and "The Blonde Abroad" are encouraging you to do? If so, you are not alone. In the assortment of African-themed classes that I teach, virtually every one of my students expresses that sentiment. I reply to these aspirations encouragingly, but also inquire what, in particular, is prompting their interest. Most often, my students and other would-be tourists respond that they'd like to venture out on safari or to experience some aspect of the "exoticness" (even if they don't always use that word) that has long been associated with the continent. Indeed, Africa's dramatic wildlife and distinctive cultures—constitutive elements of this perceived exoticness—have for centuries stimulated people's imaginations worldwide.

Beyond a genuine desire to journey to Africa to view these "attractions," very few of these aspiring tourists ever critically engage with the prospect, in great part owing to their lack of knowledge of the continent and its peoples. Even many of the countless tourists who *have* traveled to the continent fail to acknowledge or even realize that skilled African personnel employed in the tourist industry repeatedly manufacture "authentic" experiences in order to fulfill foreigners' often delusional, or at least uninformed, expectations. These carefully nurtured and controlled performances reinforce tourists' reductive impressions—formed over centuries—of the continent, its peoples, and even its wildlife. In turn, once back in their respective homelands, tourists' accounts of their travels often substantiate, and thereby reinforce, prevailing stereotypes of "exotic" Africa. Meanwhile, Africans' staged performances for their "guests" affect the lives of these "hosts," not only by generating remunerative opportunities, but also by subjecting the continent's residents to objectification, exoticization, and myriad forms of exploitation.

If you've already been turned off to the idea of traveling to Africa as a tourist, please don't be; that's not the objective of this book. Rather, this text strives to explore the enduring allure of Africa in the modern history of tourism and the dynamics of the contrasting, and often mutually invisible, touristic experiences on the continent by foreign audiences and local participants in the industry, from the nineteenth century until the present day. In so doing, through the prism of tourism the book connects African residents with the global community, and vice versa. The book also considers Western notions of Africa as an escape from the stressful, technology-laden modern world and argues that these enchanting notions reflect broader (mis)understandings of the continent. In examining these external perceptions of Africa, the book demonstrates that tourism to the continent reinforces these impressions, as well as contends that Westerners' general images of the continent often diverge from their notions of touristic Africa. Even so, many foreigners have no trouble reconciling their prevailing impressions of Africa as mired in intractable political, martial, and epidemiological crises with their romanticized, touristic notions of the continent. Over the ensuing chapters, the book explores this seeming incongruence. Finally, the book aims to deepen understandings of the durable, often mythic, appeal of Africa as a tourist destination. It also explores the range of impacts that tourism has had upon the continent and its peoples as well as upon those who make this journey.[1]

A General History of Tourism

It is, of course, impossible to pinpoint the first tourist in the history of the world. For what it's worth, the word "tourist" first appeared in print in approximately 1800.[2] But there surely exists precedent activity that could reasonably be characterized as tourism, especially if we employ historian Rudy Koshar's description of it as "any practice arising from an individual's voluntary movement between relatively permanent 'settledness' and an extended moment of leisured displacement."[3] For example, centuries prior to the advent of the word "tourism" at the dawn of the nineteenth century, an array of ancient Egyptian monuments were already inspiring sightseers, including, reputedly, such household names from Greek history as Homer, Plato, and Orpheus; wealthy Romans similarly descended upon these destinations. As historian Lionel Casson has compellingly declared, "The massive temples and tomb complexes associated with both the Old (third millennium BCE) and the New (roughly 1550 BCE to 1077 BCE) Kingdoms were as amazing to inhabitants of the ancient world as they are to us today."[4] So, was ancient Egypt, as arguably Africa's most famous civilization, the first tourist destination? Maybe, but probably not. As is often the case, our comprehension of the Western and Classical worlds greatly outpaces our understandings of other areas of the planet. Furthermore, if we keep Koshar's definition of tourism in mind, the first tourists could have set forth from virtually anywhere in the world where individuals could afford to engage in forms of leisure travel—hardly a limiting criterion.

Even if we're unable to identify the original tourists, we can still, with reasonable certainty, locate one of the preliminary forms of modern tourism in the travels of English aristocrats to various stops on the European continent, including France, Italy, and, at times, Switzerland, beginning at the end of the seventeenth century. Known as the "Grand Tour," this endeavor required considerable time and resources, thereby lending it an exclusivity to social classes of sufficient means. Even the primary objective of those who undertook these journeys—that is, to become finer, less parochial gentlemen—would be foreign to most of our contemporary motivations to engage in touristic activity. Scholarly interest in this type of travel is understandable, given that these tourists were among the few individuals engaged in travel for pleasure and there remains ample source material to reconstruct their journeys. Yet it also reflects a historical focus on the wealthy and powerful and a fascination with the development of particular, durable tourist destinations in the Western world. Regardless of the intended outcomes of travel during this period, it was also replete with challenges, including severely limited tourist infrastructure, namely, roads and inns; lurking bandits; and a menagerie of currencies and languages to negotiate. Thus, the notion of "traveling for pleasure" in this historical context was somewhat misleading, and many people only ventured out if they were compelled to do so.

By the last quarter of the nineteenth century, however, tourism had become more widespread for a variety of reasons, collectively ushering in the "golden age of travel." One factor was the expansion of the middle class in England and elsewhere, which placed tourism within financial reach for a growing, albeit still relatively small, number of individuals. Another was the power of the steam engine, which both reduced costs and expanded the distances tourists could traverse within reasonably short amounts of time. As author and publisher Alexis Gregory has declared regarding this profound impact, "Steam powered the newfangled trains. . . . Steam drove the pistons deep in the iron hulls of the largest ships the world had ever seen—and then poured through the turbines of even larger ships. It warmed radiators in vast new palace hotels where tropical palms could flourish even when ice caked the windows . . . and it drove the generators that lit up the glistening chandeliers of palaces and casinos."[5]

Although traveling for pleasure largely remained an endeavor for the leisured classes, the pioneering travel agent Thomas Cook introduced in 1841 what we might think of as modern mass tourism by organizing the first conducted tour in Europe. Some years later, in 1869, Cook arranged the first tours of the Holy Land and Egypt, often appended to the more traditional European "Grand Tour." The mythic appeal of the ancient world was considerable. As historian Eric Leed explains regarding a traveler's awed account of a tour of Greece in the nineteenth century, "It was not the sight of Athens that triggered the universal shivering, the touristic orgasm, but its mere actuality. Here, as elsewhere, the origin of the power of place is clearly in the imagination of the traveler, stocked with a literature and world of images."[6] By this time, the term "tourism" was widely understood as travel for pleasure, the evolving impressions of it reflecting its ever-increasing accessibility.

With the growth of middle classes in the Global North and, to a lesser extent, elsewhere, tourism was marked by further democratization. Technological developments expanded the geography of favored destinations while maintaining the total amount of time individuals were removed from their respective places of employment. By the Second World War, some one million people were traveling abroad each year. The introduction of the automobile and, more significantly from a global perspective, commercial air transport further facilitated mass tourism and left virtually nowhere on the earth's surface unreachable by curious travelers. Even space, the so-called final frontier, will shortly be the destination of the newest waves of tourists.

Over time, what tourism meant to its practitioners also changed, though many aspects and objectives of the experience remain remarkably similar. If travel originally entailed considerable hardships, tourism is now marketed as pleasurable, or at least as a means to pleasure. Perhaps nowhere is that more evident than on safari in Africa, which largely entails no-risk, carefully managed exposure to the continent's most dangerous species embedded in an otherwise relaxing, often luxurious experience for clients. Yet there also exist a number of individuals who willingly engage in adventure tourism around the world, replete with challenges as they test their endurance, re-silience, and fortitude while engaged in activities such as mountaineering, trekking, or rock climbing, far removed from home. Tourism has always held appeal as a means of discovery, self-realization, self-consciousness, and, to a certain extent, escape. As the famous novelist and filmmaker Michael Crichton has explained, "Often I go to some distant region of the world to be reminded of who I really am. There is no mystery about why this should be so. Stripped of your ordinary surroundings, your friends, your daily rou-tines . . . you are forced into direct experience. Such experience inevitably makes you aware of who it is that is having the experience. That is not always comfortable, but it is always invigorating."[7] This type of approach to tourism forces participants to recognize both the significant sameness and difference between oneself and the alien culture(s) into which they venture. Certainly, tourists and their hosts throughout time have both been engaged in this form of self-reflection.

Irrespective of the shifting landscape of global tourism, for some time, studying and writing about the history of tourism was an activity in which few scholars engaged, and even fewer considered the impact of tourism on host societies. But you are currently reading this very sentence because scholarly attitudes toward tourism history around the world have changed. Anthropologists and social historians have led this charge, interested not in the tourism of "men of great stature and wealth and ladies of frivol-ity and breeding," as Alexis Gregory characterized the early European tourists, but in the otherwise ordinary experiences of those travelers with lesser means. Scholars have also increasingly focused on the significance of tourism for both guests and their hosts and, in particular, on the social, economic, environmental, and political impacts of tourism in high-volume travel destinations.[8]

Unfortunately, Africans who labored in the tourism industry in the continent's past remain largely invisible. When scholars first began considering tourism in Africa, the focus was almost exclusively on the potential for the sector to serve as a vehicle for economic and human development. Africans, both within and beyond the industry, were thereby lost in a sea of financial indicators, projections, and forecasts. Even social historians, who have reconstructed the lives of a remarkable range of Africans, have granted these individuals scant attention. These significant gaps in our understanding of Africans' lived experiences in the industry are periodically reflected in this text, especially in the initial chapters. In turn, this lack of scholarly inquiry and resultant knowledge reminds us that even heightened touristic developments and activity over the centuries have done little to inform or help alter external impressions of much of Africa and its peoples.

The Enduring Appeal of Africa as a Tourist Destination

There exist myriad, varied motivations to engage in tourism, but many of them associated with visiting Africa are rather unique owing to the continent's distinctive history. Indeed, Africa has durably held considerable tourist appeal for countless outsiders. But why? One way to respond would be to attribute the continent's appeal in the Western imagination to a potent mixture of ignorance, racialism, and fantasy, dating back centuries. Following contact with populations on Africa's northern and eastern coasts, Asians and Europeans began to speculate about the human and animal populations resident in the interior of the continent. The prevailing external perception of this vast space characterized it as "spectacular, but savage, beauty, populated by exotic tribesmen" and large animals.[9] In short, every aspect of the continent—from its physical features to its peoples and fauna—was exoticized, defined by everything that Europe was *not*.

Over time, the emergence of racism as a component of the broader justification of the commerce in African slaves did nothing to temper external notions of "exotic Africa." Rather, this inhumane trade deepened these perceptions by emphasizing African savagery, barbarity, and heathenness, manifested, for example, in recurring accusations of African cannibalism. But even divergent representations of the continent as a place of serenity and innocence similarly heightened the appeal of Africa. In the eighteenth century, for example, traveler Michel Adanson, a French botanist and naturalist, wrote alluringly about the continent: "Whichever way so ever I turned my eyes, I behold a perfect image of pure nature: an agreeable solitude bounded on every side by a charming landscape." These and other accounts of the continent suggested that Africa was "the last great wilderness, and to those who listened, steeped in this romanticism, these narratives created an Africa that was both paradise and wilderness."[10]

European explorers of the continent during the nineteenth century played an important role in the next chapter of African tourism, not by establishing fundamental tourist infrastructure or even laying the groundwork for it but by representing the continent in a way that continued to pique the curiosity of outsiders. Probably no individual was more central or instrumental in this process than Henry Morton Stanley. The accounts of Africa that this deeply troubled, yet internationally famous, soldier-cum-journalist-cum-explorer generated throughout the second half of the nineteenth century amounted to nothing short of the truth for the countless readers who consumed them. Without access to Stanley's published accounts, however, Africans were unable to refute his dubious claims. Moreover, Stanley required any white travel companions to promise contractually not to write or speak publicly about their experiences until after he had published his journals. In this manner, Stanley "reduced any direct challenge to his position as the expert and guaranteed his narrative's place as the standard interpretation."[11]

Shortly after Stanley and others "discovered" Africa, European armies invaded the continent and subjugated its indigenous residents. During the ensuing period of colonial overrule, which lasted from the latter decades of the nineteenth century until roughly the 1960s, European scholars, settlers, and administrators deepened already-durable impressions of African distinctiveness, casting the continent's residents as primitive, "grown children" who embraced backward traditions and cultures. These mischaracterizations, in turn, justified the "white man's burden" to civilize these alleged brutes and legitimized the array of European colonial empires in Africa (and elsewhere). Even when representations of the continent were well-meaning, intended to broaden the appeal of Africa by highlighting its myriad agreeable features, they reinforced the supposed simplicity and primitiveness of the continent. Take, for example, an account by Martin and Osa Johnson, an American couple who traveled extensively around the continent in the 1920s and 1930s and became famous for their films, books, and photographs describing life in northern Kenya at their "Lake Paradise" home: "There are no frills to our regime. We dress to keep warm and eat to live. Simple pleasures stand out in their true values unsullied by the myriad artificial entertainments of civilization. Our diet is plain;

our costume unadorned; we rise with the sun and labor while it lasts. As a result, we find life more savory than it ever was amid the conveniences of hot hotels and traffic-jammed streets."[12]

Following the conclusion of the colonial era, Africa remained no less exotic to the external observer, nor did outsiders' imaginations of the continent grow any less fanciful, despite the expanded knowledge of Africa and its peoples that grew with the passage of time. This heightened comprehension continues to coexist with durable misunderstandings of the continent infused with the same myths, stereotypes, and misperceptions that colored earlier impressions of Africa. Popular literature, which had for centuries contributed to, or even engendered, these misperceptions, continued to play a role, as did films and, eventually, television. Indeed, television has significantly shaped perceptions of "wild Africa." Beginning in the 1970s, wildlife documentaries began appearing on public television programs such as *Nature* and, into the 1980s, *Nova*, and this pattern endures. Yet, while images of the continent's fabled fauna abound, scenes of Africans' everyday lives never seem to appear on the National Geographic or Discovery channels. Ironically, most Africans never encounter these celebrated animals, as most people live in urban areas or in places where the human population is too dense for most or all of these fauna. Rather, these animals reside mainly in expansive game reserves or parks, or on the shrinking fringes of human habitation. Yet popular culture and media sources consistently depict an undifferentiated Africa teeming with big game, a land insulated from technology and the industrialized, frenetic pace of the Global North. As conservationists Jonathan Adams and Thomas McShane have written, "We cling to our faith in Africa as a glorious Eden for wildlife. The sights and sounds we instinctively associate with wild Africa—lions, zebra, giraffe, rhinos, and especially elephants—fit into the dream of a refuge from the technological age. We are unwilling to let that dream slip away. . . . The march of civilization has tamed or destroyed the wilderness of North America and Europe, but the emotional need for wild places, for vast open spaces like the plains of Africa, persists."[13]

Into the twenty-first century, these apparent attributes—simplicity, exoticness, vastness, pristineness, timelessness—continue to collectively summon outsiders who remain curious about the continent. Naturally, this romanticized primitiveness and perceived isolation hold considerable appeal for individuals with the means to extract themselves, if only temporarily, from their hectic home environments and relocate to a place that is seemingly untouched by the disagreeable aspects of modernity.

The tourist industry, which plays an important role in perpetuating and deepening tourists' desire to travel to the continent, both encourages and facilitates these journeys. In particular, an array of savvy international tour operators and agencies, rather than tourism officials in the African countries of destination, oversee these processes. The result is often a "distorted image of wild, darkest Africa, a land of deserted beaches, tom-toms, lions, witch doctors, and bare breasts. This caricature is designed to give the illusion of adventure—but one that is carefully prepared, always controlled, and experienced with the assurance of undisturbed comfort."[14] Echoing these assertions, historian Curtis Keim astutely reminds us that "tourist Africa isn't the real Africa, just like tourist America isn't the real America. It is carefully managed, commercialized, and exoticized."[15]

One of the more recent manifestations of the "tourist Africa" to which Keim refers is the cultural tourism industry, though it too features strong links to many of the continent's long-standing allures. In this touristic endeavor, foreigners reductively objectify the African peoples and places they visit, learning about them in ways that highlight difference—the more divergent, the more appealing. For example, in order to reconcile these cultural tourism experiences with their reductive, preconceived notions of Africa, or as art historian Carol Magee calls them, "recognizable spectacles and performances," tourists typically expect to witness Africans drumming or dancing in "traditional" garb. These seemingly timeless ritualistic performances would be otherwise rare in local societies, but cultural tourists are not interested in encountering the trappings of modernity, such as cellular phones or televisions, while engaged in this form of entertainment.[16] Meanwhile, the African performers of these sessions are more than happy to oblige the touristic desire for the primitive, becoming fully complicit in the ongoing exoticization of the continent and its peoples as they pursue livelihoods in this growing sector.

Visit Africa, before the Tourists Arrive: The History of Tourism to Africa

As outlined above, it appears that Egypt may have been the first consistent African travel destination for foreigners. The Greek philosophers who reputedly visited Egypt went, as Eric Leed writes, to "drink at the fount of its wisdom."[17] In fact, many of the intellectuals in the ancient world believed that "all arts, order, government, and civilized practices originated in Egypt and spread from there throughout the Mediterranean."[18] Going forward, Egypt remained symbolically important in the European psyche, as it constituted a significant piece of the perceived foundation of Western civilization and was thereby exalted, even as European armies laid waste to its local defenders.

The next wave of foreigners attracted to the various flora, fauna, and peoples of Africa were not so much tourists as they were travelers and explorers. Household names, such as David Livingstone and Henry Morton Stanley, for example, were among those individuals who undertook significant travels to and within the continent, aided by countless indigenous porters and other auxiliaries. The sensational and often hyperbolic accounts of their travails further whetted the public's appetite for Africa. These representations of the continent and its inhabitants helped reinforce already durable images of exotic Africa and subsequently shaped the impressions of generations of outsiders.

In the nineteenth century, missionaries and, following the onset of formal colonialism in the last decades of the century, colonial administrators, big-game hunters, and anthropologists replaced explorers as the most numerous foreigners to visit the continent, stay for extended periods, and record their observations and experiences. Again, it would be misleading to depict these individuals as tourists, as their primary functions were otherwise, but just like their predecessors, they powerfully shaped popular imaginations of the continent and piqued further touristic interest in its peoples and wildlife. These updated accounts appeared on the eve of the commencement of routinized tourism to Africa, which followed the colonial subjugation of the continent and was facilitated by the establishment of transportation networks and tourist infrastructure. Although these initial touristic developments were primarily intended to service European settlers, the security provided by the array of imperial states and the expanding infrastructure rendered Africa newly opened for foreign tourism.

The continent's wildlife attracted most of these early visitors. At first, these foreigners arrived to hunt it; only later would subsequent waves of tourists arrive to shoot the fauna with cameras instead of guns. Over time, safaris transformed primarily from hunting expeditions to photography forays and, with the advent of inexpensive charter flights from many points of origin in Europe and elsewhere, this hitherto cost-prohibitive endeavor became much more accessible to aspiring tourists. Following the Second World War, colonial regimes and state-sponsored airlines promoted the African territories as viable tourist destinations, featuring the three *s*'s: sun, sand, and sea. Generating revenue from their colonial territories dovetailed nicely with the imperial powers' propagandistic aims of showcasing the ostensibly positive changes they had engineered in these settings. Meanwhile, although Africans occupied the most menial positions in these tourism industries, reliable employment and wages, coupled with less demanding and dangerous work environs, encouraged some local residents to improve their socioeconomic status via service in this sector.

Following the conclusion of the colonial era, newly independent African states attempted to capitalize on the three *s*'s to generate badly needed revenue for their largely bare coffers. Political independence arrived at a time when economic experts were widely touting tourism as a means to develop "third world" countries, and these incipient African states seemingly constituted the perfect laboratories in which to test these speculations. In response, cash-strapped African governments raced to expand whatever tourist infrastructure they had inherited from their former colonial masters, though many nations were forced to construct it virtually from scratch. Many African administrations wagered that investments in tourism would pay handsomely, even though these initial outlays were extremely risky. In practice, however, the political turmoil that engulfed many African states following independence tempered or, in some cases, entirely precluded any revenue from tourism. Oftentimes, even if violence was far removed from a particular tourist destination, would-be visitors perceived Africa monolithically, thereby discouraging travel to any part of the continent. In turn, states' gambles were proved to have been ill-advised, as they were now stuck with empty airports and vacant hotels for which they had allocated considerable amounts of their scarce funds. By the end of the 1980s, Africa was attracting only roughly 2.5 percent of all global tourist arrivals and receipts. And even then, most of this activity was centered in Northern Africa, namely in Egypt, Morocco, Tunisia, and Algeria—the southern fringes of Europe's so-called pleasure periphery.

More recently, increased political stability and strategic public-private partnerships have enhanced Africa's appeal as a tourist destination. The expansion of the middle class in an array of developing countries has also expanded the number of potential tourists to the continent. Moreover, the motivations to visit Africa, which now also include sex tourism, "voluntourism," and ecotourism, have dramatically diversified, even if many of the underlying impetuses outlined above remain firmly entrenched. African governments, communities, and individuals are all striving to benefit from this diversification and the overall expansion of the industry, while also attempting to reduce financial risks, minimize exploitation, and maintain a sense of dignity in a market that can render this objective extremely difficult. Africans' insistence on more responsible approaches to tourism, coupled with an expanding global appetite to experience the continent, has made the industry more assistive in broader development objectives on the continent than ever before, though substantial challenges remain.

Is Tourism Beneficial for Africa—Are You Helping by Visiting as a Tourist?

Even if the tourism industry is playing a larger role in human development in Africa than it ever has, considerable debate persists regarding whether it is beneficial for the continent's residents. Just like seemingly everything else in life, tourism has its proponents and its detractors. Think no further than where you reside: wherever that may be, there undoubtedly exist residents who want to expand local tourism and others who bemoan or even vilify it. Within any community, region, state, or nation, individuals will argue on both sides of this debate. Africa is no different, though over time its residents have certainly sharpened their viewpoints regarding tourism.

The Good?

First, the good. Or, the alleged good, anyway, that tourism offers Africa. Motivated by tourism revenues that were being generated in developing regions—first in the Caribbean in the 1950s and then, from the 1960s and 1970s onward, in the Pacific, parts of Asia, and Latin America—African states sought to utilize tourism as an engine for economic development. Reflective of this optimism, the World Bank and World Tourism Organization encouraged the expansion of tourism sectors in nonindustrialized countries as a means of economic growth that would produce both national and local enrichment. Even academics—many of whom are now skeptical of the industry—were initially generally supportive of this strategic approach.

Tourism also generates employment opportunities and can thereby raise household and national income levels. Even sectors of the economy that don't directly rely on tourism for their survival—for example, taxis and other forms of private transport, as well as places of entertainment—can be positively affected, generating revenues and employment opportunities owing to the influxes of tourists.[19] The industry is also generally perceived to be environmentally "clean," further underscored by the various types of ecotourism growing in popularity throughout the continent.

Finally, in many places in Africa, tourism contributes to wildlife conservation. Many of the species that tourists are particularly interested in viewing are afforded significant protections, as these faunas constitute financial assets to their host nations. For example, one study conducted in the late 1980s estimated that, in Kenya, a lion's value was approximately $7,000 per year, while the annual value for an elephant herd was roughly $610,000.[20] These figures have steadily risen over the decades that have ensued.

The Bad?

Tourism also negatively affects Africa. Perhaps most troubling from an economic perspective is the volatility of the industry, which is dependent on the whims of individuals, most of whom reside in the Global North. This relationship is at its most problematic when developing nations become overdependent on tourism, whose clientele is largely out of their control. In practice, the appeal of various tourist destinations in Africa can wax and wane, and without the development of other sectors of national economies, states are highly vulnerable to vicissitudes in the tourist market. Moreover, portions of tourism revenues and attendant local economic benefits may be lost to foreign companies that control the touristic infrastructure—known as "leakage" within the industry—as is the case with many of the hotels and other accommodations that visitors to Africa utilize. Even the generation of employment opportunities can be misleading, as overall numbers may be modest or, more importantly, the jobs extremely low paying or seasonal. Further, these positions are inherently located around particular tourist sites, thereby deepening regional employment discrepancies. These and other economic issues have prompted one observer to cynically note that "tourism is usually selected by governing elites in developing nations as much for political prestige as economic viability" and job creation.[21]

Tourism can also have deleterious environmental impacts, especially in highly visited areas, including in national parks and reserves. Pollution, overuse of limited water supplies, and damage to fragile ecosystems are just three examples from a much longer list. Anyone who has gone on safari in Africa's expansive spaces knows that the automobile traffic at certain sites can be, ironically, overwhelming.

Tourism on the continent can also erode Africans' dignity and rehabilitate colonial-era relationships between "white overlords" and "black subjects." Indeed, when heritage and traditions become commodities, a community's culture is essentially placed on sale for touristic consumption, which some scholars refer to as "symbolic colonialism." Other observers have, perhaps even more harshly, characterized this process in Africa as the "Disneyfication" of local culture. In this same vein, consider the damning statements of Tanzanian scholar I. G. Shivji regarding the fledgling tourist industry in his country in the early 1970s:

> Tourism—with its "flunkeyism" of opening and closing cab doors, with the extremely humiliating subservient "memsahib" and "sir" attitudes and, above all, the unavoidable dampening of vigilance and militancy that accompanies the necessity to create a hospitable climate for tourists—is a major component of "cultural imperialism." . . . One has only to go to some of our palatial beach hotels (only the outside of which a Tanzanian fisherman will ever see) and watch the waiters and waitresses in their immaculate uniforms, moving up and down the corridors like disciplined school children and churning out "Sirs" and "Memsahibs," to understand what an outrageous, alien structure we are harboring.[22]

So, Good or Bad?

So, then, which is it: good or bad? Well, most objective observers would agree that the tourism industry in Africa has produced mixed results. The economic benefits have been uneven—from region to region, country to country, and even within individual countries—the social impacts (negative and positive) hard to measure, and the environmental impacts, although very real, often overstated. The polemical contentions embedded in the divergent interpretations of tourism in Africa are summarized well in the following passages by scholars Garth Allen and Frank Brennan as part of their general assessment of the industry:

> Commentaries on tourism, on its developmental potential, on its casual exploitation of local peoples, on its negative effect and on its destructive impact on the environment, have often been marked by a predetermined, even supercilious hostility. The literature on tourism, at its worst, amounts to little more than a cluttered landscape of vapid moralizing and unconvincing theory, focusing on the demerits of developing tourism, rarely on the demerits of not doing so. The literature is characterized

by a series of anguished reflections on tourism's advance, with endless miseries, and where the course of things is profoundly troubled.[23]

Given this type of partisanship, it's no wonder that tourism in Africa continues to pique emotions from a range of stakeholders, often featuring competing agendas and motivations, and will undoubtedly continue to do so for the foreseeable future.

Book Content and Chapter Outline

The treatment of Africa's touristic history in this book unfolds in a series of loosely chronological chapters, intended to highlight the significance of various forms of tourism for a variety of African communities across the modern historical period. Examples from settings throughout the continent feature across the chapters to illustrate the specific touristic trends and themes that the book examines.

Chapter 1 examines the initial ventures by European explorer-tourists to the continent throughout the nineteenth century, as well as the birth of the industry in Egypt around the middle of the century. European scientific societies and governments commissioned adventurers such as Richard Francis Burton and John Hanning Speke to amass information about Africa's flora, fauna, peoples, and geography. To these ends, these travelers required large African entourages, primarily composed of porters, but also of guides, diplomatic agents, and hunters, as they traversed footpaths across the interior of the continent that were well known to their indigenous companions. Europeans who survived these journeys typically returned home to enjoy varying degrees of celebrity and often sought to capitalize on their newfound prestige by publishing memoirs that calculatedly sensationalized their African experiences; their commercial enterprise renders these short-term visitors "professional tourists." Meanwhile, the birth of the industry in Egypt placed Africa firmly on the touristic map. Intrepid men and women traveled up and down the Nile on trips organized by the pioneering travel agent Thomas Cook and facilitated by countless locals, who both formally and informally served as the backbone for the fledgling industry. Both explorers and visitors to Egypt returned to Europe with strong, often pejorative, impressions of Africa and its peoples, while their rac(ial)ist gaze and limited understandings of what and whom they had encountered also generated legion misperceptions and further exoticized the continent. Over time, these adventurous visitors prompted myriad imitators, and their re-spective governments made claims on the lands over which they had trav-eled as European nations carved up the continent in the closing decades of the nineteenth century, thereby granting this initial form of tourism a contributory role in the ensuing military invasion of Africa.

Chapter 2 considers the history of hunting expeditions in East and Southern Africa, regions that featured the most big game, beginning in the nineteenth century and extending until the conclusion of the colonial period. Among the best known of these hunter-naturalists were Frederick Selous (whose experiences in Southern Africa inspired H. Rider Haggard's fictional character Allan Quatermain), Cornwallis Harris, and Gordon Cumming. These sportsmen periodically featured in newspaper headlines, and many penned popular volumes detailing their exploits. Yet none of their undertakings would have been possible without assistance from the large numbers of African scouts, guides, guards, cooks, and porters upon whom they relied to facilitate their hunting excursions. In 1909–10, ex-US president Theodore Roosevelt joined the ranks of these hunter-luminaries via his Smithsonian-Roosevelt African expedition. Big-game hunting continued throughout the colonial period, but in a much more controlled manner, prompted by the depletion of game owing to hunting excesses. As cameras began to replace rifles on safari, colonial officials steadily set aside vast animal habitats as reserves or parks to provide sanctuary for this increasingly lucrative fauna and otherwise restricted sport hunting in a va-riety of ways.

Chapter 3 explores the range of investments that European colonial re-gimes made in tourism infrastructure in order to generate income from these African possessions. Colonial governments used both the local rev-enues and the political capital that tourism produced to reaffirm their im-perial control. In general, colonies with natural touristic assets, including big game, extensive beaches, and moderate climates, were the most appeal-ing to prospective visitors. Most of these settings were located in eastern and southern Africa, where the British and Portuguese had extensive ter-ritories, giving them a considerable advantage in touristic promotion over the French, Belgians, and other imperial powers, whose African territories were largely located in other parts of the continent or lacked the assets outlined above. Irrespective of which colonial power was touting tourism in its African territories, the minimally compensated African workers, upon whose backs the industry throughout the continent was built, maintained, and expanded, were virtually invisible. By examining Africans' struggles to navigate these exacting environments, the chapter illuminates the impact of colonial-era tourism on their daily lives. In some cases, steady wages and frequent interactions with tourists afforded these workers financial autonomy and facilitated social ascension, enabling them to circumvent limitations in their home communities predicated on age and gender. However, most African tourism workers were poorly paid, exploited by a foreign-owned industry that was intended primarily to fill the coffers of private operators and colonial regimes.

Chapter 4 examines the decisions that newly independent African states made to cultivate tourist industries in support of national development objectives. Rather than redress the most egregious colonial-era policies enacted in the name of tourism, including the forced removal of indigenous residents from ancestral lands newly designated as game reserves, most emergent African nations simply extended them. Even popularly inclined governments, such as Tanzania's under Julius Nyerere, devised creative ways to reconcile capitalistic tourist industries with state-sponsored socialism. In practice, their investments in foreign tourists' fantasies were prompted by the continuing need to generate revenue and the associated ambition to create domestic employment opportunities. Sharing these core objectives, African states across the ideological spectrum invested in tourism infrastructure, which often generated high rates of return, while actively promoting travel destinations such as Tunisia's Mediterranean beaches and Kenya's celebrated game reserves in an attempt to attract both continental and international visitors. In this manner, an array of independent African states perpetuated the tourist agendas that their colonial predecessors had contrived.

Chapter 5 examines the history of the fabled African safari. Although the word means "journey" in Kiswahili, the tourist experience packaged under that name is a thoroughly Western invention. Safaris grew out of the adventures of the original "explorers" and matured as hunting expeditions before the First World War, but they are now intended for passive observers seeking to photograph—rather than slaughter—Africa's renowned wildlife. Today, photo-tourism constitutes the bedrock of the industry in East and Southern Africa, with safari experiences ranging from self-driving tours, to catered luxury getaways, to faux colonial-era "camps" that can cost thousands of dollars a day and include hot water, gourmet meals, and bottomless flutes of champagne. The more cosseted the participants in these genteel safaris are, however, the more they operate within the "tourist bubble," in which guests are whisked directly from airports to resorts adjacent to or within game reserves and exclusively interact with an array of select, trained African staff for the duration of their stay. Many observers have criticized this insulated form of engagement with the continent as "inauthentic" and "superficial," but each year for millions of uncritical visitors from around the world seeking the ultimate "authentically" African experience, the safari remains the "trip of a lifetime."

Chapter 6 considers the experiences of tourists traveling to the continent from across the African diaspora. In particular, the chapter explores "roots" or "heritage" tourism, in which members of African diasporic communities "return" to the continent of their ancestors to "discover" and, thus, attempt to better understand both their heritage and, by extension, themselves. This form of tourism has attracted the attention of scholars interested in the following topics: the divergence between the ways in which members of these diasporic populations perceive Africa and its peoples; their range of experiences while on the continent; how these tourists negotiate these often-emotional journeys "home," only to find themselves received as foreigners and, ironically, perceived as "white"; and the ways that African guides, docents, performers, and merchants skillfully perform for these tourists, striving to fulfill these visitors' expectations of a relatable, yet no less exotic, Africa.

Chapter 7 examines more recent forms of tourism on the continent, including ecotourism, cultural tourism, "slum" or "poverty tourism," so-called voluntourism, and sex tourism. African states and tour operators readily promote these various types of visits, even if some are ethically or economically controversial. Irrespective of the financial motives of the promoters and tour organizers, these contemporary forms of tourism annually attract millions of visitors to the continent. This chapter also examines the most recent versions of trophy hunting, in which wealthy foreigners pay exorbitant fees for licenses to shoot disappearing big game. Although they fancy themselves modern-day Roosevelts, their experiences are entirely illusory: the animals are conveniently confined within private reserves, and any perils associated with the hunting of yesteryear have been befittingly removed. Although this form of tourism produces employment opportunities for local residents and significant revenue for African states and tour operators, excesses such as the illicit shooting in 2015 of Zimbabwe's beloved "Cecil the Lion" by a dentist from Minnesota can also generate unwanted attention—and, in that case, criminal charges. The chapter concludes by re-engaging with the central questions and issues raised in this introductory chapter and considering how Africa's foreign guests and local hosts might experience the tourism industry going forward.

CHAPTER ONE

Initial Touristic Incursions to Africa

> Today, it is easier to visualize the surface of the moon than it was
> prior to 1800 to imagine the reality of Africa.
>   —Bartle Bull, 1988

THIS CHAPTER follows the initial nineteenth-century touristic forays to Africa by an array of outsiders. One group included self-styled explorers, who were often commissioned to gather zoological, ethnographic, and geographical information about a largely unknown continent but who remained entirely dependent on well-traveled and knowledgeable local guides and sponsors. Yet explorers weren't exactly tourists, right? So what do they have to do with tourism in Africa? Well, a lot, actually. Many of these European interlopers returned home to market their chronicles of "daring" and "dangerous" endeavors, generating both fame and fortune for themselves and contributing to the racialized infamy of their African hosts, while further piquing public interest in the continent.

The other group of these initial travelers were hardly as intrepid, nor did they seek celebrity as a dividend of their travails. Rather, these were tourists to Egypt, who began arriving in the 1840s, accessing the rudimentary tourist infrastructure that was gradually being constructed. Later in the century, the travel agent Thomas Cook would fully extend "mass tourism" to Egypt, enabling tourists with more modest means—or "Cookites"—to mingle with European royalty in the country's various destinations. Even if these Egyptian journeys significantly diverged from the explorers' enterprise, both groups returned to their homelands with tales that further exoticized the continent and its peoples, deepening existing perceptions via their eyewitness, often embellished, accounts.

This chapter also examines these initial tourists' dependency on Africans' logistical support. European explorers would have forever been stuck in Africa's assortment of coastal centers without large numbers of facilitative, indigenous laborers, who typically endured highly disagreeable treks into the continent's interior in the name of "discovery." Similarly, in Egypt, tourists required a range of local assistance, from captains of boats plying the Nile's waters, to local guides leading guests on donkeys to an array of choice destinations, to the staff at various points of accommodation along the way. Even local belly dancers played an important role in entertaining these well-heeled guests, aiding a layer of alleged authenticity to evening meals.

The "Last Wilderness": Explorers of Africa and Their Touristic Impact

Although they were not the first travelers to reach and probe Africa, certain European explorers in the eighteenth and nineteenth centuries were responsible for significantly expanding the appeal of the continent to would-be visitors. Entering Africa at various points south of the vast Sahara Desert, they imagined themselves as heroes, penetrating "the last wilderness." Steeped in romanticism, many were also "driven by religious zeal, nationalism, simple greed, and the love of conquest."[1] Irrespective of their particular motives, they carried with them countless misunderstandings of the continent and myriad erroneous, preconceived notions of what they might find. In practice, what they sought to "discover" was quite different from what they actually encountered, yet their predeterminations greatly reduced this discrepancy. This phenomenon of encountering precisely what they expected to encounter proved to be quite durable, as accounts of Africa tended to "feed off and reinforce one another. Not surprisingly, these travelers went looking for and found *exactly* the types of things their predecessors described."[2] In turn, these spurious accounts created for receptive readers a magical place that was somehow "both paradise and wilderness, a place of spectacular but savage beauty."[3] These explorers' tales found an audience clamoring for "evidence" to confirm that their imaginations had, in fact, been accurate all along.

This blinkered desire for Africa to be a mythical land, inhabited by strange peoples and beasts, had deep origins but was also linked to more contemporaneous developments. Much as we long at times to "escape" our own lives and, perhaps in particular, modern technology, so too did the European public, even if they weren't beholden to the latest smartphone. In sharp contrast to their world of emerging machinery and industry, Africa appeared as an Eden, an unspoiled, unsullied land, upon which humans seemed to barely figure and an array of wild beasts roamed freely. Of course, none of these perceptions was accurate: the continent featured an assortment of large, sophisticated population centers, and just as in Europe, wildlife operated in natural habitats and typically avoided contact with humans.

Regardless of their various perceptional shortcomings, the series of explorers who initially penetrated the African interior were undoubtedly intrepid. They were hearty men, many of whom had a military background, and were chosen "primarily for their ability to survive an arduous journey."[4] Their masculinity was often matched by their self-promotional savvy and opportunism, as they accessed emerging publishing outlets to reach ever-broader audiences. By the middle of the nineteenth century, the expanded trade in newspapers, magazines, journals, and books enabled these authors to reach mass audiences, conveying information about the "latest expeditionary ventures in highly specific ways intended to generate more interest in these explorers—and their publications."[5] Their accounts diverged from the earlier, more sober and scientific renderings of various overseas settings. Instead, they offered sensationalized tales, "systematically misrepresenting African culture and contributing mightily to the spread of racial bias and cultural arrogance."[6] This steady stream of influential misinformation was consumed as gospel by an uninformed public. As historian Philip Curtin argues, "In general, the political classes in Europe were no better informed than ever (about Africa), but they were more confident in their information. The errors once confined to a few specialized works had now become 'common knowledge.'"[7] Even when some of these travelers-cum-writers knew that material penned by others was inaccurate, they remained silent, "as their own reputations grew when Africa was portrayed in the most extreme terms possible."[8]

Among the individuals most responsible for the spread of hyperbolic, self-aggrandizing, and condescending information about Africa and Africans was the famed explorer Henry Morton Stanley, the articulator of the legendary phrase, "Dr. Livingstone, I presume?" In fact, that experience provided the material for his first book, *How I Found Livingstone*, published in 1871. According to author Adam Hochschild, "His melodramatic flair made him . . . the progenitor of all the subsequent professional travel writers. His articles, books, and speaking tours brought him greater riches than any other travel writer of his time. With every step he took in Africa, Stanley planned how to tell the story once he got home. In a twentieth-century way, he was always sculpting the details of his own celebrity."[9]

Even the revered Livingstone was not immune to twisting his narratives to meet the expectations of his intended audiences, thereby further shaping their impressions of Africa. In his 1857 book, *Missionary Travels and Researches in South Africa*, for example, he theatrically described Victoria Falls, though he had only crafted a few, uninspired paragraphs in his journals when recording his sentiments regarding this natural wonder. Livingstone was apparently concerned that if his account was as indifferent as it had been in his journals, his various missionary projects might not attract the requisite funding. Consequently, he glowed, "No one can imagine the beauty of the view from anything witnessed in England. It had never been seen before by European eyes; but scenes so lovely must have been gazed upon by angels in their flight." Accounts that accentuated the extraordinary and exotic, while backgrounding the more disagreeable aspects of traversing the continent, piqued readers' attention and interest in Africa. And there was no shortage of readers. The first edition of twelve thousand copies of Livingstone's massive, not inexpensive, 690-page volume sold out immediately. Another thirteen thousand copies followed soon after, and three years later an abridged edition (436 pages) was published and similarly devoured by a seemingly insatiable readership.

If accounts of Africa written by Stanley, Livingstone, and others were problematic, there were no competing depictions to challenge the narrative collectively generated by these tales. Nor would contradictory accounts have fallen on receptive ears—until the end of the 1880s, that is. By that time, a number of missionaries and a handful of intrepid journalists had begun objecting to the egregious violence that Europeans were committing against Africans. Their dissenting accounts exposed these brutal and exploitative actions, thereby humanizing indigenous residents in previously unconceivable ways. In particular, the abuse in the Congo, King Leopold II of Belgium's personal territory in the heart of the continent, prompted much of this initial, condemning literature, even if few of these authors challenged the moral rightfulness of the colonial enterprise. Individuals such as the African American minister George Washington Williams, who wrote an open letter to Leopold II in 1890, were among the first to shatter the triumphant narrative that the collection of European explorers had helped generate. His critiques were echoed by others, including Dean Morel, Roger Casement, and eventually, even the famous American author Mark Twain, whose 1905 pamphlet "King Leopold's Soliloquy" delivered a biting condemnation of the imperial developments in the Congo.

Regardless, these various exposés did little to dent the mythical Africa that had been steadily forming in the minds of outsiders over the course of centuries. Instead, readers continued to consume (mis)information about the continent that stressed its wildness, wildlife, and seemingly subhuman indigenous populations, all of which fueled and deepened perceptions of its alleged "otherness."

African Labor: Vital Service Providers

For all of their bravado and heroism, none of these explorers would have been able to jaunt around the continent without a retinue of local male headmen, guides, porters, warriors, gunbearers, and, at times, female cooks to ensure their safety and sustenance. Stanley was notoriously merciless toward his African assistants, and although not all explorers were as cruel to these vital employees, they still failed to treat them as equals. Africans' role in the protohistory of tourism in Africa was crucial, as they facilitated the initial travel that prompted would-be visitors to set their sights on the continent and, eventually, begin arriving in large numbers. Without this assistance, this process would have been, at the very least, forestalled.

Treks planned through the interior, which eventually became known as safaris, were impossible without the proper manpower, namely African headmen and porters. The former procured and oversaw the dozens, or even hundreds, of the latter and also served as the linguistic mediators between the masses of African laborers and the European expedition leaders. These overseers were among the most valued and well treated of all the Africans hired for these undertakings. Talented and experienced headmen were consequently in great demand; European explorers competed for their services with other explorers, as well as with Arab trading safaris along the east coast of the continent. No less important were porters, who were regularly in short supply due to the crucial services they provided, often carrying some 60–80 pounds daily for weeks at a time in exchange for minimal remuneration. As South African author Kenneth Cameron explains, "British explorer, Richard Francis Burton, in the 1850s found Arab traders beating him to the best porters; 30 years later, Hungarian explorer, Sámuel Teleki hurried to hire his porters because Henry Morton Stanley wanted 500 for his third expedition. English explorer, John Hanning Speke, watched the price of his best porters climb to almost double as other caravans began to form."[10] This increasingly professionalized group of laborers would often serve on a safari headed into the interior and then return with a different one heading back to the coast, spending considerable time away from their homes. Neither these local laborers nor even their European expedition leaders could have envisioned that overseas tourists would one day follow in their footsteps.

To Egypt!

Egypt. Fabled land of the Sphinx, the pyramids at Luxor, the Valley of the Kings, and the Nile, the "father of African rivers" (fig. 1.1). It is not hard to imagine why tourists were initially attracted to this mysterious place and its ancient attractions. After all, Egypt retains this appeal today, continuing to draw tourists from around the world even during spells of political upheaval. As mentioned in the previous chapter, the first tourists came to this legendary land from other sites in the ancient world, but the origins of modern tourism to Egypt can be located in the early years of

FIGURE 1.1 The Great Sphinx at Giza, Egypt. *Photo taken by Joyce Munden.*

the nineteenth century. It was during this time that Muhammad Ali, an Albanian military commander in the service of the Ottoman Turks, seized control and launched modernization campaigns in a number of areas of Egyptian society, including tourism. Somewhat remarkably for his day, he recognized the economic potential of tourism, while also seeking to further consolidate power by openly welcoming European dignitaries/tourists. From this time on, tourism was to become a highly organized, vital industry within the Egyptian economy, as it remains to this day.

Muhammad Ali's touristic initiatives came at a particularly propitious moment. European and American elites were contemporaneously obsessed with Egypt, in part inspired by accounts from British and French officers serving there that highlighted the country's spectacular monuments. Meanwhile, Edward Clarke's three-volume set *Travels in Various Countries of Europe, Asia, and Africa*, published in 1813, stoked the imaginations of Westerners. Manifestations of this captivation were widely observable. As historian Eric Zuelow explains, "Victorians were so obsessed that even a cursory meander through many 19th century British or American manor houses would yield Egyptian artifacts or even mummies, while a short walk through rural cemeteries such as Highgate in London or Mount Auburn in Cambridge, Massachusetts reveals numerous grave monuments featuring pyramids, sphinxes, and the like."[11] Whether or not Ali knew of this overseas enthrallment is unclear, but his touristic initiatives resonated with the "Egypt-mania" that Western elites were fueling.

This fascination was further heightened by an array of Europeans who procured Egyptian antiquities for the British Museum in London and the Louvre in Paris. Although this type of blatant material and cultural appropriation would be condemned in the following century, at the time the tangibility of these objects merely bolstered the Egyptian craze. Thousands of people attended openings of Egyptian exhibits in Europe's capitals, prompting many of these patrons to dream of visiting the fabled North African land.

It was during this period that scholars believe the first tourist from Britain arrived in Egypt, in the form of Thomas Legh. According to Martin Anderson, Legh was a member of Parliament and "an inveterate traveler, who travelled for pleasure and did not pretend to be a scholar or explorer contributing to the knowledge of the world."[12] Legh arrived in Alexandria in December 1812 and proceeded on to Cairo in 1813. Not content with these initial endeavors, Legh longed to travel up the Nile to visit Egypt's famed temples. Although others had preceded Legh, he constituted Muhammad Ali's first encounter with a foreigner who wanted to travel for personal, rather than scientific or commercial, reasons. After granting Legh permission, Ali extended the Englishman his personal guarantee of safety to ensure safe conduct on his travels. The security and bestowed status that Legh enjoyed would convince other would-be tourists that Egypt constituted a viable, safe destination.

Following the subsidence of the turmoil associated with the Napoleonic Wars in 1815, Egypt began preparing for an increase in tourism. And it came. By the 1830s, tourists were arriving in reliable numbers and were, by all accounts, duly impressed. Consider the words of Alexander Crawford (also known as Lord Lindsay), a Scottish earl and an early participant of this touristic influx, who visited the Middle East during the mid-1830s:

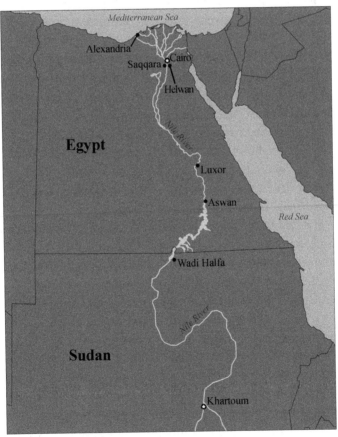

MAP 1.1 Egypt and Sudan. *Map by Maggie Bridges.*

"Whatever one's opinion of Muhammad Ali's domestic policy, travelers owe him much, for throughout his dominions (in Egypt and Syria, at least) they may travel in the Frank dress with perfect safety . . . had anyone prophesied in their days that that two Britons would, in 1836, walk openly through Cairo?" Perhaps even more optimistically, he further declared, "With English hotels at Alexandria and Cairo, and floating palaces at command for navigating the Nile, what is there to prevent our English ladies and their beaux from wintering at Thebes (Luxor) as they have done hitherto at Paris and Rome?"[13] Indeed, Britain's informal empire in the Mediterranean following the conclusion of the Napoleonic conflicts provided an "umbrella of protection" for British and other Western tourists to Egypt.[14] Overland travelers en route to India from Europe also swelled the ranks of foreign visitors to the country. Crawford's enthusiasm and the security associated with this destination combined to attract additional guests: by the middle of the century, as many as twenty thousand tourists were annually traveling to Egypt.

The revenues generated by these initial touristic flows encouraged further investment in the fledgling industry, which came in the form of improvements and expansion of transportation and accommodation infrastructure. These measures supported existing touristic flows while better preparing Egypt to accommodate anticipated increases in the numbers of visitors. When compared against the lodging infrastructure in place at the commencement of this influx, the progress is astonishing. Indeed, the earliest visitors largely depended upon the British Council or Egyptians serving in a variety of official capacities for their accommodation needs.[15] Now there was a range of hotels available. In fact, by the 1840s, tourists were vocalizing their complaints when accommodations or other aspects of the experience were *not* up to standard, suggesting that both the touristic infrastructure and, accordingly, expectations had been significantly elevated.

Before departing for Egypt, tourists learned about the country's "must see" sites via a series of guidebooks that European publishing houses were increasingly generating. These texts and travelers' personal accounts portrayed a manageable, comfortable, and exotic touristic experience—everything that Europeans wanted to hear about a place that many of them had long dreamed of visiting. These various sources of information influenced itineraries and offered prospective visitors a type of membership into an exclusive tourist club. The first tour book to appear was most likely Sir Gardner Wilkinson's *Modern Egypt and Thebes: Being a Description of*

Egypt, published in 1843. Another noteworthy text in this genre was William Makepeace Thackeray's *Notes of a Journey from Cornhill to Grand Cairo*, which had been commissioned by the steamship line P&O in exchange for an extended cruise around the eastern Mediterranean in 1844. Commenting on his stay at the sixty-room Hotel D'Orient in Cairo, Thackeray wrote, "I can't but recommend all persons who have time and means to make a similar journey—vacation idlers to extend their travels and pursue it; above all, young, well-educated men entering life."[16]

Eventually, it appears that the proliferation of these books saturated what was still a rather limited, if steadily growing, market. For example, in Isabella Romer's 1846 two-volume publication, *A Pilgrimage to the Temples and Tombs of Egypt, Nubia, and Palestine in 1845–6*, she laments that "since the facilities of steam-navigation have brought the Nile within the scope of everybody's possibility, so much has been published about the East that the subject has been completely exhausted by minds of every caliber, and books of Oriental travel have become a mere drug."[17] So too was the increased tourist traffic in Egypt off-putting to Romer. Apparently, the sight of twenty-two tour boats, including two French, two American, one Austrian, and fourteen English, on her way back down the Nile was simply too much for this aloof tourist, who wanted the Egypt experience to be much more exclusive than it had become. If only Romer knew that Thomas Cook would shortly thereafter open up Egypt to "mass tourism," she may have appreciated her comparatively less congested experience much more than she seemed to have.

Regardless of whether Cook is understood as a touristic visionary or the opener of the widely criticized mass tourism floodgates, the industry was well established in Egypt before Cook's initiatives. All the requisite components, including transport, lodging, guidebooks, and countless, indispensable locals engaged in one capacity or another to support the growing tourist traffic, were in place. Nor did the death in 1849 of Muhammad Ali, who had been so instrumental to the growth of tourism in Egypt, do anything to temper the influx of visitors. Egypt was prominently and irreversibly on the tourist map.

Thomas Cook and the Launch of Mass Tourism in Egypt

Thomas Cook laid the groundwork for the "opening of Egypt" to the masses in 1869 via an exploratory trip to the Middle East, which included stops in Turkey, Egypt, and Palestine/Syria, the previous year. Apparently, this journey went quite well (though Cook and his party were robbed in Jerusalem) and encouraged his instinct that this region of the world was a viable site for further mass, inexpensive travel. In turn, Cook announced that he would be issuing new tourist tickets connecting London with Alexandria "by the new, popular and cheap route of Brindisi (Italy) and claimed he would be able to reduce the length of travel from London to Alexandria (Egypt) to seven days, at an affordable rate of £20 sterling first class, the second class being in proportion. Travelers to the Holy Land on Cook's 1869 tour would pay £105 sterling per person for a 70-day trip."[18]

This new version of the "Grand Tour" was not without its challenges, even if the foundational touristic infrastructure was already in place. Cook openly voiced these concerns, including those related to language, the difficulty of identifying reliable local operators and laborers, the array of local coinage in circulation, and perhaps most significantly, the uncooperativeness of certain government officials. In 1869, for example, Cook would lament, "In France and Switzerland, it has become as easy to travel as in Scotland or Ireland. . . . But here, circumstances are totally different."[19]

In order to surmount many of these challenges, Cook relied on his considerable business acumen, but he also enjoyed the protection of the mighty British Empire and, correspondingly, the support of the Egyptian viceroy, Ismail, who appointed Cook's firm to run the government's Nile passenger service between Cairo and Aswan, located far upstream. It is unlikely that Cook would have been as successful as he was without these intertwined entities supporting his ventures. To ensure ongoing sponsorship, the entrepreneurial Cook remained astutely neutral when local turmoil or conflict materialized, refusing to take sides. He was consequently rewarded by the Egyptian government, which was itself somewhat strapped and thus greatly enjoying the expanded revenue streams that tourism was generating. Consequently, the state authorized Cook to open his first Middle Eastern office at the Shepheard's Hotel in Cairo; extended his Nile passenger service concession to the Sudanese border; and also granted it exclusive rights to transport government mail on the Nile.[20] With Egypt's government deeply in debt and its steamship service underwater financially, Cook's touristic efforts must have seemed a blessing. Yet Ismail wasn't entirely uncalculating or unaware of what his territory had to offer; he knew that his country was ripe for touristic development. The advent of "the steamship, telegraph, and Egyptian railway; the rapid growth of European communities in Alexandria and Cairo; and the establishment of western institutions, such as hotels, pensions, churches, restaurants, and banks, provided the foundation on which tourism could be constructed."[21]

Over time, the relationship between Great Britain, Egypt, and tourism both deepened and accelerated. The British gained increasing influence over an Egyptian government that was drowning in debt, which encouraged the latter to stay out of the way of the Cook firm, now overseen by Thomas's son, John. Consequently, the company's new director aggressively expanded its operations and generated much-needed income for the beleaguered viceroy, which declared bankruptcy in 1875. Enjoying virtually free reign in Egypt and the unwavering support of the British government and local British business and political interests, Cook & Son opened a winter season (November to March) and invested in steamships, rendering this form of transport the "master of traffic" on the Nile.[22] John Cook and the viceregal family were genuinely close, but there was little that these Egyptian officials could have done to impede these developments even if they had wanted to.

Although Cook & Son typically embraced the "business of peace" (i.e., an apolitical approach to tourism development and local affairs), the company did help the British military maintain control over Egypt following a nationalist uprising in the 1880s. As part of these efforts, the enterprise utilized steamships to convey British troops up and down the Nile to aid troops engulfed in an insurrection in the Sudan, to the south. This assistance generated significant profits for Cook & Son, and once the conflict subsided, the company plowed these funds into measures aimed to revive the temporarily disrupted Egyptian tourism industry. Perhaps the most effective, and profitable, of these endeavors was to assemble its own fleet of steamships, eventually reaching fifteen by the last decade of the century, to transport tourists of various means up and down the Nile in various states of comfort. Thus, the firm was both catering to its luxury clientele and expanding touristic opportunities to the "masses" of middle-class travelers.

By 1890, the numbers of tourists had rebounded and were increasing annually. Many of these visitors only ventured as far as the greater Cairo area, but a significant number also traveled up the Nile to visit various sites or to just enjoy the inimitable scenery that these slow-moving, weeks-long journeys featured. As travelers plied the river, they encountered a range of conveniences, including post and telegram offices. More Germans and Americans were also arriving, though British tourists continued to predominate. Cook & Son was newly targeting teachers and students, along with its more traditional audiences, and also sought out both men and women with lesser means, even if travel to Egypt remained cost prohibitive for most would-be tourists. Following the turn of the century, the enterprise enjoyed monopolistic control over Nile tourism (its only real competitor went bankrupt in 1903) and had emerged as the largest British business in Egypt.[23]

As Cook & Son tightened its touristic stranglehold on Egypt, the firm concentrated its efforts on two areas: Cairo and Luxor, a further up the Nile. In the former, the company's agents greeted tourists arriving from Alexandria, served as local guides, and issued vouchers for further train travel. The standard tour of Cairo included visits to the bazaar, the old city, the Sphinx and Pyramids, and the Step Pyramid at Saqqara; another nearby feature was Helwan, touted in Cook's brochures as "Egypt's health resort par excellence, whose sulfur springs have been praised as equal to those of Aix in Savoy (France)."[24] Tourists arriving at these sites marveled at their wildly colorful nature and the alien nature of everything and everyone they encountered. Following a visit to Cairo in the mid-1870s, for example, Englishwoman Amelia B. Edwards, commented that

> the place was like a fair with provision-stalls, swings, storytellers, serpent-charmers, cake-sellers, sweetmeat-sellers, sellers of sherbet, water, lemonade, sugared nuts, fresh dates, hard-boiled eggs, oranges, and sliced watermelon. Veiled women carrying little bronze Cupids of children astride upon the right shoulder, swarthy Egyptians, coal-black Abyssinians, Arabs and Nubians from every shade from golden-brown to chocolate, fellahs, dervishes, donkey-boys, street urchins, and beggars with every imaginable deformity, came and went; squeezed themselves in and out among the carriages; lined the road on each side of the great towered gateway; swarmed on the top of every wall; and filled the air with laughter, a Babel of dialects, and those odors of Araby that are inseparable from an Eastern crowd.[25]

There was also considerable touristic activity and development hundreds of miles up the Nile at Luxor, the site of "some of the most splendid and best preserved ruins in Egypt" and a place that has been referred to as "Cook's Upper Egyptian Empire."[26] By the turn of the twentieth century, Luxor was a bustling site of touristic activity, featuring an array of hotels and restaurants. It also offered support services that were hardly standard in Egyptian towns of the time, including a free public hospital (opened in 1891 and funded mainly by Cook), vice-consulates, postal and telegraph offices, and even resident European physicians.

But Cook & Son wasn't done. Some 133 miles farther up the Nile, the company set its sights on Aswan. At this former military outpost, the company engaged in what had become the standard touristic makeover, erecting hotels, cafés, and churches, as well as post and telegraph offices. Not content with this development, Cook eyed Khartoum, in the Sudan, even farther upstream and the terminus for tourist travel on the Nile. In this case, though, there was a twist. Because the destination was inaccessible by steamship, Cook's boats carried tourists from Aswan as far as Wadi Halfa, situated over 600 miles north of Khartoum. From there, passengers boarded luxury trains that featured dining and sleeping cars, speeding toward a city that successive waves of tourists were actively transforming. In Baedeker's 1902 edition of *Egypt. Handbook for Travellers*, for example, he praised Khartoum's 2-mile, Nile-side promenade, the missionary schools, hospital, banks, and zoological gardens.[27] Once in Khartoum, intrepid travelers could visit battle sites and tombs of local historical figures and take trips out into the surrounding desert.

Collectively, these remarkable touristic developments confirmed the establishment of Cook & Son's "Egyptian empire." Over time, the Nile had become the favorite winter resort for Westerners, as these visitors could "leave their native shores and find the comforts of home aboard a steamship and in luxury hotels bathed in desert sunshine."[28] Affirming the enterprise's accomplishments and capabilities, in 1898 a British traveler named G. W. Steevens observed, if somewhat hyperbolically, that "in Egypt, he who puts himself into the hands of Cook can go anywhere and do anything."[29]

Local Labor and Entrepreneurialism in Egypt

As swelling numbers of tourists visited Egypt, the revenues generated by their visits benefited innumerable locals, who remained the backbone of the industry's burgeoning success. Locals quickly capitalized on the economic opportunities that these foreign visitors were generating, often in creative ways. Entrepreneurial types began selling anything—even whole (stolen) mummies—that would enable these tourists to take a piece of the ancient world back home with them. Amelia B. Edwards vividly illustrates this activity in her 1874 account of her disembarkation from a boat at Luxor:

> Forger, diggers, and dealers play . . . driving a roaring trade. . . .
> You are beset from the moment you moor till the moment you

pole off again from the shore. The boy who drives your donkey, the guide who pilots you among the tombs, the half-naked Fellah . . . have one and all an "anteekah" to dispose of. . . . In short, every man, woman, and child about the place is bent on selling a bargain. . . . Private excavation being prohibited, the digger lives in dread of being found out by the Governor. The forger, who has nothing to fear from the Governor, lives in dread of being found out by the tourist.[30]

These locals were not formally employed in the sector but nonetheless carved out livelihoods based on their resourcefulness and steady interaction with tourists. For example, Harriet Martineau, a British social theorist, in an 1845 account of her visit to Egypt, described how locals had facilitated her ascent of the pyramids, initially by using a footstool and then by carrying her from tier to tier, writing, "The greatest part of one's weight is lifted by the Arabs at each arm; and when one comes to a four feet stop, or a broken ledge, there is a third Arab behind."[31] These vertical porters had established only one of many creative subindustries.

Formal employment opportunities also materialized for locals, complementing the countless Egyptians informally involved in the sector. Thousands of employees, including many who were illiterate or semiliterate, served as guides, translators, porters, mechanics, and builders for Cook & Son. The provision of assistive, remunerable services is a feature of any heavily touristed location, but the fact that this thriving subsector of the economy developed so rapidly, organically, and without local precedent is remarkable.

Among the most important of this professional class of tourism workers were the guides. Visitors relied on them to translate local languages and to help navigate, more broadly, this foreign land. Writing about her 1844 voyage up the Nile, Englishwoman Isabella Romer praised her guide, Mohammed, indicating that "his perfect knowledge of the outfit required for such an excursion has saved us a world of trouble, and his cleverness and good management in providing everything that he knew to be adapted to English tastes and habits, has really not left us the possibility of forming a wish. We had wisely prepared ourselves to expect a somewhat scrambling life of it, but most agreeable have we been surprised at finding everything going on under his auspices as smoothly as though we were in the best hotel on shore."[32]

The various members of the crews that facilitated trips up and down the Nile also played vital roles in the growth of the industry in Egypt. Among these employees were captains, pilots, cooks, and deckhands, many of whom appeared, if only briefly, in foreigners' memoirs of their Egyptian travels. Scottish tourist Norma Lorimer, who journeyed up the Nile in 1907, provides a colorful account of the darker-skinned, "Soudanese" crew of the SS *Ramses the Great*: "If there was nothing else to watch all day but the antics of our Soudanese crew, it would be sufficient for me. There is the ostrich-feather broom boy who watches for a speck of dust to brush away, and the brass boys who lift up rugs and mats to find some hidden treasure in the way of knobs to polish, indeed there is a boy with a grinning smile and flashing teeth for every mortal occupation you can imagine."[33]

Unfortunately, our knowledge of these African tourism laborers is essentially limited to mentions in travelers' written accounts of their experiences. Yet their contributions were vital to an industry that was, in many respects, fueling the overall development of the country. In 1889, for example, tourists spent an estimated $2.5 million in Egypt, this figure increasing fourfold over the next twenty-five years.[34] Even though Egypt remained under Britain's thumb throughout this transformational period, both the country itself and many of its citizens were directly or indirectly benefiting from the sojourns of these curious foreigners.

IT MIGHT seem like a stretch to characterize the initial European explorers who began venturing to sub-Saharan Africa as tourists. Indeed, their motivations were divergent, while few aspects of their journeys were marked by leisure or general pleasurability. Yet their sensational accounts precipitated subsequent tourism to the continent. In fact, although the touristic forays to Egypt outlined in this chapter were substantively different, they were motivated, even if only indirectly, by these explorers' fantastical tales.

Once would-be travelers' safety concerns were addressed, Africa became a natural, proximate outgrowth of the touristic activity in Europe that had been jumpstarted by the Industrial Revolution. The constituent sweeping technological developments sharply delineated work and leisure times, newly furnished many individuals with the income required to engage in travel for pleasure and, eventually, produced a class of industrial and administrative elites who received paid holidays. In many respects, the tourists that the Industrial Revolution generated were just the latest Westerners to arrive in these African stops, following in the footsteps of explorers, missionaries, merchants, and soldiers. Many of these individuals were hunters who, like the early visitors, shared their experiences with eager audiences back home. In devouring the accounts of these hunters, many would-be tourists were inspired to travel to Africa, ushering in the next wave of foreign visitors to the continent.

CHAPTER TWO

Hunting in Africa

Invisible Guides, Big Game, and Bigger Egos

> *I speak of Africa and golden joys; the joy of wandering through lonely*
> *lands; the joy of hunting the mighty and terrible lords of wilderness,*
> *the cunning, the wary, and the grim. . . . There is delight in the hardy*
> *life of the open, in long rides rifle in hand, in the thrill of the fight with*
> *dangerous game. Apart from this, yet mingled with it, is the strong*
> *attraction of the silent places, of the large tropic moons, and the splendor*
> *of the new stars where the wanderer sees the awful glory of sunrise and*
> *sunset in the wide waste spaces of the earth, unworn of man, and changed*
> *only by the slow changes of the ages from time everlasting.*
>
> —Theodore "Teddy" Roosevelt, 1910

ROOSEVELT'S WRITINGS, which are featured in the foreword of the former US president's 1910 book *African Game Trails: An Account from the African Wanderings of an American Hunter-Naturalist*, capture perfectly the sentiments that generations of Western big-game hunters held toward the continent. Following closely behind the explorers whom we examined in the last chapter, these hunter-tourists cast Africa as an exotic, "lonely land, unworn of man," teeming with big game, which was apparently exclusively theirs to fell. Implicit in this approach to, and perpetuation of, "the myth of wild Africa" was the absence of Africans, a commonly invoked claim that Europeans employed to justify their eventual colonial occupation. But even though Africans were obviously present, the continent's big game was clearly not for them. Rather, it awaited its foreign slayers, who treated Africa as little more than a playground for their own exploits, egos, and excesses. Given this allure, Africa's incomparable fauna helped stimulate flows of foreign hunter-tourists beginning in the nineteenth century. Like Teddy Roosevelt, who arrived in East Africa in 1909 on what ultimately became an epic, if notorious, expedition, these hunters primarily arrived from the Global North, were deep-pocketed, and had little concern for their African assistants, who might as well have been invisible, even though they were vital in assisting these outsiders as guides, scouts, guards, gun bearers, porters, and cooks.

This chapter examines the history of hunting safaris in sub-Saharan Africa from the middle of the nineteenth century through the end of the colonial era, which culminated in the decades following the Second World War, and then onto the silver screen, where this endeavor durably survived. Accounts from the hunter-sportsmen and, on occasion, sportswomen who engaged in these touristic "shooting expeditions," as they were known until the first decade of the twentieth century, periodically were featured in newspaper headlines or in other popular culture outlets in Europe and North America. In 1909–10, Roosevelt officially joined the ranks of these hunter-authors via regular dispatches from his East African expedition. This (in)famous undertaking resulted in the deaths of over twelve thousand animals; many of their preserved remains are on permanent display in the Smithsonian Museum of Natural History, in Washington, DC, and the American Museum of National History, in New York. Roughly two decades after Roosevelt's safari, the iconic novelist and paragon of machismo Ernest Hemingway famously shared aspects of his 1933 hunting experience in East Africa with readers via his introspective work *Green Hills of Africa*.

Big-game hunting continued throughout the colonial period, but in a much more managed fashion following the creation of game reserves and the adoption of conservation guidelines, prompted by the excesses of Roosevelt and others. Not surprisingly, European colonial officials declared these newly delineated reserves the exclusive domains of white hunters, even though many of these lands were the ancestral hunting grounds of African communities. Colonial regimes criminalized further hunting by indigenous communities in these spaces, newly deeming their long-standing sustenance strategies "poaching." These hunting policies constituted another component of the institutionalized racism that touched every part of indigenous life in imperial Africa, rendering these continental residents not only exploitable and invisible but also crucial to the various European colonial projects.

The Early Hunters: Africa as Eden

If many of the initial explorers of Africa became celebrities in Europe and North America, the ensuing foreign hunters engaged in a similar brand of self-promotion, carefully cultivating an image of white men taming an exotic, savage land. They fashioned themselves sportsmen and, over time, "created an ever more elaborate code of hunting conduct to fit the blood sport with the ideals of chivalry and Christian behavior."[1] To both disparage Africans and differentiate themselves from their indigenous counterparts, European sportsmen branded local hunting practices as "barbarous and unfair," evidenced, for example, by Africans' utilization of poison to kill game, which was condemned as "unmanly" and "abominable."[2] European tourist-hunters arrived in Africa to refashion how the endeavor was to be "properly" conducted, and by whom. To achieve the exclusive access to big game that Europeans desired, hunting by Africans had to be denounced and, ultimately, abolished. To this end, in their written accounts, European hunter-authors distorted and maligned Africans' relationship with nature, characterizing it as destructive, while these outsiders simultaneously trumpeted their own supposedly decorous, noble exploits. In fact, they often outright lied, or at least exaggerated, to curry favor with audiences back home as well as with European colonial officials serving in Africa. These two audiences were, of course, acutely receptive, and eager to "learn" about alleged African barbarianism and, conversely, the courageous, masculine feats of their racial brethren negotiating this "hostile land."

As is often the case, it's difficult to pinpoint the initial occurrence of a particular touristic endeavor in Africa, and hunting is no exception. But it is safe to say that foreign tourists were arriving to the continent to engage in hunting expeditions of varying types and lengths by the 1830s. Although he may not have been the first, Cornwallis Harris, an Englishman born in 1807, is considered one of the pioneers of this undertaking. Irrespective of whether he had any predecessors, an account of his exploits provides significant insight into the early days of hunting as a form of tourism in Africa.

Stationed in India upon joining the British East India Company, Harris was sent to Cape Town, South Africa, in 1836 to recover from a severe fever. Undeterred, he was determined to turn his "two-year convalescence into a prolonged hunting expedition deep into the interior of uncolonized Africa," thereby becoming perhaps the first foreigner to engage in an African hunting safari.[3] In August 1836, Harris set out with William Richardson, who had been a copassenger on the voyage from India. At this time, game was exceedingly abundant. According to one, albeit somewhat hyperboliz-ing, observer, "Animals were so plentiful that elephants foraged in herds of hundreds. At times, antelope covered the savannah like a carpet. Lions were literally pests. One might see 150 rhinoceros in a day. Dedicating a lifetime to foxes and pheasants, or at best to stag and boar, European sportsmen saw in giraffe and elephant the animals of paradise. To the European hunter, Africa was Eden."[4]

Harris, Richardson, and their African retinue, along with innumerable oxen, repeatedly encountered this copious game. And although they slew many of these animals, amassing an unparalleled collection of trophy heads that would eventually be brought to London, they were also mindful of the zealousness of many of the European settlers who were already thin-ning certain populations, including two antelope species: the blesbok and hartebeest.

Harris's safari team also consumed, rather than discarded, much of what they slew. An account from November 1836, some three months into the expedition, graphically describes an evening spent around a huge bonfire feasting on a Cape buffalo, which, when wounded, had twice charged Har-ris: "With a four-foot spread of horns, the animals made a handsome meal, while the diners, gorged to the throat, and besmeared with blood, grease and filth from the entrails, sat nodding torpidly around the carcass, sucking marrow from the bones."[5]

In general, these safari endeavors were not for the faint at heart. Days began at dawn, as hunting was both sport and sustenance and was often marked by extended periods of fruitlessness, even during this early period. Oxen also had to be fed and overseen, ammunition fashioned, water secured for man and beast, and both weather and dangerous animals—large and small—negotiated. At this time, in sharp contrast to contemporary safaris, hunting was also extremely dangerous. The firearms available to hunters of this period and the lead ammunition they used were insufficient to stop large game in their tracks unless the animal was hit at extremely close range and directly in the brain. For example, Harris recorded one rhino that required twenty-seven hits before it collapsed, and a bull elephant that required a re-markable fifty.[6] Harris's likely embellishment aside, the hunting of big game "often had the character of a small battle, with many men shooting at many animals, instead of the cleaner approach of one-to-one hunting."[7]

Following the completion of Harris's five-month safari in January 1837, he was in a unique position to be able to compare hunting in the wilds of

Southern Africa and India. And he didn't hold back. He duly warned his fellow tourist-sportsmen that "safari life in Africa was far harder and more dangerous, more wild and demanding, than the pampered life of the great Indian *shikars*, the lavish hunting expeditions attended by large retinues, preceded by carpenters and specialized servants and housed in sumptuous tents." Notwithstanding these cautionary words, he implored fellow hunters to "welcome the toils, trials, and, troubles that beset the wanderer in the African desert."[8]

Just as the explorers did, Harris put pen to paper regarding his travails, thereby establishing his own celebrity while piquing touristic interest in Africa. Harris's *The Wild Sports of Southern Africa*, published in Bombay in 1838, constituted the first book ever exclusively devoted to game hunting in Africa. Remarkably, because of its popularity in both India and Britain, by 1852 four further editions had been released. Feeding this public interest was also Harris's 1840 work *Portraits of the Game and Wild Animals of Southern Africa*, which featured over thirty colored engravings, as well as descriptive text. Although a hunting safari in sub-Saharan Africa was beyond the financial means of most of the readership of these texts, these written accounts further fueled the mounting fascination with the continent.

Stories and Souvenirs: Generating Touristic Interest in Africa

As the written corpus of tales from explorers and hunters grew, Africa increasingly filled the European imagination and, for a small number of travelers, became a tangible reality. The authors of these texts spawned imitators, who journeyed to the continent to confront and attempt to surmount the numerous challenges that Africa reportedly featured. Hunter-tourists sought to experience what Harris and others had or, at least, to have an adventure that included the more appealing and inspiring dimensions. These new visitors "turned to sketching and diaries to document their days in Africa," further bringing these experiences to ever-expanding audiences in Europe.[9] Yet there was also a darker side to this zealous quest to dominate the continent's fauna, especially when coupled with European settlers' further pushes into the African interior. In Southern Africa by the 1840s, for example, big game was already "virtually exterminated south of the Orange River, which runs east-west roughly across central South Africa, or, like the elephant, forced to retire to the north . . . the last lion shot south of the Orange River was in 1842."[10] These worrying developments were among the earliest signs that this approach to hunting was unsustainable.

Further exacerbating this trend was the overseas demand for African hides, feathers, ivory, and, somewhat oddly, hippo teeth, which could all be found in Europe's finest gathering places and establishments. One colorful account of these trends indicated that "Mzilikazi [the Matabele king, b. 1790, d. 1868], the ladies of Paris, and the Bushmen [a pejorative term for indigenous Southern Africans] were all decorated in the savage feathers of Africa, while the clubs of London rang to the sound of ivory dice and billiard balls and to the chatter of false teeth, which had once been the dentures of the hippo of the Orange River."[11] Today, many people would squirm with disapproval at the frivolous usage of these animal products, especially given how low stocks of these once-plentiful animals are. But during this period, the animal populations from which these items derived seemed inexhaustible. Indeed, rather than contemporaneous Europeans displaying a moral aversion to, for example, ivory billiard balls, they deemed them prestigious objects, items that also served to further whet a taste for Africa among individuals with means and even among those without.

One hunter who apparently believed in the boundless supply of African big game was Gordon Cumming, a solider and socialite from the Scottish Highlands, who commenced an astonishing *five-year* hunting safari, beginning in 1844, across much of the central and eastern interior of South Africa and present-day Botswana. Given the duration of this undertaking, it would be misleading to characterize this former military officer as a tourist, but his experiences served to further pique the interests of would-be visitors to Africa. While hunting in the Limpopo River valley, Cumming apparently shot multiple hippos and rhinos each day and arbitrarily killed crocodiles, disregarding most of the hides that this fallen wildlife offered. Unfortunately, even if other foreign hunters of the day weren't as aggressive, they joined Cumming in this type of casual killing, deeming the game to be unlimited.

This excess notwithstanding, Cumming was committed to consuming at least a portion of what he killed, which was not always the case with other foreign hunters. In particular, elephants provided a significant quantity of meat for his safari outfit. Cumming apparently favored the back feet and, "like the epicures of ancient Rome, sliced trunk." To prepare these delicacies, the feet were carefully placed in "close-fitting pits filled up with hot ashes, not coals, lest they burn the meat, and then covered with a fresh fire from the top."[12] Cumming allegedly "ate how his dogs did," even supposedly consuming locusts when game was not available. According to one

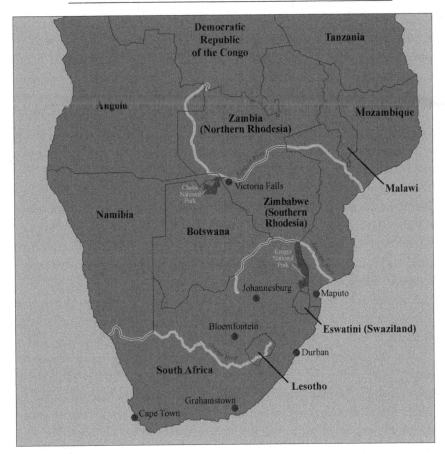

MAP 2.1 Southern Africa. *Map by Maggie Bridges.*

account, "one day, hot and thirsty after a long chase after a female oryx, the most exhausting antelope for a horse to run down, Cumming finally shot her, and then sprang from the saddle as she fell and drank the warm milk from her teats."[13] Certainly, no one could accuse him of a lack of enthusiasm in his approach to consuming everything edible that the fallen game had to offer.

His personal exploits aside, the most important touristic aspect of Cumming's extended undertaking was the promotional activity associated with his 1849 arrival back in England. In true Cumming fashion, there was nothing subtle about this endeavor. Eventually joining him in England were some 30 tons of "Africana," including, remarkably, the Cape wagon he had used while on his hunting adventure. Cumming subsequently traveled the country, exhibiting many of these items, as well as his impressive collection of specimens. In an act that was neither surprising nor novel for the time, he also included in this touring exhibit his "loyal Bushman," Ruyter. Almost forty years had passed since Alexander Dunlop had brought Sarah Baartman, the "Hottentot Venus" (the label "Hottentot," like "Bushman," is a pejorative term for the KhoiSan peoples, who are indigenous to Southern Africa), from South Africa to England for public display as part of a money-making scheme. As historians Clifton Crais and Pamela Scully have argued, "People came to see Baartman because they saw her not as a person but as a pure example of this one part of the natural world."[14] Her arrival even prompted a popular ballad, which went as follows: "We'll go no more to other shows / while Venus treads the stage / We'll go no more to other shows / while Hottentot's the rage." In displaying Ruyter to curious audiences, Cumming was similarly exploiting a racial spectacle that could be relied upon to draw large audiences in mid-nineteenth-century Victorian England.

Arguably even more important in terms of generating touristic interest in Africa was the 1850 publication in England of Cumming's journal. Entitled *The Lion Hunter of South Africa*, it was so popular that it briefly exceeded sales of the works of Charles Dickens, who was already an international literary titan by this time. The following year, a large exhibit featuring many of Cumming's African trophies was a major attraction in London, while he continued to "lecture widely and also established a popular private museum near Inverness, Scotland, where he finally settled."[15] Upon his death in 1866, the Barnum and Bailey Circus even incorporated some of these items in its African sideshow. Ultimately, the appeal of Cumming's Africana outlasted even his protracted safari.

The Essential Contributions of "Invisible" Africans

If Africans have been largely invisible from this reconstruction of the early years of foreigners hunting the continent's big game, that's because they were essentially absent from contemporaneous accounts of these touristic exploits. Virtually all of these European hunters, just like the explorers and missionaries who had preceded them, had sizable African support teams, members of which crucially served as, inter alia, porters, gunbearers, guides, repairmen, and cooks. Indeed, in the early days of safari, a single paying client might require, on average, as many as thirty porters. Yet these individuals rarely feature in any significant way in these foreign hunters' written accounts, owing to a potent combination of racism and self-promotion that didn't allow for coprotagonists. Although these authors often acknowledged their African staff as vital and even praised select individuals for their bravery, loyalty, commitment, or hearty constitution, these functionaries mainly served as part of the backdrop on a literary stage intended for a singular, white male.

Even attempts to offer complimentary words often ended up condescending. Take the case of William Charles Baldwin, who often hunted alone but occasionally bought African slaves while on safari to temper his loneliness. As he began to grow closer to them over the course of their travels, esteeming both their endurance and their stoic indifference to hardship, he would allegedly occasionally celebrate with them following a successful hunt, thereby breaking the taboo associated with drinking with "Hottentots." Yet, just as he admired their "skilled mimicry," he also allegedly remarked that "a Tottie half-seas' [i.e., drunk] is the most merry [*sic*] fellow in the world."[16]

Beyond serving in a support capacity on these safari outings, Africans also played a key role in a transformational event in April 1860, which would forever change the hunting safari experience on the continent. On this occasion, the Orange Republic, in central South Africa, celebrated the visit of Prince Alfred, the second son of Queen Victoria, to the territory by organizing a massive hunt near the administrative capital of Bloemfontein. Local Barolong peoples were recruited to assemble in a vast circle and drive any game inward that they could. Over the course of their efforts, a remarkable 20,000–30,000 animals "were hemmed in by the human cordon, with upwards of 5,000 killed, as part of the 'largest one-day hunt in the history of Africa.'"[17] As one observer has commented, "As much as any single day could, it marked the end of the first generation of the old white hunters, and beginnings of the elegant safari, when local [white] professional hunters escorted privileged Europeans on organized hunts into the bush."[18] These white guides both needed and resented these affluent foreign hunters, prompting one to remark that his clients "treated him like a butler," while another bemoaned, "I'd rather be a men's room attendant."[19] Nevertheless, legendary names such as Frederick Selous and Teddy Roosevelt would eventually come to be associated with this new, more tourist-friendly version of the African hunting safari, especially with the onset of the colonial era from the 1880s.

Hunting in Colonial Africa

As touristic hunting in Africa was growing in both popularity and accessibility, the continent was also experiencing massive political transformation. In December 1884 and into the initial weeks of 1885, representatives from an array of European nations with imperial designs gathered in Berlin to quite literally carve up Africa into a series of colonial empires. No African leaders—or Africans of any sort, for that matter—were invited to the proceedings. Although American representatives were present, they were primarily interested in protecting Liberia, the United States' slave resettlement project on Africa's western coast, and were otherwise uninterested in empire on the continent. However, America was the exception. Officials from an assortment of European states, which had made prior claims on African territory, horse-traded with their fellow representatives during their stay in the German capital. Territorial claims and negotiations with local African leaders had long preceded the gathering in Berlin, but if the commencement of the durable process of European colonial overrule of Africa could be reduced to a single moment or event, it would be this conference. The final agreement determined that imperial powers had to demonstrate "effective occupation" of the land they claimed in order to legitimize their authority. This stipulation prompted widespread military conquests, though European armies had already invaded a handful of lands before Berlin; collectively, these incursions came to be known as the "scramble for Africa." Although many Africans resisted the onslaught, they were badly outgunned, and within a few decades, Africa had been carved up into a series of European colonial empires.

The lack of formal European control over the entirety of Africa hadn't exactly been a prohibitive impediment to foreign hunters before Berlin, but entering new lands had often required some type of negotiation with local African rulers to secure the requisite permission to proceed. With the onset of European imperial overrule, hunters could now largely dispense with these formalities.

Although a successful European invasion of Africa had for centuries been unthinkable, medical advances, including the ability to mass produce quinine to protect against malaria, and the Industrial Revolution's propulsion of military technology enabled these invading forces to utilize these newfound advantages to lethal effect. This technological superiority was perhaps most profoundly and succinctly captured in Hilaire Belloc's poem

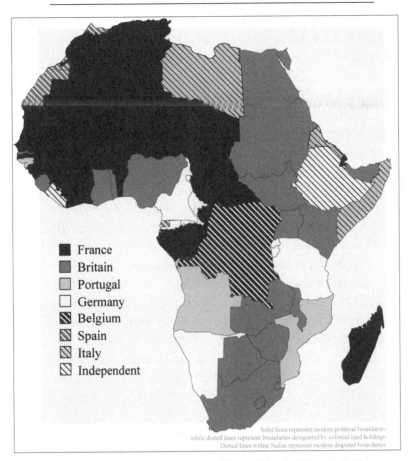

Solid lines represent modern political boundaries,
while dotted lines represent boundaries designated by colonial land holdings.
Dotted lines within Sudan represent modern disputed boundaries.

MAP 2.2 European colonial empires in Africa. *Map by Maggie Bridges.*

"The Modern Traveler," which includes a passage that highlights the supremacy that European armies enjoyed owing to their access to the Maxim gun, the first recoil-operated machine gun, which had been invented in 1884: "Whatever happens, we have got / The Maxim gun, and they have not."[20] Local rivalries, European duplicity, the devastating demographic impact of the outflows of slaves, and a number of other factors doomed those Africans who opted to try to defend the continent, each eventually falling to these foreign invaders.

If these far-reaching developments ravaged African societies, thrusting them into a decades-long subservience that was enforced via real and potential imperial violence, these changes constituted a boon for the fledgling safari industry. Prime hunting grounds were newly accessible, while colonial regimes sharply curtailed hunting by Africans, now labeling what locals had done for centuries or longer as "poaching." Moreover, European commercial hunting operators could proceed knowing that the security of their staff and clients was virtually absolute, while Africans could be coerced to provide vital labor to these outfitters. Although paid hunting safaris had begun rather humbly, they emerged as a legitimate industry in the southern and eastern parts of the continent, where the British and, to a lesser extent, the Portuguese held extensive colonial territory. These newly opened lands attracted some of the world's highest-profile figures, eager to engage in the African hunting experience as the colonial era in Africa matured from its origins in the nineteenth century into the first half of the ensuing century.

Some two decades before Teddy Roosevelt's hunting expedition, the 1891 safari of Lord Randolph Churchill illustrates the elevated status and means of both the paying clientele and the various safari operators in Africa. A British parliamentarian and high-ranking government official, Churchill retreated to South Africa in 1891 to try to recover his deteriorating health, attributable to the contraction of syphilis as well as a series of political setbacks. But, even in this subdued state, there was nothing discreet about his safari experience: Churchill had calculated that a highly publicized expedition could return him to political, or at least social, prominence. Thus, he prepared for a long safari, intending to file with the press a series of accounts of his observations and exploits. For Lord Churchill, like many others who followed him, "the safari was not so much a wilderness hunting adventure as it was a stage, a set on which to earn attention and applause."[21]

Consequently, to where and for how long Churchill traveled—the Cape Colony, the Transvaal (northeastern South Africa), and Rhodesia (Zimbabwe), covering some 2,500 miles and six months—was not nearly as important as were his dispatches from the field. This correspondence was published by the British newspaper the *Daily Graphic*, for a princely sum of £100 per article, all of which was aggregated and republished in 1892 as *Men, Mines and Animals in South Africa*. The safari included four Cape wagons with some 20 tons of provisions, including tinned meat and pressed vegetables from London, twenty-four rifles and shotguns, and, most remarkably, a piano!

Upon the conclusion of the safari, in December 1891, Churchill reached Cape Town and stayed with Cecil Rhodes, the mining magnate and South African politician. When friends inquired why he had stayed with his host, as he supposedly did not enjoy Rhodes's company, Churchill declared, "My dear fellow, it's the only place in this God-forsaken country where I can get Perrier-Jouet '74 [a coveted champagne]."[22]

This degree of lavishness was rapidly becoming normative, manifested in and spurred on by "celebrity" expeditions such as Churchill's. A different type of individual was now venturing to Africa as a hunter-tourist. These sportsmen were among Europe's elite, and they were soon joined by their American counterparts. By the end of the century, this undertaking was no longer the exclusive domain of the "pioneering, unpaid hunters who lived for the free, wild life of the chase."[23] Per author Bartle Bull, the new hunters were tourists, "essentially on a sporting holiday. . . . Some, despite Randolph Churchill's disdain, were women, and often far better in the field than he. Gradually, the white faces at the camps came to represent two different worlds, as overseas clients paid a new breed of [white] professional hunter to introduce them to the African bush."[24]

Luminaries: Frederick Selous and Teddy Roosevelt

One of these new professional hunters was Frederick Selous, who was more of a commercial safari leader than a tourist-hunter. As with Selous's predecessors, tales of his exploits further piqued curiosity about Africa, prompting at least some consumers of his written adventures to travel to the continent themselves. A renowned hunter and guide, Selous also advanced scientific knowledge of areas that now compose the country of Zimbabwe. If Selous was the adventurer, though, the famed novelist H. Rider Haggard was his publicist, so to speak.

Haggard first arrived in South Africa in 1875 at the age of nineteen and would establish himself as a low- to mid-level bureaucrat before returning to England in 1882. These years had a profound effect on his life, helping fuel the creative imagination that would inspire his Africa-based literature. Stirred by Selous's exploits, including harrowing escapes from man and beast, and further intrigued by contemporaneous discoveries of extraordinary mineral wealth in Africa's soils and of its great civilizations, such as Great Zimbabwe, Haggard created the fictional hero Allan Quatermain. The character was a white hunter who featured most famously in *King Solomon's Mines* (1885), a book that Haggard dedicated to "big and little boys," as well as in a series of other novels. As Bartle Bull has contended, Haggard's works became a "magic inspiration for generations of young Englishmen, turning their interests to the adventures of empire; in the long English winters, controlled by the disciplines of boarding school and bound in by

Victorian and Edwardian convention, the seeming freedom of Africa, with its warm horizons and impossible animals, became a bright magnet."[25] In fact, Quatermain was featured in more than fourteen novels, and his influence and inspiration reached far beyond the British Isles. Haggard's work has been translated into at least nineteen languages and made into at least seven movies, while *King Solomon's Mines* went through thirteen printings in its inaugural year in the United States. A 1950 film version was immensely popular, winning an Academy Award for Best Color Photography.

Although Selous had no idea that he would play such an important role in African-themed popular culture for Western consumption, by the 1880s, his reputation as a hunter and guide was firmly established. He had by then been hired as a paid safari guide, most notably "discovering" on a journey in 1888 the limestone caves and blue subterranean lake at Sinoia in Mashonaland (part of contemporary northern Zimbabwe), which is now a National Park. In 1881, he had also published *A Hunter's Wanderings in Africa: Being a Narrative of Nine Years Spent amongst the Game of the Far Interior of South Africa.* By the arrival of the new century, the "global hunting fraternity recognized Selous as the greatest outdoorsman of his time."[26] Ultimately, he played a key role in ushering in the professional hunting safari that would come to flourish in colonial Africa and remained active in the industry into the second decade of the twentieth century.

Big President, Big Personality: The Immediate and Durable Impact of the Roosevelt Safari

There was arguably not a more ardent admirer of Frederick Selous than Teddy Roosevelt. By 1897, when Roosevelt was serving as the assistant secretary of the navy, he and Selous had already established a "rich, personal correspondence, with Roosevelt unusually deferential."[27] Moreover, Roosevelt regularly gathered his four sons and read aloud to them his favorite passages from Selous's *A Hunter's Wanderings.*[28] After Roosevelt assumed the presidency in 1901, he hosted Selous in the White House, further motivating him to visit Africa. As Roosevelt prepared to step aside upon the conclusion of his second term, he set his sights squarely on the continent. The larger-than-life president, at fifty years old, was ready to fulfill his own African dreams, and in so doing help precipitate the "booming trade in American safari clients, which became the financial core of the safari business."[29]

As the United States lacked an African empire of its own, Roosevelt was poised to bring "exotic" Africa to the American masses through his dispatches to various newspapers and *Scribner's* magazine. The resultant income helped finance the expedition, which traversed the modern-day nations of Kenya, Uganda, South Sudan, Sudan, and the Congo, augmenting the funding that business magnate Andrew Carnegie had already provided and would continue to provide following the commencement of the safari. In Roosevelt's own words, by heading to Africa he was preparing to visit "these greatest of the world's great hunting grounds," helping open up the continent just as intrepid sorts had done in the American West.[30] This proclamation infused the expedition with a magnitude that Africa seemingly warranted and further fed the Western idealization and imagination of the continent. Yet these written accounts from the field were not the only items that would be conveyed back to America. The Smithsonian Institute and American Museum of National History contracted Roosevelt to collect species that could then be displayed or at least preserved in these museums' holdings (fig. 2.1).

FIGURE 2.1 Specimens from Roosevelt's African safari being worked on in the taxidermy workroom in the National Museum of Natural History.

In order to realize his ambitious plans, Roosevelt, like his predecessors, required assistance from large numbers of Africans—eventually totaling more than two thousand over the course of his year-long safari—who served as trackers, gun bearers, guides, porters, tent boys, horse boys, cooks, skinners, and soldiers.[31] His safari, for some time thereafter the largest ever undertaken in Kenya, employed 265 porters alone, who collectively formed a line over a mile long, all trailing the unfurled American flag that fronted the caravan. The copious and cumbersome supplies and provisions restricted the safari to roughly 10 miles per day. Yet, even in a rare moment when Roosevelt attempted to compliment the Africans who hauled this massive collection of safari miscellany, Roosevelt patronizingly referred to them as "strong, patient, childlike savages," using language that would have been consistent with many contemporaneous Westerners' impressions of the continent's indigenous residents.

For all of Roosevelt's legitimate conservation credentials, forged and burnished through the establishment of the US Forest Service and the creation of several national parks, he seemingly left these distinguishing sentiments behind in America as he took aim at Africa's wildlife. Although he repeatedly declared that he would not "do any butchering," that's exactly what he did. Among other violations of contemporaneous hunting protocols, Roosevelt and his son, Kermit, who joined him on the expedition, often took shots from long distances without first stalking the prey. Thus, they often wounded, rather than killed, the animals even more than would otherwise be expected, as the ex-president had bad vision and was apparently an unreliable shot. In general, he and Kermit shot many more animals than were required for the collection of specimens Roosevelt was contracted to amass. The most egregious example of this habitual overshooting was the slaying in southern Sudan of nine white rhinoceros, including four cows and a calf, and the wounding of two other calves. Roosevelt was allegedly aware that these magnificent animals had already been hunted to extinction in Southern Africa and were on the verge of disappearing from the East African landscape as well, but he claimed that although his license only allowed for six, he wanted to gather two family groups for the museums, each featuring a calf. In fact, Roosevelt and Kermit shot approximately one third of all the white rhinoceros they encountered, such that even to this day the site of this undertaking is known as "Rhino Camp."[32]

Although Roosevelt may have awed his American sponsors with this haul, the fraternity of African-based, white safari guides and hunters was appalled. Some of them generously attributed Roosevelt's immoderation to his "Americanness," which in this context indicated that a hunter was "more interested in good results than good technique."[33] Conversely, local European hunters by and large embraced the chase, the endeavor itself, rather than focusing on the kill. The underlying idea was that the hunt needed to be at least somewhat fair and the hunter engaged in a struggle between man and beast in which the latter stood at least a fighting chance. To this end, stalking was encouraged, shooting females was discouraged so as not to jeopardize reproduction and replenishment, shooting game at waterholes was anathema—especially at night—and wounded animals were to be finished off rather than simply left to stagger off and die. Hunting was newly imbued with a scrupulousness and sense of honor, or at least integrity, that men such as Roosevelt casually disregarded.

Excesses: The Golden Age of Safari

Even though Roosevelt's actions may have contravened local protocols, accounts of his exploits spawned waves of tourist-hunters to follow in his footsteps. Scholars agree that no single visitor did more to precipitate an explosion in the safari industry than did the former US president, who has been described as "the archetype of the new safari client."[34] These newly arriving sportsmen flocked to an assortment of British colonial sites in East Africa, primarily including Kenya, on whose Athi Plains it was said that one was more likely to be hurt by a bullet than a lion, but also Tanganyika (Tanzania) and Uganda, helping prompt the proliferation of regional safari operators. These local guides included Baron Bror Blixen, the husband of Isak Dinesen (Karen Blixen's pseudonym), and Dinesen's lover, Denys Finch Hatton, all of whom were featured in the highly acclaimed film, *Out of Africa* (1985), which starred Meryl Streep and Robert Redford and was based on Dinesen's 1937 book of the same name.

Although these East African destinations experienced a touristic setback during the First World War, the region was again ascendant during the ensuing Roaring Twenties. The wealth generated by the booming postwar Western economies led many affluent hunter-tourists to the eastern and southern regions of the continent. East African safaris, in particular, exemplified luxury, which one observer described as "dinners served on linen tablecloths accompanied by fine wine while tracking big game though the bush."[35] Furthermore, safaris were no longer truly dangerous for the client, as the professional hunter and his African staff were now charged with insulating these foreign visitors from all manner of risks.

The Kenyan city of Nairobi greatly transformed as a result of the hunting safari. It had been founded as a railroad depot in 1899 yet within eight short years had become a tourism hub for big-game hunting and was made the capital of the colony. Subsequently, Nairobi, and Kenya more generally, acquired a hedonistic reputation among foreigners, manifested by a joke that circulated in England: "Are you married, or do you live in Kenya?" This decadent atmosphere correspondingly gave birth to a new kind of luxury in the bush—what has been dubbed the "champagne safari."[36] Lord Cranworth, an English baron and local resident in Nairobi at this time, would remark regarding the local safari boom that it was a time when "princes, peers, and American magnates poured out into the city in one continual stream."[37]

Before the Great Depression, this process of touristic infusion and corresponding local development and settlement continued to accelerate, with both existing and newly arriving settlers further invigorating this swelling colonial space. As part of this process, hunting increasingly became a commercial endeavor. Foreign clients came to expect "not merely trophies, but high times, an African extension of the privileged life that entertained them, or bored them, in Biarritze and St. Moritz, in the West End and Newport. Like polo and yachting, safaris combined excitement with luxury."[38]

This social and recreational intemperance naturally spilled over into the hunting fields, including on the famed Serengeti plains, which stretch across Tanzania into Kenya. Probably the most egregious example of this profligate comportment was the case of two American hunters, Leslie Simpson and Stewart Edward White, who, while on safari in the 1920s in Tanganyika, killed a total of 323 lions between them, prompting the alarmed British colonial government to limit hunters to five lions each.[39] Local hunters even derisively coined an affliction, "American trigger itch," to describe this overindulgence. The Scotsman, John Alexander (J. A.) Hunter, experienced exactly this type of behavior while he was leading two American clients to the Ngorongoro crater in Tanganyika. Apparently, they shot until their guns were too hot to hold and at night slept with revolvers tied to their wrists, prompting Hunter to declare, "It's not the wild beasts that are the problem. It's the clients."[40]

The introduction of the motor vehicle into the safari also fueled this age of hunting overkill. Forced labor schemes in the colonies compelled Africans to, among other things, construct roads, allowing foreign tourist-hunters to more easily reach the most remote animal habitats. Cars were first introduced on safari in the 1910s and were more common in the 1920s, and by the 1930s their impact had been made abundantly clear to local officials. In 1932, for example, the Kenyan game warden declared that "transport over almost all of the shooting country in Kenya is now mainly mechanical; the foot safari is a thing of the past." As one car-aided, candid hunter rued, "My trophies represent neither skill nor courage."[41] Moreover, the famous English safari guide Philip Percival lamented that owing to lions' propensity to remain still, fixedly watching the cars that were used for hunting, "When the motorcar entered the field, lion hunting as a sport went out. True, the sportsman is not in the car, but for all the sport there is in it he might just as well be."[42] Further, many clients took to shooting game from automobiles, never leaving the vehicles, which predictably prompted outrage among local, professional (white) hunters. In general, the motorized hunt could not have been more different from the expeditions that the initial foreign hunters, such as Cornwallis Harris and Gordon Cumming, had undertaken. No doubt, these two pioneers would have been rolling in their graves at the sight of a motor car approaching a prized specimen so that its cossetted passenger could make the kill.

Although this type of client may have appalled hardened outdoorsmen, hunter-tourists who embodied the masculinity and nobleness of the hunts of yesteryear also continued to arrive in Africa. Not surprisingly, given his oversized allocation of masculinity and ego, the renowned novelist Ernest Hemingway was one of these individuals. The Great Depression notwithstanding, in 1933 the already-famous author secured the sizable sum of £4,400 from his uncle to finance a ten-week hunting safari, which he would undertake with his wife, Pauline Pfeiffer. Just as Teddy Roosevelt had done some decades previously, Hemingway hired Philip Percival as his safari guide.[43] In fact, there were many connections between the iconic author and the former president. The safari strongly affected both men, as each "saw similarities to their beloved American West, and both had ideas of 'manliness' that were rooted in hunting and guns."[44]

Percival made an enduring impact on Hemingway, prompting the author to model two characters in his works on this professional hunting guide, while both the Englishman and American called each other "Pop." Hemingway impressed Percival, too. At times, the guide paid the author the "professional's compliment" of permitting Hemingway to hunt with his personal gun bearer, M'Cola. In turn, these African staff members, including M'Cola, also impressed Hemingway. The author later remarked that M'Cola took good care of him in the bush, while from another African on safari Hemingway learned a bush trick he shared with his hunting friends in Wyoming, which entailed "cutting open the stomach of a dead reedbuck and turning it inside out, thereby making a sack to hold the liver and kidneys, which was then sewn up and carried over the shoulder on the end of a pole."[45]

Like so many other hunter-authors, the principle touristic impact that Hemingway's safari experiences had was delivered via his writings, in this case a book entitled *The Green Hills of Africa* and two short stories, "The Short Happy Life of Francis Macomber" and "The Snows of Kilimanjaro." Although *Green Hills* was not nearly as popular as the short stories, its "picture of the land and the safari are wonderfully vivid and to know what a hunting safari was like in 1934, there is no better source."[46] More significantly from a touristic perspective, many readers first heard of Kilimanjaro through Hemingway and many "formed their entire idea of safari life and East Africa through these two stories."[47] Arguably even more importantly, both stories would eventually make it to the big screen, further popularizing these representations of Africa.

While Hemingway and others brought a mythical, exotic, and wild Africa to reading audiences, some particularly affluent members of this crowd brought themselves to Africa—to hunt, yes, but also to engage in a wide variety of debauchery. A group of these hedonistic settlers, some of whom were safari guides, converged on the Wanjohi Valley in central Kenya, known as "Happy Valley," and were correspondingly coined the "Happy Valley set." From roughly the 1920s to the 1940s, this largely British community became notorious for the serial infidelity in which its members engaged, their pervasive drug use, and, in general, their decadent lifestyles.

Although this assortment of foreign elites was largely incestuous, they also welcomed foreign safari clients and spouses and, at times, seduced some of them. In practice, safari, hunting, and licentiousness were closely intertwined, embodied by individual members of the set, such as Bror Blixen, who has been described as "a gregarious rogue, a man's man and a lady's man, delighted to drink and seduce all night, and stalk and shoot all day. As one of his clients once warned another client, when on safari with Blixen it was best to bring an extra woman so that he would be too busy to sleep with your wife."[48] Surrounded by the finest luxuries, breathtaking landscapes, droves of African servants, and abundant game, visitors were treated to an otherworldly experience. Bartle Bull captures this milieu well, writing, "With the entire colony as one extended shooting estate, with polo and naked Africans visible from the same veranda, surrounded by an exoticism that made it easy to feel the abandon of a perpetual costume party, the Happy Valley set danced in a fantasy. But for some safari clients, they added a scandalous glamor to the excitements of Africa."[49]

The Happy Valley set's dissolute reputation seemed to suggest to safari clients that anything was permissible in this context. The Scottish safari guide J. A. Hunter, for example, had, as one of his first clients, a French count who "believed that each man should do what he did best." For the count, that apparently meant drinking, and the implication was that for Hunter, that meant hunting. It is unclear what that meant for the accompanying countess. But according to Hunter, "One night, the Countess raised the flap of my tent and seated herself on my cot in a lace nightgown, holding a beer glass of whiskey in one hand. 'Countess,' I inquired, 'Where is your husband?' 'Hunter,' she replied in annoyance, 'You Englishman [*sic*] ask the strangest questions.'"[50]

Another excessive dimension to this period was the exploitative and abusive nature of African laborers' participation in the hunting safari industry. The conditions under which these workers toiled were acutely difficult. Although technically illegal, floggings were daily occurrences, with Europeans regularly employing the notorious hippo-hide whip to "remind" Africans of the imposed racial hierarchy. So strong was this connection between hippo and whip that the Swahili word for hippo, *kiboko*, became in European dictionaries the word for "whip." Commenting on Teddy Roosevelt's infamous 1909 safari, an American visitor, Edgar Bronson, casually justified this form of punishment: "Mr. Roosevelt will have to close his eyes or accustom himself to occasional severe floggings . . . for without it no safari could be held together for a fortnight."[51] African laborers endured this abuse for scant material award. For example, before the First World War, porters earned roughly £1 per month, and even though some skilled safari workers (e.g., gun bearers and cooks) could potentially earn four times that, the trekking season was limited to three to five months, rendering all of these jobs seasonal.[52] By contrast, a European female clerk made roughly £10 per month. If wages had been color blind, the hunting safari industry would have been financially unviable.[53]

With the steady establishment of road and other transport networks in the initial decades of the twentieth century, the African porter was a rapidly disappearing figure, even if he continued to provide vital service to hunting safari outfits. For example, as late as 1928, one safari set out with "100 porters, two skinners, two mess boys, and a head man."[54] Going forward, transportation advances, coupled with the transition away from hunting excursions, greatly reduced the numbers of Africans employed on safaris. Those who remained in the industry, however, increasingly professionalized, primarily working as trackers and guides but also as cooks and servers at safari lodges, regularly interacting with sojourning clientele. Even so, racist, or at least racialist, sentiments continued to cloud these interactions. European settlers routinely informed foreign tourists that Africans were lazy, aiming to reinforce the racial hierarchy vital to the perpetuation of the various colonial projects. Similarly, carrying their own racial baggage, many of these foreign visitors uncritically consumed these characterizations, regardless of how assiduous the Africans who were servicing them were.

The Gradual Decline of the Hunting Safari

Perhaps the only silver lining for Africa's fauna during this period of social and sporting excess was that, from the 1930s, colonial officials reactively tightened game laws and introduced a series of conservation initiatives. These local administrators recognized that hunting at existing rates was unsustainable and was rapidly stripping the colonies of a valuable touristic resource. Without restrictions on hunters, wildlife populations would soon be irreparably depleted or, in some cases, permanently exhausted. This shift in administrative sentiment by no means precluded or even deterred foreigners from traveling to the continent to shoot Africa's legendary game. However, the financial impact of the Depression, which deprived many would-be tourist-hunters of the funds they needed to engage in this expensive pursuit, coupled with the raft of new policies and laws intended to conserve Africa's wildlife, meant that adjustments had to be made. As outlined above, local observers also grew alarmed at the increasing usage of the motor car to track and kill game, a clear transgression of regional hunting protocol. Over time, these factors collectively prompted the gradual replacement of the rifle with the camera to "shoot" African fauna, fundamentally altering the very meaning of the term "safari."

Conservation efforts in Africa had, in fact, commenced well before the 1930s. African hunters had been sustainably hunting various species for millennia, while even from the initial decades of the Dutch settlement at the Cape in South Africa in the 1650s, farmers were limited to a single rhino, hippo, and eland each year. But going forward, concerns over Africa's big game had been notably muted, with attendant consequences. In the early 1930s, however, the European colonial powers agreed upon the Convention Relative to the Preservation of Fauna and Flora in their Natural State, more succinctly and commonly known as the London Convention of 1933. Given its scope and ambition, it has been referred to as the "Magna Carta of wildlife conservation," while historian Edward Steinhart has declared that it was "the high point of institutionalized global nature protection before the Second World War."[55] The resultant limitations placed on human settlement and the establishment of many of the region's national parks, which provided sanctuary for animals, were among the many aspects of the convention that prompted these laudatory proclamations.

Yet these conservation measures also negatively affected many Africans, who had no voice in their formulation. In particular, colonial regimes forcibly removed many communities from areas newly designated as wildlife reserves without adequate compensation for their lands. Furthermore, these relocated peoples consequently lost access to vital resources, such as "grazing fields for cattle, hunting grounds, medicinal plants, firewood, and thatching grass."[56] Losing access to this land also had spiritual dimensions, as their ancestors, who according to local belief systems played important, ongoing roles in the well-being of the community, were both interred and ever-present in these spaces. Consequently, these relocated residents were "alienated from their natural environment and also lost some of the accumulated knowledge and cultural values associated with it."[57] Just as Europeans had previously maligned African hunting techniques, they now justified these forced removals by denigrating indigenous conservation and environmental practices.

As European conservation measures accelerated following the conclusion of the Second World War and colonial governments deemed big game significantly more lucrative alive than dead, hunting safaris continued to decline in number. To be sure, they persisted in certain settings, but the "Golden Age of Safari" had incontrovertibly passed. Beyond colonial officials' financial calculations and associated policies, increasingly absent were some of the important motivations for hunting. As colonial regimes began to recede, the glamor and appeal of the hunting safari diminished. Indeed, as colonialism gradually faded, "the illusions associated with the hunting safari could no longer be maintained."[58] More importantly, over time the safari had largely been reduced to "just hunting" and a "lot less like the ultimate experience of Western man dominating African nature."[59]

The Survival of the Great Hunting Safari on the Big Screen

Even as the African hunting safari declined, Hollywood breathed new life into it on the big screen. These films helped keep the endeavor alive in the nostalgic imaginations of moviegoers worldwide and prompted at least some of them to book vacations to the continent, eager to experience a time long past. Building upon the success of the 1950 release of *King Solomon's Mines*, MGM Studios produced the box office sensation *Mogambo*, starring Clark Gable, Ava Gardner, Donald Sinden, and Grace Kelly, with Gable cast as a big-game hunter. The film was shot primarily in Kenya but also in the French Congo (Republic of the Congo) and Uganda. A three-hundred-tent expedition formed for the production constituted the largest safari in Kenyan history. To nourish the massive operation, Sinden recalled that "Ten White Hunters were seconded to our unit for our protection and to provide fresh meat."[60] Underscoring the connection between real-life hunters on the ground in Africa and Hollywood's rendition of this enterprise was the presence on the set of Bunny Allen, a renowned British hunter and safari guide based in Kenya, who offered on-site technical advice just as he had done for *King Solomon's Mines* and *The African Queen* (1951) and would do for other films; he also served as Clark Gable's stunt double. Ultimately, Grace Kelly won a Best Supporting Actress Golden Globe Award for her performance in *Mogambo* and the film was nominated for two Oscars, including Best Actress in a Leading Role for Gardner and Best Actress in a Supporting Role for Kelly.

Some three decades later, the 1985 film *Out of Africa*, directed by Sydney Pollack, may have provided the hunting safari in Africa its greatest and most touristically significant treatment. By this time, the hunting safari was largely relegated to history, as even Kenya had banned the shooting of all big game in 1977. However, this film brought the undertaking back to worldwide audiences and reinvigorated the nostalgia for a colonial context never to be duplicated. Robert Redford was cast as Denys Finch Hatton, a big-game hunter, while Baron Bror Blixen, played by Klaus Maria Brandauer, was much more interested in safari than he was in either of his avowed livelihoods: running cattle and coffee farms. Production required a staggering ten thousand actors and cost roughly $30 million, but the film was wildly successful, winning seven Academy Awards, including Best Picture and Best Director. The Oscar for Best Cinematography was perhaps the most important from a touristic perspective, as the stunning landscapes generated significant interest in traveling to Kenya and, more broadly, to Africa to engage in camera safaris. This romantic, idealistic portrayal of colonial-era Africa generated a "tourism bump" among visitors who, however unrealistically, deemed that they could somehow re-experience that long-past time and place.

OVER THE course of its existence, the hunting expedition in Africa underwent significant transformation. Initially, local white hunters traversed lands largely or completely unknown to Westerners, felling seemingly inexhaustible big game as they proceeded. Over time, these types of intrepid individuals, who had typically carved out livelihoods selling ivory and hides, were hired to lead wealthy foreign clients in tightly managed, typically shorter, hunting expeditions, marking the birth of the hunting safari and the associated white safari guide, all relying on multitudes of African functionaries to facilitate these experiences. Gradually, however, shifting attitudes among colonial officials and moral sentiments among tourists rendered the camera the preferred method to "shoot" Africa's famed wildlife. Colonial officials realized that conservation of this fauna meant more to their balance sheets than did the slaying of these animals. Under constant pressure to increase contributions to the various metropolitan governments' coffers, European colonial administrations in Africa also sought other ways to generate revenue via tourism, none of which involved the extermination of a valuable resource. It is to these efforts that we turn in the next chapter.

CHAPTER THREE

Profits and Propaganda

Tourism in Colonial Africa

South Africa is one of the most modern and progressive sections of the world . . .
luxurious hotels and railroads, delightful golf and yachting clubs, superb motor
roads, and all the comforts and conveniences of modern civilization. . . .
But there is also the immensely picturesque native side . . . so alluring to the
tourist . . . the quaint Kraal life . . . wild war dances . . . weird, age-old tribal
customs . . . the dignified Zulu chief and his retinue of dusky wives . . . stalwart
warriors with their spears and shields . . . the primitive musical instruments . . .
women's fantastic headdresses . . . the superstitious mummery of the witch doctor.
And all this within easy access for the tourist, as are all the other matchless
wonders of South Africa . . . and many other wonderful features of this . . . land
of charm, contrast, mystery, beauty . . . and an ideal climate.

> —A South African government advertisement placed in the
> American magazine *Travel*, promoting the country's dual
> "modern" and "primitive" touristic appeal, October 1929

There was a difference between me and others in my neighborhood because
what I could afford, others could not. Although my salary wasn't much, I
could still count on tips. And, I was actually able to build myself a house.
I could also buy clothing for my mother—scarves and fabrics—so, again,
there was a noticeable difference between my mother's grooming habits and
appearance and those of other guys' mothers.

> —Rodrigues Pelembe, an African hotel employee, who worked in
> the early 1970s in Lourenço Marques (now Maputo), the capital
> city of Mozambique, identifying some of the tangible benefits that
> employment in the colonial-era tourist industry afforded him, 2017

FOLLOWING THE consolidation of imperial control over most of Africa in the decades following the Berlin Conference of 1884–85, when a handful of European nations carved the continent into colonial empires, overseas tourists began to trickle into these "exotic" domains. Over time, some of these trickles turned into streams, with visitors flocking to a series of destinations, including the Kenyan savanna, Victoria Falls, and Cape Town. In order to cultivate and facilitate these influxes of tourists, who were not interested in hunting safaris, colonial regimes either built the requisite tourism infrastructure or encouraged private investors to do so.

Before the Second World War, touristic promotion was primarily intended to generate revenues to help offset the considerable operational costs of empire. However, as the maintenance of empires grew increasingly untenable from the 1950s onward, colonial administrations welcomed both the financial and propagandistic value that tourism produced to perpetuate their presence in Africa.

One particularly attractive destination throughout this imperial period was South Africa. In addition to its temperate climate and physical appeal, it also featured the big game that increasing numbers of tourists wanted to observe and photograph rather than hunt. Even the introduction of the racially oppressive apartheid regime in 1948 did little to dent these inflows. In fact, the South African state actively marketed the country as a viable and pleasurable destination, and tourists duly responded, arriving in ever-increasing numbers. Only in the late 1970s, following the civil unrest sparked by the uprising in Soweto, a Johannesburg township, and its violent aftermath, did tourists begin to pause, questioning their own safety and the morality of the country's administration. Yet foreign visitors continued to arrive all the way up to the complete dismantlement of apartheid in 1994, although in smaller numbers.

Invisible in these various touristic processes were the African laborers, such as Rodrigues Pelembe, whose testimony appeared at the outset of this chapter. These workers comprised the foundation of the industry but were generally underpaid and forced to endure both physical and mental abuse by their white overseers, consistent with colonial-era racial conventions. However, in comparison to toiling in the mines or on settlers' farms, which constituted the livelihood for millions of Africans over the course of the colonial period, these employees faced much less dangerous working conditions. Further, for some of these laborers, steady wages and regular interaction with foreign tourists generated opportunities for social ascension.

This chapter examines the inception and expansion of tourism in colonial Africa, including apartheid-era South Africa, otherwise unassociated with the various hunting exploits considered in the preceding chapter. In most settings, tourist industries were generated from scratch. As colonial regimes increasingly acknowledged the financial potential of tourism, they invested resources in its development. The British and, to a lesser degree, the Portuguese enjoyed colonial possessions that featured more of what tourists wanted, namely big game, beaches, and moderate climates. Conversely, West Africa, the site of most of France's colonial territory on the continent, lacked these reliable attractions; its North African colonies, with their extensive beaches, were the exception to this generalization, though big game was largely absent in these possessions. Eventually, colonial administrations also identified the propagandistic utility of tourism in support of and, following the Second World War, in defense of their colonial projects. Tourism offered an opportunity to showcase "responsible colonialism" to a global audience. Finally, the chapter considers the African laborers who facilitated the establishment and growth of colonial-era tourism industries on the continent, always operating in the background as they navigated the assortment of exacting imperial milieus.

To Africa? Tourism to Colonial Africa before the Second World War

When the delegates from the various European imperial nations sat down at the table in Berlin to delineate their African empires, they weren't claiming lands based on their respective touristic potential. Beautiful beaches or abundant big game, the hallmarks of contemporary African tourism, were completely peripheral to these representatives' imperial designs. Yet as we have seen, tourists—first the intrepid variety, followed by more cautious types—will go virtually anywhere, especially locations perceived as exotic. The first tourists to Africa traveled in the footsteps of explorers, hunters, missionaries, and merchants. As with earlier travel to the continent, tourism to Africa during the early colonial period was an endeavor that entailed considerable cost. Transportation remained both slow and expensive, rendering this undertaking exclusively for the well-to-do, though it did retain its luxurious features. As one observer has contended, though perhaps somewhat hyperbolically, "Under the protection of colonial powers and due to the perfect organization of travel agencies . . . these tourists traveled in complete luxury, enjoying the same guaranteed facilities as did European travelers in the resort towns of Interlaken (Switzerland) or Baden-Baden (Germany)."[1]

At the dawn of the twentieth century, there was little touristic activity on the continent, irrespective of how plush this endeavor might have been. Those visitors who did satisfy their curiosity generally traveled to places with sizeable white settlements, invariably located in the far northern and southern stretches of the continent and in a series of highlands. These locations featured moderate climates, thereby attracting European settlers in larger numbers. Consequently, these sites featured the fundamental components of touristic infrastructure, including transportation networks, lodging, and restaurants, while still offering a taste of the unfamiliar.

Following the end of the First World War, which in Africa included battles, rebellions, and unrest in an assortment of locations, international tourism began to take root, albeit modestly. These visitors were wealthy but also reasonably intrepid. Moreover, they often felt as though they were engaged in an endeavor that harkened back to an earlier day, penetrating the seemingly impenetrable "Dark Continent" and then returning home to impress friends and family with tales of their exploits. In many respects, they likened themselves to the Europeans who had preceded them in the previous century, while still demanding the comforts and conveniences that affluent travelers of this era expected.

In fact, this dualistic exercise of linking oneself to a more adventuresome, "primitive" past while embracing (Western) modernity, was common for early twentieth-century tourists. These travelers surrounded themselves with luxury, invoked empire, and enjoyed its myriad benefits, while casting their endeavors as embedded in a sea of African wilderness, surrounded by primal, indigenous subjects. Arguably, no setting highlighted these contradictions more exemplarily than colonial-era Victoria Falls, which featured vantage points from both Northern and Southern Rhodesia and was cultivated as a tourist destination as early as the turn of the twentieth century. Among the touristic infrastructure that British settlers on both sides of the Zambezi River established was the bridge, an "engineering wonder," which passed over the river in full view of the falls and the flagship Victoria Falls Hotel. In this resort setting, imperialism mixed with tourism to generate powerful propaganda related to the prodigious accomplishments of the British colonial project. In particular, it evoked the "Cape to Cairo" railway axis, the avowed ambition of English imperialist and gold and diamond mining magnate Cecil Rhodes. As geographer JoAnn McGregor has compellingly argued, "The striking combination of symbols of the power of nature and of triumphal British science along an important imperial axis gave an excessively jingoistic flavor to understandings of the Falls landscape. When the first train pulled into the Victoria Falls in April 1904, it flew a Union Jack and bore a board below its headlamp reading, 'We've got a long way to go.'"[2]

It was this heady mixture of progress and ambition, tempered with a much smaller dose of realism, which characterized the growth of Victoria Falls as a tourist destination. The natural wonder also appealed to visitors who were eager to access "authentic Africa," which in this case featured an untamed river, dramatic waterfalls, and a dimension of adventure. Local settlers were eager to capitalize on these perceptions, hastily opening hotels, restaurants, and curio shops. These locals "imagined, and then designed, a 'Real Africa,' where visitors could enjoy European comforts while they experienced Africa at its wildest."[3] This dialectical coupling of "civilization" and "luxury" embedded in an "untamed," "pristine," and alien land, embodied by throngs of "primitive" and "uncivilized" indigenous residents, suited both travelers and the various individuals and entities keen to profit from this enticing touristic admixture.

Once again, Thomas Cook & Son was among the agencies that were quickly on the scene, having sensed the potential touristic revenues associated with this emerging white playground. For the company, the opening of the railway line and resort was "an event second only in importance to the completion of the Cape to Cairo line itself."[4] In fact, Cook & Son attempted to parlay the imperial bravado of Cecil Rhodes's dream into touristic profits in 1922, when it organized the first commercial tour between Cape Town and Cairo, claiming that "the spirit of wild places can only be grasped on trek."[5] Meanwhile, the agency continued to tout Southern Africa as a salubrious, "European" destination, while successfully invoking Niagara Falls to cast its counterpart on the Zambezi as an equally appropriate "place of romance for lovers and honeymooners."[6] These successful marketing efforts drew, among others, the famed novelist Agatha Christie and her first husband, Archibald Christie, in 1922.

At the core of the regional touristic infrastructure was the landmark Victoria Falls Hotel, completed in 1904 (fig. 3.1). This facility was promoted as a place of luxury, replete with an array of comforts and amenities, which multiplied following a series of renovations during the 1920s. The hotel appealed to well-heeled men but also to women interested in "braving Africa." Notably, the logo of the hotel, which featured the Lion of Africa and the Sphinx of Egypt, invoked two of the continent's most recognizable

FIGURE 3.1   The Victoria Falls Hotel, c. 2005. *Photo by author.*

icons, while the white staff was particularly cosmopolitan: the first owner was Pierre Gavuzzi, who had worked at both the Carlton and Savoy hotels in London; the chef was French; the barman a Chicagoan; and the first waiters were Arabs. The hotel confirmed the Falls as a modern resort while "deploying symbols of a global tourist industry and of empire."[7]

As the official travel agent for the Cape Government and Rhodesia Railways, Cook & Son chronicled the construction of the hotel in its magazine, *The Excursionist,* and began offering tours to the site from Cape Town. A 1904 piece entitled "By Rail to Victoria Falls," generated by the agency declared that the tourist could "enjoy European luxury even here in the heart of Africa."[8] Some two and a half decades later, in November 1930, the agency was again employing similar promotional rhetoric, depicting the hotel as the natural accompaniment to one of Africa's most remarkable natural wonders: "There is a splendid and natural hotel at the Falls and during the season the fashionable throngs in the grounds and on the verandas are more reminiscent of a European spa than of a retreat in the interior of Africa."[9] Once again, the continent was being marketed as a destination that featured both comfort and ruggedness, modernity and primitiveness.

Unlikely Promoters from America: Edith Wharton, Martin Johnson, and Osa Johnson

Colonial governments and travel agencies weren't the only entities fueling the accelerated touristic activity in the decades immediately preceding the Second World War. A group of Americans, including the famous author Edith Wharton and the married couple Martin and Osa Johnson, played an unlikely role in this process. Wharton's contributions revolved around the French territory of Morocco while the Johnsons showcased Kenya in both film and books. In both cases, these American promoters of tourism in Africa brought the continent's peoples, landscapes, and wildlife alive for highly eager audiences.

By the time Edith Wharton traveled to Morocco in 1917, one year before the French colonial regime's official launch of tourism in the territory, she was already a famous author. Wharton was an avid supporter of France and, as a Francophile, had been living there during the First World War. In part, her travel to Morocco was to support the embattled French state and also to justify its occupation and control of the territory. Her 1920 book, *In Morocco*, would bring her experiences and observations in Morocco to Anglophone audiences everywhere, as well as serving as excellent propaganda for France. From a touristic perspective, the book helped promote Morocco as "a land of the Middle Ages, with old imperial cities, beautiful Moorish architecture, colorful, earthy people, and an intense physical environment, an Arabian Night fantasy world" a characterization that would prove highly durable.[10] As historian F. Robert Hunter argues, these images of Morocco are "presented in their most vivid and complete form" in Wharton's book, giving "American and British readers a compelling, almost irresistible reason for visiting the French colony."[11]

Wharton brought her readers back in time by linking Africa's ancient history to contemporary Morocco, suggesting that "there was no break in the links between past and present."[12] To highlight these "unbroken" connections, she crafted descriptions of the Moroccans that suggested their stark differences from more modern (i.e., Western) peoples. In Marrakesh, for example, she described "fanatics in sheepskins glowering from the guarded thresholds of the mosques, mad negroes standing naked in niches of walls raining incantations on passers-by, and fierce tribesmen with inland arms in their belts and the fighters' tuft of wiry fair escaping from camel's-hair turbans."[13] When not exoticizing Moroccan culture and its peoples, Wharton also assured readers that recent transportation and communications developments meant that tourism in the territory was swift, safe, and reasonably comfortable, important factors in a would-be traveler's destination deliberations.

Martin and Osa Johnson (fig. 3.2) arrived in Kenya shortly after Wharton left Morocco and would have a similar impact on their audiences. Hailing from Chanute, Kansas, the Johnsons traveled the globe, subsequently writing accounts of and generating films about their far-flung experiences. Africa was squarely on their map. The couple first traveled to the continent in 1921 as part of a year-long expedition, which yielded the feature film *Trailing Wild African Animals* (1923). They returned to the continent in 1924 for a three-year stay in northern Kenya at a place they called "Lake Paradise," at Mount Marsabit, near the Ethiopian border. Martin's 1928 book, *Safari: A Saga of the African Blue*, included photographs taken during this extended trip, while footage taken while at Lake Paradise featured in the films *Martin's Safari* (1928), *Simba: King of the Beasts* (1928), and Osa's *Four Years in Paradise* (1941). Collectively, this cinematic and literary output burnished Africa's already well-established "exotic" credentials. The couple also advanced notions of Africa as a place to escape from modernity, thereby

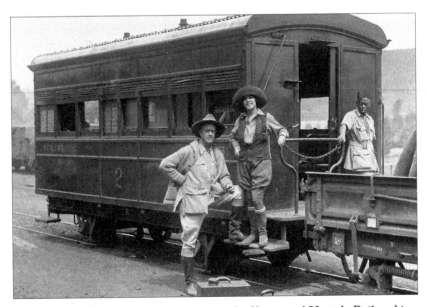

FIGURE 3.2 Martin and Osa Johnson on the Kenya and Uganda Railroad in Nairobi, 1925. *Used by permission of The Martin and Osa Johnson Safari Museum.*

reinforcing its reputation as a site of primal simplicity. Three more trips to Africa followed, with the Johnsons increasingly engaging in flights over notable natural features and faunal assortments. They subsequently generated a collection of films and written publications related to these more recent African adventures. In 1935, the couple even appeared together on a Wheaties cereal box; Osa was only the second woman (following Elinor Smith, also a female aviator, the previous year) to be featured on this iconic packaging. This peculiarly American form of celebrity suddenly had an African connection.

Although the Johnsons' efforts brought Africa to audiences around the world, for most of the 1930s, the Great Depression slowed the influx of foreign visitors to the continent. Moreover, the remoteness of many African sites and the hazards involved, even minimized as they were, ensured that touristic flows remained modest. That would all change, however, after the Second World War.

To Africa! Tourism to the Continent following the Second World War

Following the devastation and turmoil that marked the global conflict, European nations with imperial territories in Africa scrambled to reconsolidate control. They also sought to generate increased revenues from their overseas possessions, eager to rebuild their tattered homelands and pay war debts. To this end, colonial regimes increasingly identified tourism as a potential motor for economic development, as well as a sector that would help diversify economies that were primarily predicated on commodities and various natural resources. In the aftermath of the conflict, European countries with imperial territory in Africa also faced a new global community of war-weary nations that was more skeptical of empires and increasingly inclined to extend freedoms to populations that had historically been denied them. Consequently, colonial regimes increasingly eyed tourism as a way to both generate revenue and maintain control over their imperial territories by using the industry as propaganda to showcase the alleged benefits of their colonial projects and, in some cases, highlight the opportunities that the sector was providing for indigenous residents. Thus, from the late 1940s until the waves of decolonization that peaked in the early 1960s, these colonial regimes laid the groundwork for a viable, sustainable tourism industry on the continent.

Following the conclusion of the Second World War, European nations with territories in Africa, excepting Spain and Portugal, were badly ravaged.

The major European imperial powers, namely France and England, recovered reasonably quickly. However, all the colonizing nations faced increased pressure from both the United States, eager to promote supposedly "universal" freedoms around the world, and the Soviet Union, which condemned colonialism as an inherently exploitative system. While France and Great Britain could relatively easily push back against this two-pronged admonishment to substantively reform or abandon their empires, lesser imperial powers, such as Portugal and Belgium, recognized the propagandistic possibilities that tourism offered as a way to counter this mounting criticism. Interestingly, although both Lisbon and Brussels began to promote tourism to their African colonies, only the latter understood the campaign as purely promotional. In practice, the Belgians were not sincerely interested in foreigners traveling to its African possessions; rather, the touristic undertaking was solely intended to perpetuate empire. The numbers of visitors underscore this indifference. During the mid-1950s, the Belgian Congo attracted roughly ten thousand tourists annually, rendering the industry only the twelfth most important sector in the colonial economy. Conversely, Mozambique, the "gem" in the touristic crown of Portuguese Africa, drew hundreds of thousands of visitors a year during that period, with revenues from the industry buoying the economy.[14]

The strategic blending of tourism and propaganda proved to be highly efficacious. Would-be visitors were treated to films and travel brochures that highlighted the alleged civilizing missions of the various colonial projects, juxtaposed with alluring beaches and wildlife. Those tourists who subsequently traveled to Africa generally encountered sanitized versions of indigenous subjects' daily lives under imperial overrule. For example, visitors might observe an entertaining local dance performance, but would be kept far away from worksites at which forced laborers were toiling six days a week from sunup to sundown as part of their "development" under colonial rule.

Of course, most tourists only saw what they wanted to see, anyway. After all, one rarely goes on holiday seeking to witness social injustice or exploitation. It was through these powerful filters that the foreign tourist gazed at Africa. For example, following a visit in 1950 arranged by the *East African Standard* newspaper for American and British journalists to promote tourism in the region, a Mr. Bob Althuler of the American magazine *Feature* remarked, "I was surprised at the absence of cannibals, the industry, and foresight of the British, and was surprised that they did not exploit the

Natives, but really try to do what is best for the Africans and the country itself."[15] One could hardly have bribed an observer—and one with a large readership, no less—to provide a more praiseworthy advertisement for the British colonial project under the guise of tourism. Without knowing anything about Mr. Althuler's racial sentiments, the notion that Europeans were present to "do what is best for the Africans" (i.e., the so-called white man's burden) pervaded Western thinking and continued to provide the perfect cover for the array of acutely exploitative colonial projects. These types of touristic visits for journalists and others who could effectively publicize the "good work" that the Europeans were allegedly doing in far-flung lands were commonplace. In turn, these blinkered pieces drew ever-expanding numbers of tourists to Africa, eager to experience all that the continent had to offer, as long as, of course, it wasn't particularly disagreeable.

Although colonial regimes allocated funds for this increasingly important sector and aggressively devised ways to spin imperial projects into propagandistic exercises in "indigenous welfare," the fledgling industry on the continent also benefitted from external developments. As we established earlier, sea travel to reach various destinations in Africa required both extensive time and financial resources, which few individuals had at their disposal. And although the late 1920s and early 1930s marked the advent of commercial air travel, most tourists to the continent continued to arrive by sea. However, by the late 1950s, and certainly in the 1960s and beyond, technological advances in aviation facilitated commercial jet aircraft travel. Even if the costs remained prohibitive for many would-be tourists, the drastic reduction in travel time enabled many others to visit the continent. The *Sabena Revue*, the magazine of Belgium's national airline, trumpeted in 1959 that this new form of air travel had "solved a double problem: lack of time, and lack of money."[16] The introduction of the Boeing 747, the first wide-bodied jet, in 1970 further facilitated touristic flows to the continent.

Meanwhile, colonial officials were busy ensuring that these throngs of visitors had something to see, namely, Africa's famed wildlife. As colonial officials began to take stock of dwindling game populations, they grew increasingly alarmed that they were poised, in this new touristic context, to potentially lose such a valuable resource. In response, they accelerated a process that dates to 1925 with the founding of Prince Albert National Park (Virunga National Park) in the Belgian Congo and Kruger National Park in South Africa the following year, establishing an expanding number of game reserves to preserve their profitable fauna. As we learned previously, these designations often entailed the forced removals of indigenous settlements as, in the touristic imagination, Africa's game did not live in proximity to the continent's residents. These engineered landscapes needed to be vast and unpopulated, spaces where animals could roam freely, uninhibited and untainted by the presence of local populations. But, of course, the primary intent was never conservation. If that was the case, colonial officials would not have arranged for the construction of extensive roadways and Western accommodations and facilities within these reserves and parks. In short, the animals needed to be conserved so that they could be observed— observed profitably, that is.

Boosting Tourism: Generating Organizational Infrastructure

Sensing the economic potential of tourism and the foreign exchange it would generate, colonial administrations began to establish formal entities to organize their touristic efforts. Following a 1947 conference on tourism in East Africa, for example, the East African Tourist Travel Association, or EATTA, was formed. This entity was truly imperial in nature, as it aimed to coordinate tourist activity across Great Britain's four East African territories: Kenya, Tanganyika, Uganda, and Zanzibar. The association also worked closely with businesses that played important roles in the tourism industry, including shipping, airlines, banks, and hotels. EATTA was only supposed to be a ten-year experiment, but the agency wasn't disbanded until 1965, after independence had swept across the region. Regardless, over the course of its existence, tourism ascended to the fourth largest "export" industry in the area, while in Kenya, which dominated this regional market, tourism was second only to coffee.

The Belgian and Portuguese governments took similar initiatives, creating the Office du Tourisme Colonial and the Centro de Informação e Turismo, respectively, though these entities were much more closely associated with these regimes' primary political objective: the perpetuation of empire. For officials in Brussels and Lisbon, the colonial stakes were higher than they were for Britain and France; without their empires, Belgium and Portugal were but small states. Moreover, citizens of both countries derived significant pride and validation from their colonial missions. Thus, these newly created touristic entities were also actively generating imperial propaganda and enjoyed close links with their respective Ministries of the Colonies and, in the case of Portugal, with the country's vaunted secret police force, the PIDE.[17] For Belgian and Portuguese officials, these measures constituted a novel, yet vital, form of soft diplomacy that would grow increasingly important as the decolonizing "winds of change" first began to whirl across the continent.[18]

The Belgians and Portuguese also extended their touristic initiatives to the United States. Both governments established information offices in New York to promote tourism and portray to American audiences their respective colonial projects in a positive light. Between Washington, DC, and New York, the home of the fledgling United Nations, Brussels and Lisbon lobbied via their own administrative channels, while the Portuguese also hired public relations firms to manage their charm offensive. The United States was increasingly seen as a vital battleground on which to attempt to win the hearts and minds of both the American public and the federal government, as well as New York–based United Nations dignitaries from around the world. Following the 1955 Bandung Conference in Indonesia, at which dozens of African and Asian countries and nationalist movements pledged to oppose colonialism and neocolonialism (the perpetuation of asymmetrical colonial-era power relationships), efforts to cultivate American empathy intensified. If not already in place, tourism now constituted a vital weapon in the fight to maintain colonial empires in Africa.

Boosting Tourism: Generating Transportation Infrastructure

Helping to prompt the touristic explosion of this period was the reduction of airline fares and the introduction of "package" tours to satisfy the growing demand for African holidays. For example, in 1952, the British Overseas Airways Corporation (BOAC) became the first airline to introduce a passenger jet into airline service via its London-Entebbe (Uganda)-Johannesburg route, and soon after introduced "tourist class" fares to East Africa for residents of the United Kingdom and East Asia, a benefit extended to all passengers the following year. BOAC also began offering "packages" to residents of the United States, France, United Kingdom, and Switzerland. The core elements of these travel bundles were airfare and accommodations. Yet, even as carriers expanded their services, demand typically outpaced supply, as the various colonial destinations struggled to construct the requisite hotel infrastructure. In fact, at its inception in 1948, EATTA officials had ominously declared, "The shortage of accommodation and the inadequacy of existing hotels, in particular, represents the greatest single factor restricting any increase in tourist traffic in East Africa."[19] Some three years later, the Ugandan governor expressed similar concerns in a letter to the British Colonial Office, declaring, "We are not entirely satisfied that the facilities for tourists are as satisfactory as they should be, either in quality or in capacity to handle a large tourist trade."[20]

Even if these colonies struggled to furnish hotel beds suitable for Western tourists, these challenges did not stop foreign visitors from coming. To facilitate this increased touristic traffic, colonial administrations encouraged private investment in hotel construction but also raced to construct the requisite aviation infrastructure. For example, after significant renovations and the expansion of its main runways, Uganda's Entebbe airport reopened in 1951 and could now boast the longest runway on the continent. In response, carriers to the region began eschewing Nairobi, the long-standing terminus for flights to Eastern Africa, in favor of Entebbe. Meanwhile, a new airport in Dar es Salaam, Tanzania, opened in 1954, even as Kenya officials were plotting to reassert the colony's regional aviation supremacy with a new airport of its own. Some four years later, Embakasi airport, which featured a runway slightly longer than Entebbe's, was unveiled. Regionally, smaller airports were constructed at all the major national parks and beach areas, creating a network of linked touristic destinations.[21]

Tourism to (Apartheid) South Africa

During the majority of the time that European colonial powers were expanding touristic services across the continent, South Africa was, in fact, not a colony at all. But it had been. The first European settlement in South Africa dates to 1652, in what eventually would become Cape Town. Previously, European ships rounding the Cape of Good Hope had stopped in the area to trade for supplies, primarily fresh food and water. Identifying the strategic position of this site, located near the meeting point of the Indian and Atlantic Oceans, the Dutch East Indies Company identified the Cape as an ideal location for a more permanent commercial outpost. Much like the story of European settlement in America, relations between the indigenous and recently arrived communities were initially cordial, though wariness featured on both sides. Subsequently, owing to the lucrativeness of the Cape station, Dutch settlers forcefully encroached upon adjacent lands, driving the resident indigenous populations farther into the interior. Eventually, the ascendant British took a fancy to the Cape due to its strategic location. In the 1830s, the British finally dislodged the Dutch, who, due to their significant temporal and geographic distance from the Netherlands, had by then begun self-identifying as "Boers" (the Dutch word for farmers) or "Afrikaners." Seeking to escape British overrule, these Boer trekkers, or voortrekkers, set out riding in covered wagon trains with all their possessions, including slaves. Ultimately, they settled in the central portion of South Africa. In the 1860s, however, unfortunately for these relocated trekkers, diamonds were discovered on their newly settled lands. Not one to pass up opportunities for profit and power anywhere in the world, the British army soon followed. Having recently defeated the powerful Zulu kingdom, though not after a series of stunning defeats, the British assumed control over the diamond fields and, eventually, the nearby areas in which gold was discovered in the 1880s.

During the Victorian era (1837–1901), South Africa initially drew tourists who perceived the country to be a type of expansive, open-air health resort. In particular, British civil servants and military personnel on leave from India were attracted by the supposed "salubrity of its climate," its various watering and bathing spots, and its scenic landscapes.[22] An 1845 guidebook to South Africa printed in Bombay, India, for example, features several bathing points along the Cape Peninsula, as well as possibilities of "short and easy tours with comfort and pleasure and without distress even to ladies" through the scenic passes of the Cape to visit the rural settlements and the hot baths in the nearby valleys.[23] It was during this period that the first inns began appearing, giving birth to a rudimentary, if promising, tourist infrastructure and associated industry.

Over the ensuing decades, South Africa's reputation as a healthy space attracted increasing numbers of foreign visitors. Beyond the Cape Colony, Grahamstown, in the Eastern Cape, earned a reputation as a "health and holiday resort with game shooting, trout fishing, and steep wooded valleys."[24] Even the Karoo, a relatively barren area in the South African interior, could boast an internationally famous health resort at Matjiesfontein, which attracted sojourning European socialites and even British cricket squads.[25]

Following the South Africa War (1899–1902), which pitted Afrikaner settlers against the British Empire, the colony grew even further in stature on the tourism map. In fact, rather than suppressing touristic inflows, the conflict helped market South Africa as a prospective destination. In 1900, for example, during the fighting, Thomas Cook & Son organized the first steamship excursion to South Africa. Over the ensuing decades, following South Africa's nominal independence in 1910 and full sovereignty in 1931, the country became a frequent stop for cruise ships from the United

States and various places in Europe and also served as a point of embarkation for trips to Mozambique, an emerging Portuguese-controlled tourist destination. As was the case elsewhere in colonial Africa, the modern and primitive were strategically bundled, with some exoticness sprinkled in to further entice would-be tourists. For example, one marketing brochure from this era described the country as follows: "For all the furbelows of modernity, there is an ever-present nearness to life in the raw. At one hour of the day the sightseer may be seated on the lounge of a fashionable club or hotel, with around him all the emblems of refined living, and the next he may be intrigued to find himself at a native kraal, face to face with the primitiveness of Bantu life."[26] During this period, South Africa steadily transformed from a health resort into a highly diversified destination in the tourist imagination.[27]

Arguably, the most important touristic development in South Africa before the Second World War was the establishment of Kruger National Park in 1926. Although British and Boer authorities had established game reserves as early as the 1890s, it was not until the 1920s that these conservation sites were also considered potential tourist destinations. Kruger was exemplary of this evolution in thinking. This expansive space quickly established a global reputation for its resident big game. Similar protected spaces followed, including at Hluhluwe, in the far eastern stretches of South Africa, though Kruger remains, to this day, the most famous and largest of these animal reserves.

As was the case throughout Africa when white-minority governments established nature reserves, South African authorities similarly erected fences to demarcate these new lands for conservation and forcibly removed black residents from them. The South African regime strove to create "marketable constructions of 'wild nature,' which required these spaces to be emptied of humans and, attendantly, human history."[28] Authorities astutely surmised that increasing industrialization would push urban dwellers to strive to escape from their hectic lives and find solace in "zones of primitive space and time."[29] Travel writer Carel Birkby's 1937 book, *Zulu Journey*, is exemplary of this allure. Via his travels through Zululand in eastern South Africa, readers were invited to "escape from a sick civilization in London or New York. Travel through Zululand . . . and forget your fogs and skyscrapers as you encounter as strange a set of living characters as Rider Haggard ever invented."[30] For local officials, this seemingly primeval place, void of the trappings of the industrializing West, could not be "sullied" by the presence of Africans. This manufactured virginity serves as a reminder that seemingly "natural" spaces also have histories, even as they appear "timeless, pristine, and outside the human world."[31]

Following the end of the Second World War, South Africa experienced a radical sociopolitical turn. Coming to power in 1948, South Africa's Nationalist Party implemented apartheid, a social, political, and economic system characterized by institutional racism and acute racial segregation that included the dispossession of land and citizenship. Although more extreme and systematized than anything that preceded it, apartheid was built upon decades of racially discriminatory policies and practices in South Africa. From 1949 until the early 1990s, South African society was divided into four racial groups: European, African, Asian, and mixed-race. Peoples of European descent operated at the top of a racial hierarchy that permeated all aspects of society, including education, housing, interpersonal relationships, and so forth. Despite their vast numerical superiority, black South Africans had the fewest legal rights and the least access to social services and institutions, and they remained the most vulnerable and exploited members of society. As the decades elapsed, the country exploded with violence as the security apparatus endeavored to suppress calls and associated action for democratic rule. Torture, terrorism, and brutality eventually became routine in apartheid South Africa.

Somewhat surprisingly, it was during the apartheid era that the South African regime earnestly embarked on a campaign to promote tourism to the country. Although the newly ascendant apartheid government initially focused on implementing policies that codified racial discrimination, it eventually turned to tourism as a source of potential revenue. At first glance, this decision may seem absurd, but keep in mind that the entirety of colonized Africa featured similar racialized power structures. In fact, it's arguable that this social dynamic, in which whites generally enjoyed comfortable existences owing to the servility of the black underclasses, greatly appealed to tourists from the Global North. Moreover, the subjugation of Africans in colonial contexts meant that tourists could safely observe, even engage, them without any apprehension.

Meanwhile, the increased availability and affordability of long-distance air travel facilitated the arrival of growing numbers of foreign visitors to South Africa. The touristic infrastructure grew apace, with hotels proliferating, including upmarket accommodations. Even the 1960 massacre in Sharpeville, a township near Johannesburg, during which police fired on thousands of unarmed black protesters, killing 69 and injuring 180, seemingly had little impact on the inflows of international guests. Although Sharpeville didn't deter prospective tourists, the independence of an array of African nations in the region, such as Zambia, Botswana, and Tanzania, and the attendant flight of white settler populations—an important component of South Africa's touristic traffic—meant that Pretoria had to look further afield for potential visitors.

A potent combination of government initiatives to organize and manage the industry, an economic boom in the 1960s that facilitated further touristic development, and the steady introduction of longer-range commercial jets and expanded air routes rendered South Africa more than able to compensate for the reduction in regional tourism. Touristic films screened internationally—53,828 in 1970 alone—as well as carefully orchestrated scenes of the country produced by Satour, the state tourism agency, which had offices in London, Paris, Rome, Frankfurt, and Amsterdam, also helped draw foreign visitors in ever-larger numbers. By the early 1970s, South Africa had become the most popular tourist destination in sub-Saharan Africa, featuring a touristic infrastructure capable of supporting the hundreds of thousands of visitors it hosted annually. One local media outlet, echoing earlier promotions, rhetorically asked, "What can we offer the international tourists?" and answered, "Tremendously wide open spaces, a favorable climate with long sunshine hours, magnificent scenery, a wildlife that is one of the richest and most accessible in the world and a fascinating mix of cultures—plus the fact that it's all undiscovered and the long trip gives social prestige to the tourist when he gets back home."[32] Of course, South Africa had long ago been "discovered" by its indigenous populations, but the appeal of the exotic in the advertisement is unmistakable.

Although South African authorities were enjoying the revenue that foreign tourism generated, they were simultaneously anxious about the social disruption that it might foment. Apartheid South Africa was a meticulously engineered society, potentially vulnerable to unsettling influences such as foreigners who might challenge the prevailing racial hierarchy either implicitly or explicitly, or even unwittingly violate one of the myriad petty laws, regulations, or policies enacted to ensure strict racial segregation. Officials strove to insulate Calvinistic, conservative, white South Africa from foreigners' righteous sentiments or disruptive behavior, as these authorities believed had happened in Spain and the Caribbean, upon which relatively less affluent travelers with allegedly dubious morality had descended. To maintain revenues while minimizing potential tourism-induced disorder, authorities courted high-income visitors, referred to by tourism officials as an "aristocratic cachet." It was presumed that these tourists, owing to their station and associated social outlook, would be mindful of the country's social order. Theo Behrens, former South African secretary of tourism, reasoned that "the government was of the opinion that wealthy tourists were more likely to be politically conservative and influential in the 'right' circles and would comment favorably on their visit to South Africa upon their return to their home countries."[33] Only much later, prompted by the foreign exchange and the sizeable revenues that tourism generated, would the regime attempt to attract a wider range of visitors to travel to South Africa.

By the early 1970s, tourism was the fifth largest earner in the country's economy, but this progress was shattered in 1976. The Soweto massacre, during which security forces killed at least 176 black citizens, primarily students, who were protesting the imposition of Afrikaans, the language of the National Party, for school instruction, deeply tarnished South Africa's international reputation. Until Soweto, apartheid hadn't served as a significant deterrent to visitors. For example, worldwide tourist arrivals increased 7.2 percent from 1965 to 1970, but for South Africa this growth was 11.4 percent. However, the slaughter at Soweto arguably marks the country's irreversible slide into international isolation and, eventually, its status as a global pariah, which deeply distressed the tourist industry. Although the Ministry of Tourism correspondingly launched an international "reassurance campaign" following Soweto, the impact of the tragedy was insurmountable. Only the United States seemed intent on backing the apartheid regime, a perceived stalwart against the spread of communism in Southern Africa and, thus, a major American ally. This political support notwithstanding, the decline in tourist arrivals reflect the country's growing isolation, as following an all-time high in 1975, the number of visitors tumbled some 27 percent in 1977, despite significant efforts at "damage control" by South African tourism officials.[34]

While the remaining colonial territories surrounding South Africa steadily gained their independence during the 1960s and 1970s, and Zimbabwe, in 1980, and Namibia, in 1990, subsequently followed suit, the country experienced violent civil unrest as the intransigent apartheid regime clung to power. States of emergency, negative international media coverage, and the mounting global condemnation of apartheid collectively dissuaded tourists from visiting the embattled nation. Although some foreigners continued to arrive, the writing was clearly on the wall. In response, in one of the apartheid government's many desperate efforts to turn the tide, it permitted the development of casino hotel resorts in some of the supposedly independent, exclusively black "homelands," or "Bantustans."[35] The most notorious of these establishments was Sun City, which enticed both domestic and international visitors with the prospect of interracial sex (illegal under apartheid law), gambling, and other resort attractions. Subsequently, an international group of rock stars, Artists United Against Apartheid, would belt out damning lines about the resort in their song, "Sun City," including the refrain: "I, I, I, I, I, I ain't gonna play Sun City." With Bono, Ringo Starr, Lou Reed, Bob Dylan, George Clinton, Bob Geldof, Peter Gabriel, Keith Richards, and dozens of others crooning about the evils of apartheid, South African tourism officials faced a very formidable opponent.

Under extreme international and domestic pressure, the apartheid regime finally released Nelson Mandela from jail in 1990, marking the formal beginning of its end. Over the next four tumultuous years, the nation crawled toward its first open, democratic elections. Mandela emerged victorious and while the world watched this historic political development, the country's tourism industry quietly recalibrated its efforts, preparing to promote the "new" South Africa.

The Invisible Backbone of the Industry: African Labor

For all the governmental promotion of tourism in colonial Africa and both public and private investment in the sector, like so many other industries on the continent during this period, it would have been unviable without the contributions of countless African laborers. These seemingly invisible workers formally served in a wide range of capacities, including as safari guides; big-game trackers; restaurant and lodging staff; and the builders— often as forced laborers—of hotels, resorts, and transportation infrastructure that facilitated increasing touristic flows. Other Africans participated in the tourist economy informally by selling fresh food to hotels and restaurants, while others peddled local crafts and curios to tourists or to European shop owners, who then hawked these items to visitors. There were even cases in which Africans managed their own shops, selling directly to tourists. Regardless, the institutionalized racism that pervaded colonial Africa rendered all individuals active in the sector vulnerable and ripe for exploitation. Consequently, their wages were lower, often significantly, than those of their European counterparts in the industry.

They also often suffered racially motivated verbal, and at times physical, abuse while toiling in an array of occupations. For example, Fernando Cunhica, who in 1967 at nineteen years old began working in the kitchen of a Mozambican restaurant popular with tourists, explained that "they [the Portuguese cooks] used to beat us and call us *preto ordinário* [stupid black]. Some would rub pepper in their hands and then slap us in the face. If you protected your face, they would punch you in the stomach, but we had to bear all that. I needed the job. . . . If they teach you [something] today, tomorrow they don't want to repeat it."[36]

Even if Africans weren't abused physically, their employers and the European settlers with whom they shared colonial space generally disrespected them. A 1907 article from the *Livingstone Mail*, printed in Livingstone, Zambia (a former British territory), adjacent to Victoria Falls, provides an exemplary case. The piece reported the deaths of two African men working for a local merchant who were attacked by a hippo as they crossed the Zambezi River. Not surprisingly, the article refers to the African workers as "boys," which reflects the disparaging attitudes that Europeans typically held toward African men.[37] The author continued, "Someday, a still more serious accident will happen—a boat load of tourists, or perhaps, a Director of the Chartered Company—will be drowned and the nuisance will be taken in hand. . . . There is no reason why these dangerous monsters should be permitted to imperil the lives of visitors and the property of residents."[38] It is hard to imagine a scenario in which victims of a tragedy, in this case fatalities, could be blamed any more egregiously for a hypothetical touristic incident.

In treatment arguably even more demeaning than the condemnation they suffered at the hands of European residents and employers, African workers were often humiliated by the very tourists they were servicing. As Pedro Manhiça, a former hotel employee in colonial Mozambique, remarked, "I think the hotel industry is good but it requires a lot of patience around the guests and staff because some even, you know, threatened you. . . . They often insulted you, but you still had to say 'I am sorry, I am sorry, I am sorry,' no matter what. You had to be humble."[39] These forms of physical and emotional abuse rendered life in the colonial-era industry doubly challenging for African employees.

Nonetheless, tourism industry workers did not engage in large-scale strikes, sabotage, or other forms of high-profile defiance that marked other sectors, namely mining, during the colonial period in Africa, even if they regularly demanded any withheld or lower-than-agreed-upon wages.

Although life as an employee in the colonial-era tourism industry wasn't ideal for Africans, it offered relative advantages. For example, employment in a restaurant as a cook or server presented far fewer risks to one's personal well-being than did working as an underground mineworker, as millions of African men did during the colonial period. Moreover, the steady wages they earned often facilitated social ascension in local societies. With limited opportunities for social mobility available under indigenous social systems, working for Europeans in the tourism sector was an appealing, if still less than ideal, option.

In the Victoria Falls region, this is exactly what happened. The chance to accumulate material wealth motivated innumerable Africans to offer their labor to Europeans who were busy trying to develop Livingstone as a tourism hub. In the late nineteenth and early twentieth centuries, African workers, many of whom were former slaves, constructed the site's foundational tourism infrastructure, including hotels, restaurants, and stores. In this setting, although their wages were suppressed and they routinely experienced poor treatment, they "enjoyed an openness that was novel for them. The wardrobe and recreation choices they made reflected a desire to define and enact an urban social life and sense of community, imagining and articulating new identities."[40] In turn, this heightened social status influenced relations with friends, family members, and neighbors.

Other times, Africans realized social mobility via regular interactions with foreign visitors. Daily exposure to and eventual proficiency in European languages and customs facilitated this ascension. The case of Vasco Manhiça who, in the early 1960s at the age of twelve, began working as a message boy for the Inhaca Hotel in colonial-era Mozambique and who now manages a major business hotel in the center of Maputo, is exemplary: "Twelve years old was not really the right age to start working. . . . But, things came so fast. Within three years, I was already a head receptionist, because I was very clever. . . . Slowly, slowly, I started to deal with the clients and they let me try to learn their languages, because it was very important for me to communicate with the guests. . . . Actually, at school, I had a few English classes, but not enough that I would say, 'yeah, my English was from school.' Rather, it was from dealing every day with the hotel clients."[41]

There were also intangible benefits to working in the tourism sector. For example, Luís Macáucau, who began in the hotel industry in colonial Mozambique in the early 1970s, explained, "It was an honor to work in the hotel industry because we used the basic principles of tourism: courtesy, delicacy, and hospitality. . . . We had pride working there because you learned to eat well, and better . . . you were proud to work in the hotel industry because you were identified as a man who dresses better."[42] Citing similar immaterial advantages, José Manhique, a former hotel employee in the same setting, indicated that "tourism not only brings monetary gains, but also brings foreign culture, which shapes the citizens of our country . . . tourism for me is a science that shapes our personal behavior . . . in terms of culture, Mozambican citizens gained something with tourism, such as a change in attitude and culture."[43] In these and other ways, tourism enriched African societies, though the exploitative dimensions of the industry arguably outstripped any benefits the sector may have delivered.

In some settings, particular African workers were exalted by their European superiors, namely those who were employed on safaris as guides, trackers, or gun bearers, or who worked in security in the range of parks and reserves established throughout the colonial period. For example, in the aforementioned *Zulu Journey*, set in South Africa, Carel Birkby offered the following account of his encounter with Induna Mali, an ethnic Zulu game guard: "Of all the game guards, the most famous is Mali. He is a silent, skillful tracker, a deadly shot and terror of poachers. With his khaki uniform, his blue leggings and motor-tyre sandals, his Baden-Powell hat and his beard, Mali is a picturesque figure."[44] Employees such as Induna Mali were vital to touristic-conservation efforts in Africa during this period, even though these workers were only permitted to serve as game guards, the lowest occupational tier of this hierarchy. A similar example of this racial power dynamic features Harold B. Potter, the game conservator in Zululand, in eastern South Africa, during the 1930s and 1940s, who viewed his game guards "paternalistically in his capacity as benevolent manager of the 'estate of nature' at Hluhluwe."[45] These African laborers apparently remembered Potter fondly, even though he also oversaw the erection of fencing around the reserve, as well as some forced removals in the area, recalling the responsibility "with which they were entrusted, symbolized by their uniforms and the rifles they were given, as well as their boss' appreciation of their shooting skills as a qualification for employment."[46]

Upon the conclusion of the colonial period in Africa and the attendant exodus of most Europeans, Africans with competence or longevity in the industry utilized their training and experience to sustain tourism sectors. Upon assuming power, socialist governments often appointed these industry veterans to supervisory positions at hotels, game reserves, and other tourist destinations. Even in more capitalistic settings, some African employees eventually advanced to managerial positions and other positions of authority and responsibility, which would have been unfathomable during the period of colonial overrule. Consequently, certain African tourism workers not only experienced social ascension during the colonial era but were well positioned upon independence to further advance their careers in the tourism industry.

IN MANY important respects, developments during the colonial period laid the foundation for the tourism industries that the newly independent African nations inherited. Conservation efforts had been launched, the continent had been permanently linked to the rest of the world via long-haul air travel, and domestic and regional road networks had been constructed. Moreover, the exoticness that colonial governments habitually used to promote tourism had further deepened Africa's allure in the touristic imagination, while indigenous laborers who had been meaningfully exposed to various subsectors within the industry could apply their work experience in postcolonial Africa.

For all the propitiousness associated with the tourism industry as African nations realized their independence, the new governments often did little to rectify past injustices. These new states, for example, opted not to return residents to "conservation" areas from which colonial authorities had forcibly removed them, while even the most leftist regimes justified capitalistic ventures to protect touristic revenues while simultaneously condemning various forms of colonial and neocolonial exploitation. Although working conditions in the industry generally improved, many Africans continued to operate on the informal fringes of the sector. In this sense, the newly independent states largely perpetuated rather than disrupted the touristic agendas and associated processes that their colonial predecessors had devised. It is this next era of tourism on the continent that the ensuing chapter examines.

CHAPTER FOUR

Paradoxes of Independence

Modernizing by Promoting Primitivism

> *In many ways tourism is the worst form of neo-colonialism.*
>
> —Alan Hutchinson, scholar, 1972

> *Tourism, which encourages the peaceful encounter of man with man, enables men to know men in their own surroundings—enables them to learn to appreciate their civilization and their culture. These exchanges, more than all others, are of a nature calculated to create affinities from which will arise true understanding among peoples of the world.*
>
> —Mr. Ley, the former manager of the state-run Tanzania Tourist Corporation, 1973

WAS MR. LEY correct in his sanguine assertions about tourism? Or was the much more critical Mr. Hutchinson? As African nations gained their independence in the 1960s and 1970s, the first generation of leaders were forced to make these very determinations. Some of them, desperate to diversify revenue streams away from a dependence on commodities, embraced tourism, pouring state resources into the promotion and marketing of their countries and investing in touristic infrastructure. Others, in the face of more pressing needs, were either unable or unwilling to allocate funds to develop or expand tourism sectors. Still others, especially Marxist-socialist governments that had been forced to take up arms in their struggles for independence, were suspicious of the enterprise, condemning it as a bourgeois endeavor intended for the wealthy at the expense of the poor.

There was, as is so often the case, no one-size-fits-all answer to this dilemma. Nor was there consensus regarding the overall impact of tourism in Africa. Writing in 1979, in the aftermath of the decolonization of the continent, development scholar Reginald Green explained that "studies done by those involved in tourism tend to be remarkably positive, and those carried out by academics tend to be dominantly negative. When prospects are considered, even less agreement can be found—in the extreme, the same type of touristic development in the same country is presented as both a gift of the gods and the work of the devil."[1] Regardless of the divergence in opinion, for those countries that already featured established tourism industries, such as Kenya, the decision to expand and invest in the sector was reasonably straightforward. Conversely, for most African nations, the prospect of launching an industry virtually from scratch was either financially impossible or at least irresponsible. Most African leaders wanted to establish or expand tourism industries, but this undertaking was not always feasible, or at least not immediately.

Regardless of how quickly these new administrations moved to facilitate the growth of this sector in their respective nations, they generally proceeded in similar fashion. African governments now oversaw a range of natural touristic assets, including beaches, hunting reserves, national parks, and conservation zones. They typically nationalized portions of the industry or simply inherited touristic infrastructure, such as hotels, from departing European proprietors. Yet, even as the new governments assumed control of these natural and built assets, they retained some of the most grievous policies enacted in the name of tourism by their colonial predecessors. For example, rather than return indigenous residents who had been forcibly removed from their homelands to make way for game reserves by colonial regimes, most African governments either maintained these spaces as resident-free zones or, in some cases, expanded them in the name of tourism and conservation. Moreover, even as African laborers in the industry enjoyed more favorable working conditions with the conclusion of colonial rule, management positions often fell to Westerners who had the training and experience that locals were denied throughout the extended period of imperial overrule. Within the realm of tourism, there were sharp divergences from the colonial era, but arguably just as many continuities.

One important continuity from the colonial era was the ongoing inclination to promote Africa as a primitive place, even as governments and tourist agencies assured would-be visitors that they would enjoy all the comforts of modernity during their stays. Quite simply, these promoters knew what would attract foreign visitors. The intertwining of primitivism with modernity resonated with tourists, who wanted to experience a trip back in time without experiencing any of the discomfort or inconvenience that this "time travel" would otherwise feature. Although visitor flows increased in the decades following independence and touristic revenues helped buoy struggling African nations, promoting the continent as a primeval destination reinforced notions of its alleged backwardness. In this respect, these new nations were uncritically mimicking impressions of the continent that their European predecessors had so carefully cultivated.

In the decades immediately ensuing the conclusion of the colonial era, newly independent nations successfully, if gradually, increased touristic inflows to the continent, though other global destinations continued to outpace the growth that Africa was experiencing. Policies enacted by these states had both positive and negative material impacts on their citizenries. Prudent investment in tourism could generate both employment opportunities and increased revenues for the state. Indeed, both African men and women successfully pursued livelihoods in this rapidly shifting touristic environment, even if wages remained relatively low. However, the hasty or unconsidered allocation of scarce state resources could just as easily prove financially ruinous for the citizens of these incipient nations.

At other times, even judicious investment could be wasted owing to civil conflict—a fate that plagued the continent during the turbulent 1970s and 1980s. Not only did warfare often destroy vital infrastructure and arrest touristic inflows, but the negative impressions it generated took ample time to reverse, further handicapping these states' efforts to attract visitors to produce badly needed, post conflict revenues. Linda Richter, a scholar of human development, has argued, "Even national disasters such as earthquakes and hurricanes do not have the lasting and devastating impact of political unrest on tourism."[2] Moreover, geographical ignorance can cause would-be visitors to stay away from a perfectly stable nation solely because it happens to be located on the same continent as a strife-plagued country. I've experienced this phenomenon firsthand as a leader of study abroad trips to Africa. In one case, a parent wanted to remove her son from a trip to South Africa owing to an Ebola outbreak in West Africa, while before a departure to Ghana, a grandmother cautioned a female student to "be aware of [Somali] pirates," apparently unaware that Somalia and Ghana are approximately as far apart as Seattle, Washington, is from Buenos Aires, Argentina!

How Do We Do Tourism? Weighty Considerations in Postcolonial Africa

For African governments that actively sought to cultivate or expand their tourism industries, a host of challenges loomed that were far more formidable than even the most geographically challenged grandmother. Newly installed governments faced grim economic realities, including heavy dependence on the export of a range of commodities. These undiversified economies were at the mercy of fluctuating international commodity prices, which were highly volatile during the period that followed independence. As promising as the development of a tourism industry might be, there were clearly more pressing issues that required the allocation of scarce resources to raise the standards of living for a country's citizenry. For example, a 1970 editorial by Tanzanian citizen O. B. Kopoka asked, "Why make things so comfortable and easy for tourists? If they have to do their mischief, let them do it in the greatest discomfort ever. At any rate, give us bridges first."[3] For many African governments, these realities served to deprioritize tourism as a possible economic engine, causing tourism planning across the continent to lag behind other areas of the developing world. For example, as late as the 1990s in Zambia—home to one side of the tourism mecca that is Victoria Falls—tourism was officially "classified as a 'social' sector and regarded as being of little consequence for economic development planning."[4] Another deterrent was the considerable initial investment that tourism development often requires, rendering the sector financially beneficial only in the longer term. For example, a study on tourism in East Africa conducted in 1981, almost two decades after independence, concluded that total government investments in the tourism sector in none of the constituent countries had yet realized a profitable overall net return.[5] Nonetheless, an array of assertive African governments forged ahead, determined to develop this sector of their economies, even if it caused hardships elsewhere on their economic and social landscapes.

African administrations interested in the development of the industry also had to decide exactly how involved they wanted to be in this process. There were, in practice, many options or roles that a government could play in this sector. The least expensive was to create a business- or investment-friendly operating climate for the private sector to facilitate touristic development. A government might also assume a more prominent role in the promotion of its country as a tourist destination, for example by shouldering the financial outlay of the transportation infrastructure needed to support the industry, including roads, airports, ports, and various utilities, as well as heritage preservation. Finally, an administration might assume control over the entire industry, irrespective of how financially impractical that might be.[6]

Developmental economists generally agree that the state needs to be actively involved in touristic development, especially during the initial stages, before transitioning to a supportive or facilitative role, often in collaboration with private sector stakeholders. However, many economists argue that governments are ill-suited for entrepreneurial activity and do not respond well to market changes and demands; rather, these experts contend that tourism is the domain and, arguably, the inherent role of the private sector. Yet as Kenyan scholar John Akama has averred, "In most less developed countries where tourism has evolved and flourished as a major economic sector, this socio-economic phenomenon has been achieved primarily through direct government support and involvement in the development of the tourism sector."[7] Akama's home country of Kenya, as well as Egypt, Tunisia, and Morocco, provide examples of this type of statal involvement. These governments have established tax incentives for private investors and developers, provided soft loans, and even worked with companies to operate tourism and hospitality facilities and services.[8] Specific examples of successful public-private operational partnerships during this period include the Sheraton Hotel in Kampala, Uganda, and the Hilton and Intercontinental Hotels in Nairobi. Over time, the widespread privatization of state-owned hotels clearly indicated that the private sector more efficiently managed this component of the broader industry than did African governments.[9]

A Case Study of Kenya: An Industry Leader

Following independence, many African administrations elevated the importance of tourism by either enhancing existing agencies that oversaw the industry or establishing new entities. In Kenya, for example, the government upgraded what was the Department of Tourism to the Ministry of Tourism and Wildlife and charged it with overseeing all matters pertaining to the development and management of the tourism industry.[10] The Kenyan government then created a parastatal organization, the Kenya Tourism Development Corporation, to invest public monies into the sector, funds that were often secured via loans from major international donors, such as the World Bank. In turn, the government invested heavily in tourism and hospitality facilities, namely those around Kenya's leading tourist areas, including along its Indian Ocean coastline and among its most popular wildlife parks and reserves, such as Maasai Mara, Amboseli, and Tsavo.[11]

In the mid-1970s, the government also opened the Utalii Hotel Management and Training College, built with Swiss expertise and funding, which to this day continues to train students for careers in the tourism industry. In its national development plan for 1966–1970, the government argued that "Kenya's tourism income is proportional to the development of tourism facilities, and the more the country spends on the development of this sector, the greater the flow of tourists will be."[12] It also opened up tourism offices in Europe, the United States, and Japan and encouraged foreign investment, passing the Foreign Investments Protection Act, which included special tax relief, including depreciation on buildings, to encourage privately funded hotel construction.[13]

Some observers ultimately bemoaned these measures, as even these seemingly progressive initiatives were not immune to the country's notorious corruption. For example, following the opening of the aforementioned Utalii College, Swiss private capital, especially in the highly profitable seaside resorts, enjoyed highly disproportional access to investment opportunities in the country. Despite pervasive corruption, though, these measures collectively proved to be successful. Into the 1970s and 1980s, Kenya attracted increased foreign and multinational investment in its burgeoning tourism industry and more than tripled annual tourist arrivals from independence in 1963 until the mid-1980s.

The Case of Tanzania: An Aspiring Kenya

In neighboring Tanzania, similar changes were afoot. Upon achieving independence in 1961, the government began utilizing state funds to develop the industry, including the construction of the Kilimanjaro Hotel, which opened in 1965 in the capital city of Dar es Salaam. For the remainder of the decade, though, tourism development took a back seat to the much more dramatic and sweeping changes the country was attempting to institute. In Tanzania, the socialist revolution was underway. Despite some promising aspects of these radical reforms, they ultimately hampered more than accelerated the economy, and by the middle of the 1970s, with diminishing agricultural productivity, deteriorating terms of trade, and chronic foreign exchange shortages, officials re-engaged with tourism's significant potential.[14] Thus, by the late 1970s, a parastatal agency had been formed to lead the development of the tourism industry, replacing a series of inefficient entities that had preceded it. A sizable loan from the World Bank facilitated the expansion and renovation of touristic lodging, while the recently created Air Tanzania Corporation established a flight schedule that linked Dar es Salaam with Kilimanjaro International Airport, which provided easy access to the internationally renowned game parks in the country's northern stretches.[15] Air Tanzania's fleet was upgraded via a Japanese bank loan, and, smelling profits, KLM, British Airways, and Ethiopian Airlines all initiated direct flights to Kilimanjaro, Dar es Salaam, and Nairobi. Virtually overnight, the number of park visitors jumped by roughly 20 percent.[16]

What makes the Tanzanian case so interesting is that investment in the industry was done against the backdrop of an aggressive brand of socialism led by the "father of the nation," Julius Nyerere, who served as the country's first leader from independence in the early 1960s until 1985. Nyerere preached national self-reliance, while denouncing neocolonialism and capitalism.[17] Much of the citizenry embraced his political philosophy and, thus, openly questioned the government's seemingly capitalistic touristic ambitions. In a particularly pointed letter to the editor of the *Standard* newspaper from May 25, 1970, these concerns are clearly evident:

> Is the development arising from investment in the tourism industry helping to create a socialist Tanzania? Is the expenditure justified in view of our ultimate objectives? It is estimated that to provide one bed for a tourist costs between 50,000 and 75,000 Shillings. This is more than five times average Tanzanians collectively earn in their lifetimes. The question inevitably must arise whether there are not more urgent priorities for Government investment than luxury hotels. . . . Further, we need to consider whether the economic, social, and cultural patterns resulting from a concentration on tourism are those that are desirable in our nation.[18]

Reflecting widespread views, another Tanzania observer, signing his letter, "The Socialist," wrote to the same paper roughly a month later, objecting not only to the economic issues cited above, but even more so to the cultural and perceptual implications of touristic development:

> In a brief survey of foreign tourists at the parks in the north, a sample of 20 persons revealed that about half were attracted by the lions while the other half was attracted by the Maasai

tribe! This Maasai attraction is subject to a variety of interpretations, one of which is that the outsiders take it as a reminder of those days when Africa was supposed to touch the "Dark Ages of African History" popularly described in bourgeois history textbooks. This sort of thing has a debasing effect. . . . Tourism is a profit seeking enterprise which has so far forgotten the important maxim that "We are not a company seeking profits, but a nation seeking development."[19]

Ultimately, widespread public faith in Nyerere overcame these concerns, and, as outlined above, the country engaged in tourism development, assisted in this process by its world-renowned big game, long Indian Ocean coastline, and picturesque Zanzibar archipelago. Even as Nyerere criticized Western nations, maligned neocolonialism, and advocated for global socialism, he needed tourists from those very same (capitalistic) nations to travel to Tanzania to generate badly needed revenue so that he could extend the socialist revolution. The irony was clearly not lost on the above letter-writers.

Gambia: A Small Nation with a Much Larger Touristic Impact

Across the continent in Gambia, the trajectory of the tourism industry in the aftermath of independence played out somewhat similarly, although without the socialist dimensions. After Gambia gained its sovereignty from Great Britain in 1965, Swedish tourists almost immediately "discovered" this West African country. As the number of foreign visitors grew, the country began to develop the industry in earnest. In 1972, Gambia secured both technical and financial assistance from the United Nations Development Programme (UNDP) and the International Development Agency, using this support to launch the ambitious "Tourism and Infrastructure Project" (1975–80). The objective was to provide the basic infrastructure required for tourism, which included setting aside land west of Banjul, the capital, along the Atlantic beach fronts, and designating it as a Tourism Development Area.[20]

From these auspicious beginnings, the Gambian government reached out to foreign investors to help develop the industry without ever completely relinquishing control over it. As in Tanzania, the state generated basic transportation infrastructure and facilities to train laborers to work in the sector, while "granting generous incentives to investors, and, at times, even acting as full guarantor for loans to secure financing for hotel construction."[21] The government streamlined the approval system, enabling commercial applications and associated processes to advance more rapidly. Gambia also established a Ministry of Information and Tourism, which included the Tourism Advisory Board and the Tourism Area Development Board, to oversee touristic activity domestically and in target markets abroad.[22]

Eswatini (Swaziland): Marketing and Protecting Tradition

In Eswatini (formerly known as Swaziland), the government was similarly making strategic moves to develop its tourism industry. This Southern African nation is unique in sub-Saharan Africa in that it features a monarchy, with "real power resting with the king and a council of chiefs and elders in direct descent from those who had wielded power in the pre-colonial era."[23] The state welcomed foreign investment and proved to be a reliable partner for such enterprises as Sun International Hotels, a South African company that enjoyed a commanding position in the industry in Eswatini in the decades following independence.

Of particular importance is the country's emphasis on tradition, exemplified by the durable monarchy. This insistence on tradition is manifested in the nation's tourism industry, as well, in which ethnic Swazi culture is stressed and showcased. As the government is an important player in the tourism industry, it is actively involved in selling Swazi "tradition" to attract foreign tourists.[24] As development scholar David Harrison has contended, in this way "tradition becomes an advertising gimmick, presenting potential tourists with 'exotic' people in colorful costumes and spectacular ceremonies."[25] During a recent trip to Eswatini, I found myself presented with this exact package while visiting a "traditional" Swazi village in the country's Ezulwini Valley region, which is run by the state tourism entity. I took the photo below, and many more like it (fig. 4.1). Just as the other tourists did. Just as the performers encouraged us to do. Tradition, as it often is in Eswatini, was on full display.

Tunisia: Promoting Africa as Europe

While most African governments and tourism operators were busy promoting Africa as thoroughly alien from visitors' homelands, the North African country of Tunisia was actively advertising itself as an extension of Europe, just across the Mediterranean. This former French colony

FIGURE 4.1 Tourism at the Mantenga Cultural Village, featuring local performers and foreign tourists. *Photo by author.*

gained its independence in 1956 and by the 1960s had launched a strategic tourism development plan. From the onset, government officials concluded that the country would be best served by portraying itself as a European, rather than an African or an "Arab," destination, part of a broader Mediterranean space that included Europe. The country's first leader, Habib Bourguiba, who ruled from independence until 1987, declared that the "reorientation of Tunisia toward the West will represent progress and prosperity, the very objectives to which an independent Tunisia aspires."[26] To this end, the government invested in high-rise hotels, most of which were located along its roughly 800 miles of Mediterranean coastline, intended to accommodate masses of sojourning Europeans seeking "sun, sea, and sand," a familiar refrain. Europeans were made to feel at home in these touristic enclaves, which featured customs and activities with which they were familiar while limiting contact with indigenous Tunisian culture. In turn, tourism became the country's second leading source of foreign exchange, firmly situating Tunisia on the "pleasure periphery of Europe," as the North African shores became known from the 1970s.

In 1980, *National Geographic* magazine featured a profile entitled "Tunisia: Sea, Sand, Success." Yet, even if the country's tourism strategy may have brought the desired influxes of visitors (i.e., "success"), the uneven development, extension of European culture and values into conservative Tunisia, and the touristic disregard for local culture led to discontent among many Tunisians. For these disenfranchised citizens, the tourism industry was exemplary of everything that ailed the country. The presence of scantily clad visitors, and even naked sun-bathers, on the country's beaches; open affection between male and female visitors; excessive alcohol consumption; and foreign women seeking sexual encounters with local men, known locally as the *bezness*, offended many Tunisians, who deemed these and other examples of Western culture an assault on local values and comportment.[27] The government's secularization of society and the predominance of French and Italian programming on television further "reinforced the pervasiveness of European culture and the prioritization of European 'leisure imperialists.'"[28]

By the mid-1980s, domestic struggles, regional conflict, and dated touristic facilities had reduced the numbers of foreign visitors. But by then the damage had already been done. An overall decline in economic conditions, coupled with the marginalization of the country's Arabic and Islamic heritages, prompted the organization of a powerful Islamist movement to challenge the Tunisian government. As part of its agenda, the movement also maligned the country's tourism development strategy, seeking instead to redirect the economy "away from the reliance on tourism and to promote an alternative construction of Tunisia's identity and external image."[29] The leader of the movement, Rashid Ghannouchi, famously declared that "Tunisians are not tourists who live in a hotel." Ultimately, the government, using heavy-handed tactics, prevailed in this contest over nothing less than the identity of the nation. But while this contestation persisted, tourism had been thrust into a difficult position, uncomfortably situated at the heart of national debate.

Conservation as a Revenue Generator: Examples from Tanzania, Zimbabwe, and Rwanda

One touristic asset that many newly independent African countries enjoyed was the presence of big game. Like their colonial predecessors, these governments aimed to protect this wildlife in order to generate touristic revenues. States initiated a range of new conservation measures, including

the establishment and expansion of park and reserve networks, the enact-
ment of stricter hunting regulations—or even an outright ban on the sport,
as happened in Kenya in 1977—and the implementation of increased security in an effort to reduce poaching. Although the illegal slaughter of
animals continues to be a problem in contemporary Africa, the other measures were largely successful in protecting the fauna and thereby increasing
touristic flows.

Tanzania was one of the countries that rushed to protect these animal
resources, particularly within and around Ngorongoro Crater and Serengeti
National Park. Regarding the former, for example, the country's 1976–1981
national development plan declared that "the Ngorongoro Conservation
Authority will have the responsibility of administering and conserving
natural resources, effecting a balance between man and his environment,
conserving soil, and conserving natural resources for the benefit of future
generations."[30] Capturing this commitment to protect the environment, in
1981 the general manager of the Tanzania Trust Corporation outlined the
country's vision for tourism and its inextricability from the conservation
of natural resources: "We hope to make tourism the first or second most
important earner of foreign exchange. . . . We are offering local subsidized
programs so that our people can get to know and appreciate their own
country and therefore feel more responsible for its preservation; otherwise
poaching will only increase."[31]

Another country that strove to protect these valuable resources was
Zimbabwe. As a former colony that had hosted large numbers of European
settlers, the nation did not attain independence until 1980, following a protracted struggle against a renegade white-minority regime, the so-called
UDI (Unilateral Declaration of Independence), which seized power in the
mid-1960s after England indicated it planned to decolonize the territory.[32]
Central to the fledgling nation's conservation efforts was the Parks Department. Interestingly, the key personnel in the unit did not change with the
transition from colony to sovereign nation, which ensured continuity in
policy. This development is somewhat astounding given that many other
governmental departments were indigenized, understandably so given the
long fight to overthrow the UDI. But in many other ways it's not overly
surprising, as touristic strategies remained largely consistent as colonies of
all types made the transition to independent states. Across this political
divide, African governments continued to strive to attract visitors to generate revenue; wildlife, including elephants, rhinos, and lions, constituted

an excellent way to achieve that objective. In Zimbabwe, this important task remained the purview of the Parks Department, which, in addition to overseeing and regulating the industry, also ran tours and owned various accommodations in national parks and safari zones.

The Parks Department also established divergent entry fees for foreign visitors and local residents. Department officials argued that Zimbabweans "contribute to the maintenance of national parks through taxation, therefore they're entitled to an entry discount when compared with overseas tourists, who only pay into the system when they are visiting."[33] At least in theory, this system meant that the parks remained accessible for locals, who "have a real and usable right of access to enjoy their own natural heritage at a reasonable rate."[34] Perhaps most importantly, the system tempers criticism regarding tourism as an endeavor exclusively designed for foreigners, rather than for members of local populations with, presumably, lesser means. Thus, it is not surprising that many African governments have adopted some version of this system, which results in minimal losses of admission fees—at higher rates, many locals simply would not enter the parks—while generating much goodwill among the electorate, or at least blunting potential criticism.

Farther north on the continent, a very different type of wildlife was key to Rwanda's conservation-as-tourism strategy. Following independence from Belgium in 1962, the small central African nation moved to protect its most valuable faunal asset: mountain gorillas. By the mid-1960s, the American primatologist Dian Fossey was actively studying these gorilla groups, made famous via her 1983 book, *Gorillas in the Mist*. Further popularizing this wildlife was a 1988 feature film starring Sigourney Weaver, which was based on the book and was nominated for five Academy Awards. In part due to Fossey's pioneering efforts, poaching of these gorillas declined over the course of the 1970s. Grimly, these primates were "killed for their skulls, which were then sold to collectors and museums, and their hands, which became ashtrays for the tourist trade, while live young were captured for sale to foreign collectors."[35]

Starting in 1979, advocates for the gorillas teamed with the Rwandan government to devise the Mountain Gorilla Project (MGP), which married conservation efforts with the country's tourism objectives. Before the launch of the MGP, scientists had learned that the state had been planning to set aside 12,000 acres of land in Virunga National Park for cattle grazing, which would have drastically reduced the gorillas' habitat. Reflecting on the reaction to this proposition, one of the leaders of the MGP, Bill Weber, explained that "faced with a proposal to put in 5,000 heads of cattle and take another 5,000 hectares of the park, tourism made total sense. Just on a purely economic basis, you didn't have to put in that many tourists to outcompete the cattle."[36] Accordingly, entry fees were set sufficiently high in order to generate ample revenue while limiting the total number of visitors.

Significant obstacles remained, however, before these touristic monies could begin to flow. For example, Fossey strongly opposed this form of tourism, as gorillas are highly susceptible to human diseases, such as influenza, against which they have no immunity. She even fired several shots over the heads of a group of Dutch tourists who were visiting, uninvited, in the area in which she worked. The gorillas also need to be habituated to the presence of sizable numbers of humans, which can otherwise cause these animals undue stress. This acclimation takes time and renders them more vulnerable to poachers, as they obviously cannot discern between humans interested in admiring them and those who aim to kill them.

These challenges notwithstanding, with funding from the African Wildlife Foundation, the Flora and Fauna Preservation Society, and the People's Trust for Endangered Species (PTES), as well as support from the Rwandan government, the MGP was well established by the mid-1980s.[37] The government was amenable to the project, but did need some convincing. Weber explained:

> We found that foreign technical consultants had locked into class A tourism, in which you must travel in a zebra-striped minivan through grasslands and watch lions yawn. When we went in and said we think there are people who will want to come here and walk around the mountains, they really thought we were nuts, and the head of the Rwandan parks service at first turned it down. He said it just wasn't workable. And the next time we suggested it, he asked if I thought there were enough crazy *mzungu* [whites] who will want to come crawl around Green Hills National Park. . . . We felt it was safe to say something like one thousand tourists per year and pretty soon you might get two thousand.[38]

Before long, the number of visitors was many times the figure Weber cited, while the success of the MGP spawned similar enterprises in the neighboring Congo, in 1985, and in Uganda, in 1993. Ultimately, the partnership between the Rwandan state and the MGP served both conservation and touristic objectives. It can also, however, be understood as an example of neocolonialism given that the initiative was conceived by Westerners and funded by foreign agencies. Regardless, it is arguable that without this intervention, including the associated incentives and revenue that this form of tourism generates, Rwanda's gorilla population would almost certainly have perished.[39]

The Material Impacts of Tourism Initiatives on Local Populations

Although newly independent African states strategically developed their respective tourism industries to generate much needed revenue, these sectors typically impacted their citizenries somewhat minimally or, at best, unevenly. Even so, in every nation in which the industry was expanded, jobs naturally followed. For example, one study suggested that in 1972 there were some forty thousand Kenyans employed in that country's industry, though that figure is most likely exaggerated.[40] Irrespective of the accuracy of the report, as was the case during the colonial period, Africans were largely employed in entry-level jobs that featured low wages, while more lucrative positions, at least in the period immediately following decolonization, were commonly staffed by foreigners and smaller numbers of educated or experienced Africans. Because colonial laws had prevented Africans from serving as proprietors of touristic businesses and denied them managerial opportunities, there was minimal expertise among local populations at the dawn of this new era. Only later did Africans who had been employed in the industry during the colonial period typically transition into more senior posts.

In fact, scholars and others with an interest in the industry following decolonization were hotly debating these labor realities for Africans in the sector. On one side were individuals promoting tourism as a vehicle for national development, based largely on economic indicators. Conversely, detractors adopted a more critical approach, noting that any "national development" that might occur would be quite limited, benefitting only a small group of elite stakeholders and foreign investors, while doing little for the "average African." In many ways, these debates persist: governments and private investors continue to actively develop tourism industries to improve their own financial well-being and, indirectly, the welfare of the populations of these countries, while myriad observers continue to question the economic, social, and environmental impacts of tourism.

Even the conservation of animals can be a contentious issue. Earlier, we learned how various African governments were utilizing resident faunal populations to generate touristic revenue, but these endeavors, though widely applauded by international conservation groups and visiting tourists alike, rarely take into consideration the impact on local populations. During the colonial period, we know that many communities were forcibly removed from lands to create national parks and game reserves, despite a demonstrated record of sensible and sustainable resource management, which balanced survival and conservation. Following independence, African governments might have returned these communities to lands they had previously inhabited. However, the lure of touristic revenue was simply too great, prompting a Maasai member of Kenya's Parliament to accuse the government in 1968 of "adopting a land use policy that put wild animals first and human beings second."[41] Even in the 1970s, when many national development projects had gone awry and growing numbers of citizens, including farmers and landless peasants, were actively lobbying to access these proscribed spaces, governments refused to allow communities to (re)settle, or even enter, these areas.

More Gorillas, More Jobs: The Case of Rwanda

Even when African governments disregarded local concerns, some of the conservation plans they pursued still generated employment opportunities for proximate communities. An example of this scenario comes from Rwanda. As we read earlier, the Mountain Gorilla Project, or MGP, constituted a major conservation initiative that also promised to produce significant touristic revenue for the country. Before the MGP was launched, the Rwandan Office of Tourism and National Parks employed only a handful of administrative employees and twenty guards to safeguard the valuable gorillas. Roughly a decade into the project, the guard ranks had increased to seventy, or one guard for every 2 square kilometers, making the gorillas' territory "one of the best protected areas on earth."[42] Moreover, tourist revenue generated by the MGP facilitated training and equipment purchases for this increasingly professionalized staff. The initiative also generated a host of other employment opportunities for locals who began servicing the increasing number of foreign visitors. There was, however, one problem. Amplified security meant that local people lost access to certain natural resources in the park, including firewood and water, that they had previously utilized. Moreover, the Rwandan government rejected a revenue-sharing proposal, wanting to keep the significant tourism "revenues for the central treasury, even as it identified rural communities as the engine of national development."[43] Regardless, surveys of regional residents indicated that, over time, they increasingly recognized the value of the MGP, even as they lost control over the local environment and the access to resources that they had once enjoyed.

Livelihood Opportunities in Paradise: The Case of the Seychelles

Not all tourism on the continent revolves around fauna. The Seychelles, a 115-island Indian Ocean archipelago, attracts foreign visitors due to the country's beaches, sunshine, tropical waters, and, according to its tourism industry, its "otherworldliness." With by far the continent's smallest population—which even today remains under one hundred thousand people and was just over sixty thousand at the time of its independence in 1976—it's tempting to think that the development of the country's tourism industry would greatly benefit the Seychellois population. To some extent, that's accurate. But it's also a bit more complex than that.

The development of meaningful touristic infrastructure in the Seychelles began in the early 1970s, just prior to independence from the United Kingdom. In 1972, the first international hotel opened, with another following closely behind in Victoria, the capital city. A handful more of these establishments opened in the ensuing years, providing employment opportunities for "all adult males."[44] Yet the close relationship between touristic development and the generation of jobs also featured a particularly problematic dimension: just as employment rates could be boosted among the miniscule population via a single large-scale construction project, so too did jobs evaporate when these projects concluded. In spite of this challenge, given the islanders' predicament—the Seychelles feature only minimal, mountainous land and are devoid of any mineral resources—government officials naturally eyed sustained touristic development as an attractive economic solution.

Initially, there were few dissenting voices. On one hand—a much larger hand, for what it's worth—the governing Seychelles Democratic Party touted tourism's potential and, to some extent, the benefits it was already delivering, including widespread employment, high(er) wages in the sector, opportunities for social mobility, improved transportation networks, and important linkages to the broader world, from which the islands had long been isolated.[45] Meanwhile, on the (much smaller) other hand, some

Seychellois began to question the assumption that tourism was an exclusively positive development for the islands. Among other concerns, they cited "soaring land prices, rapid inflation, shortages of staple commodities such as fish and vegetables, increasing volumes of imports, domination of expatriates and foreign capital, increasing poverty and malnutrition, the neglect of agriculture," and perhaps most damning, the transformation of the local population into a "nation of waiters."[46] Various African citizenries, governments, and civil society organizations would echo these very same concerns in the ensuing decades.

So great was this swelling discontent regarding the development of tourism in the Seychelles that the coup d'état that the country experienced in 1977 was born partially out of this dissatisfaction. When Prime Minister France-Albert René overthrew the country's first president, James Mancham, he instituted a one-party state, condemning the economic dependence on tourism and declaring that rather than continue the foreign influx of capital and tourists, he wanted "to keep the Seychelles for the Seychellois." As with prior government officials across the continent, these sentiments highlighted the intersection of politics, national sovereignty, and touristic development in the aftermath of independence.

Despite their rhetoric, many socialist leaders of newly independent African states found the potential revenue from tourism irresistible. The Seychelles was no exception. Over the course of the 1980s, the industry continued to expand and it became clear that even Seychellois on the lowest rungs of the sector's employment ladder came to see the industry as vital to the country's well-being. For example, in a 1991 interview, a local maid working in a tourist guest house remarked, "What can the Seychelles do without tourism? A few fish here, a few coconuts there—how can Seychellois live on that?"[47] In general, Seychellois society appeared to tolerate the trade-off: although the country was often overrun with tourists, these visitors generated tax revenues and livelihood options for the resident population. Moreover, Seychellois favored these new "clean" employment opportunities in the tourism industry over more traditional, "dirty" pursuits, such as agriculture and fishing.[48] And, unlike in other African settings, employment in the sector was permanent rather than seasonal, as the tourism season spans the calendar in this climatically temperate archipelago. Finally, as in many other places on the continent during these initial decades following independence, foreign visitors seemed content with remaining in the various international hotels and resorts, minimally interacting with, and thereby only minimally disrupting, local cultural practices and mores. For example, in 1991, on an average visit of roughly ten days, foreign tourists remarkably consumed only two meals outside of their hotel restaurants, while engaging, in general, in very few excursions that would take them away from these accommodations. This phenomenon may be less surprising given the government's aim to entice primarily affluent visitors by keeping lodging rates artificially high and banning camping and youth hostels.

Entrepreneurial Women: The Case of Gambia

Finally, the example of the development of tourism in Gambia in the aftermath of independence reminds us that African women were also key figures in this broader history. Gambian women were initially able to find work in the formal portion of the sector, for example in tourist hotels, but in far lower numbers—only about 20 percent of the staff at these establishments were female—than their male counterparts. Moreover, most of these women held the lowest-paying positions: kitchen hands, cleaners, and laundresses.[49] In response, Gambian women moved to capitalize on the expanding curio and handicraft markets for the influxes of tourists who, to avoid the rainy season, primarily arrived between October and April. Not to be excluded, Gambian men also sought livelihoods in this arena, focusing on woodcarvings, leather goods, and various types of jewelry. But women cornered the market on dyed cloth (tie-dye and batik) and apparel, generating types and styles intended for the touristic, rather than domestic, market. In particular, they focused on cuts and styles that appealed to Western tourists, while still retaining enough "Africanness" in their products to satisfy these visitors. These entrepreneurial women even strategically adopted terms to describe their wares that they had picked up from the initial waves of tourists, who had been primarily Scandinavian.[50]

Gambian women's dominance in this arena was attributable to their resourcefulness and creativity rather than predicated on traditional gender roles. Indeed, in Gambia, both men and women customarily produced dyed clothes of various types, but Gambian women utilized their conventional roles as petty traders to monopolize the market. In practice, the women "producing and selling indigenous tie-dye and batik to the tourists were primarily former petty traders who had learned how to be artisans as well, though not in the traditional context, but in a modern one where the emphasis was on trading and not on production."[51] Beyond setting up shop near the major hotels, in 1968, the capital city of Banjul became the site of the largest tourist-specific market, "The Banjul Craftsmen's Market." Despite the gender-exclusive name, women were also able to pursue livelihoods selling their wares in this forum to sojourning clientele from the Global North.

The Cultural and Psychological Impacts of Tourism

As increasing numbers of tourists began arriving in Africa following independence, the economic and developmental impacts of these visitors were, as outlined above, intensely debated, and, in many respects, this contentious discussion continues. With the dramatic changes in social dynamics that marked the new, postcolonial era, foreign tourists also began to have significant cultural and even psychological impacts upon their hosts. During the colonial period, these visitors' activities, and, more importantly, the actions of Africans who were employed in the industry, were closely monitored or even circumscribed. However, in many settings following independence, foreign tourists and members of local populations could more freely interact, prompting many Africans to adopt alien behaviors and Western styles. Local observers of a more conservative bent typically lamented the "destructive" or "distortive" influences that foreign visitors had on local practices, customs, beliefs, and comportment. Others, however, in particular younger Africans in urban settings, readily embraced these styles and behaviors, gradually eroding their parents' and elders' control over them.

One of the most profound impacts of this nature occurred in Eswatini (Swaziland) following the country's efforts to develop its tourist industry in the aftermath of independence. As explained previously, Eswatini is still ruled by a monarchy, a powerful indication of its conservative culture. In fact, this adherence to tradition is a means by which the monarchy legitimizes itself and its hold on governmental power. Thus, the "modern" thinking and behavior that foreign tourists brought to the nation inherently threatened the status quo. Indeed, some contemporaneous observers contended that the influx of tourists was having deleterious effects on the local population, including an increase in "begging, prostitution, and other forms of 'immoral' activity attributed to the arrival and influence of these visitors," though, in practice, these activities long predate the arrival of foreigners brandishing cameras and prodigious disposable income.[52] Further, the government's decision to invest in a series of casinos generated backlash among conservative Swazis who condemned the perceived unsavory components of casino culture—namely, gambling and drinking—as threatening to local society.

These social concerns notwithstanding, young Swazi women were quick to embrace new styles introduced by foreign visitors. One example was the newfound practice of wearing trousers, especially jeans, which generated considerable and widely aired hostility.[53] In response, the kingdom briefly banned these pants—even for tourists—before subsequently rescinding this interdiction. Owing to the conservative nature of Swazi society, though, periodic calls or even outright bans have been instituted regarding various clothing choices for women, mostly revolving around the baring of skin. Ironically, as the country strove to package its "traditional" culture for the consumption of foreigners, it reacted aggressively toward any corrupting influences on local society that were ascribed to these very same (coveted) visitors.

A similar phenomenon played out in Kenya, with younger members of the population most likely to embrace foreign visitors' styles, mannerisms, and values. As one observer opined in the 1980s, "These young people adopt the 'modern' way of life by imitating not only Western clothing, but also the behavior and lifestyle of European and American visitors, including their ethical and moral codes. A particular side of touristic demonstration is 'nudism,' i.e. walking in bathing suits around town, which is in sharp contrast to local Muslim ethics."[54] It is, of course, impossible to attribute these social changes solely to young Kenyans' physical exposure to Western tourists; yet, before widespread access to film, television, and, of course, the internet, most Africans learned about other peoples through personal interaction.

If many Africans—and, in particular, older and more conservative individuals—bemoaned these cultural developments, many younger members of society held a divergent perspective for a host of reasons. For some, interaction with tourists constituted a chance to practice foreign languages, which could, in turn, facilitate employment. For other Africans, including the Seychellois, who apparently enjoyed talking with tourists, these interactions offered a type of "substitute for overseas travel and, thus, provided in its own way a source of prestige through the knowledge gained from and about the tourists and the countries from which they came."[55] Seychellois also allegedly found that talking to visitors was actually therapeutic, as they could "talk more freely to tourists, whom they would not see again, than to their fellow islanders. Such 'confessional' conversations were difficult with other local people, because of the danger of either mockery, malicious gossip, or even being reported to the authorities for political 'offenses.'"[56]

Beyond the behavioral influences that these foreign visitors had on host communities across the continent, tourism often had a psychological impact, as well. In many ways, interpersonal colonial-period power dynamics between foreigners and Africans were re-created or simply perpetuated in this otherwise novel era. As accusations of neocolonialism abounded throughout the developing world during these decades, these kinds of asymmetrical interracial interactions provided ample ammunition for individuals seeking to condemn the cultural and psychological impacts that international tourism was having on Africans. For example, in 1970, Tanzanian citizen S. A. Kibona argued that "when you go to Europe you are supposed to talk, drink, walk, dress, eat, and laugh like them. When they come here, we treat them like little gods. This inferiority complex and subordination truly erodes our nationalism and identity. I feel it is high time we started exporting our cultural values even if it means losing some fancy tourists. We may lose financially in the short run, but we shall be gaining in stabilizing our cultural evolution."[57] Given the lingering pain of the colonial period, it is not surprising that so many African would resent this "re-invasion" of the continent, with its attendant subordination, submission, and mimicry.

In some respects, Africans themselves played a central role in the perpetuation of these interactional dynamics. For example, to develop fledgling tourist industries, local organizers tapped the "exoticness" of various resident communities, often along ethnic lines. An emphasis on tradition—and the revenues it promised to deliver—made this commodification of culture palatable for African tourism officials, but it also debased the communities and performers selected to present these cultural forms. Commenting on Eswatini in the decades following independence, for example, David Harrison has contended that "the message conveyed to potential tourists is that Swaziland is a country of exotic people, with unfamiliar customs and colorful costumes, which is locked in the past. The logical conclusion is to consider the entire country a showpiece, a living, moving, breathing storehouse of tradition."[58] This type of criticism notwithstanding, governments elsewhere on the continent replicated this touristic approach. Writing contemporaneously about this phenomenon in Kenya, scholar Philip Bachmann observed that "one has the impression that African culture, as it is propagated by Kenyan officials, has become a mere vehicle to boost the tourism industry. Because the tourists like it, traditional dances are arranged in hotels and elsewhere, while [ethnic] Maasai warriors—both living Maasai and carved ones—are posed at tourist crossroads."[59]

AS AFRICAN nations gained their sovereignty, they desperately needed funds to provide the services that their citizenries newly demanded. Given the continent's alluring fauna, flora, and peoples, coupled with its warmer climes and appealing natural features, including extensive beaches, government officials naturally identified tourism as a potential revenue generator. In some countries, governments perpetuated colonial-era marketing. However, in many other locations, states had to commence the development of tourism industries essentially from scratch, which included generating their own promotional messaging and materials.

Although African officials certainly made mistakes, and these sectors undeniably benefited members of national citizenries unevenly, these initial efforts eventually bore fruit, at least from a quantitative perspective. The emergence of international "mass tourism" included an uptick of visitors to the continent starting in the 1960s, especially to Morocco, Tunisia, and Egypt, on the Mediterranean coast, but also to other destinations, such as Kenya, Gambia, and South Africa. By the 1970s, the list of popular sites also included Rwanda, the Seychelles, and Mauritius. Into the early 1980s, the five most popular destinations—Egypt, Tunisia, Morocco, South Africa, and Kenya—accounted for an astounding 73 percent of all international tourist arrivals to Africa.[60] It is important to note, though, that even as traffic to Africa increased, traffic to other global regions rise during this period. For example, in 1974, there were 196.7 million international tourist arrivals globally, of which only 3.9 million, or 1.98 percent, occurred in Africa. A decade later, in 1984, those figures were 300 million and 7.5 million (2.5 percent), respectively.[61]

Foreign visitors to Africa were treated to a place packaged as timeless and tradition-bound, even as the continent's newly independent nations raced to modernize a range of services. For example, a tourist brochure from 1980s Swaziland (Eswatini) boasted that it was a land in which "Ancient Traditions Mingle with Up-to-the Minute Amenities: Swaziland is a fascinating blend of contrasts and contradictions, old traditions mingling with 20th-century technology."[62] This combination of "ancient" and "modern" was exactly what most tourists wanted. As one observer in the early 1980s commented, "Tourism to Africa is an escapist drama."[63] These visitors imagined a particular Africa, one that existed in sharp contrast to their homelands in the Global North, and African tourism officials and tourist operators happily obliged, packaging purported tradition and exoticism for guests while assuring them they would be continuously ensconced in comfortable surroundings.

In myriad ways, the tourist experience in Africa was expertly stage-managed by its various stakeholders, and, in practice, no touristic undertaking was more carefully manufactured for foreign visitors than the safari, itself a touristic invention. It is to this endeavor—one of the principle activities about which would-be tourists to Africa dream—that we turn in the ensuing chapter.

CHAPTER FIVE

The Touristic Invention of the African Camera Safari

We drove around Etosha and saw some amazing things, including a herd of elephants not even 50 feet away. One of the bulls told us in no uncertain terms that we were in his way. . . . I told our amazing guide that I wanted to see some baby elephants playing in the water . . . what do you know, that's what happened next! . . . We were very fortunate—I think we saw in one trip what would normally take 10 trips to see.

—A blog post by Jen Black, of Idaho, following a 2014 safari in Namibia's Etosha National Park

On a Thorn Tree Safari, you abandon civilization and all of its discontents and journey across miles of natural wilderness, traveling millions of years back in time. Here in Kenya it is still possible to view the world as our primitive ancestors saw it, in its natural state, without the influences of modern civilization. On safari you will see nature unfold as it always has. . . . A Thorn Tree Safari is an enjoyable adventure that combines wild nature with civilized luxury.

—Contemporary promotional material for Thorn Tree Safari, a Kenya-based operator

JEN BLACK may, indeed, have been "fortunate" to have had such a remarkable experience, even if she was not on one of Thorn Tree Safari's "wild," yet "civilized," outings. In fact, most folks with whom I talk about their visits to the continent cite the camera safari as their primary motivation and, moreover, indicate that they would not have traveled to Africa at all had they not been slated to observe and photograph the wildlife in its natural environment. And this sentiment is perfectly understandable. After all, the prospect of viewing an array of magnificent animals in their natural habitats, far removed from zoo settings or the array of "drive-thru" safaris that are so common in the United States, is undoubtedly appealing. In fact, some studies have revealed that tourists are even willing to pay additional amounts of money while on safari to protect this wildlife.[1]

Irrespective of the particular site of the camera safari, the core components of this undertaking are reasonably similar. Tourists are generally driven around in a "safari vehicle" by an experienced guide, who simultaneously serves as chauffeur, spotter, and amateur zoologist. The vehicle periodically stops so that passengers can take photographs of any wildlife in view, with the duration of the engagement dependent on the particular animals within sight and their proximity. The tourists are then returned to a nearby resort, where they enjoy the creature comforts of the Global North, including high quality cuisine, cold beverages, satellite television, and abundant air conditioning, serviced by a variety of African staff (fig. 5.1). Collectively, these elements produce the internationally recognizable "African safari."

FIGURE 5.1 Safari lodge, just outside Etosha National Park, in Namibia. *Photo by author.*

There are, however, also important variations in the camera safari experience. For example, one might drive oneself or go on a "walking safari" through one of Africa's multitude of game parks or reserves. Moreover, accommodations can be "deep in the bush," broadly within a game park's boundaries, or just beyond them. Safari experiences also vary dramatically in price, generally depending on the degree of exclusiveness and luxury, with some outfits charging thousands of dollars per evening, per person. Irrespective of these differences, the fundamental experience is intended to be universal: tourists witness a seemingly pristine landscape, devoid of indigenous residents, populated by "exotic" game, and protected by earnest stewards who are committed to the conservation and well-being of the park's faunal inhabitants.

Although we are all familiar with the African camera safari, it does not have a particularly long history. After all, some of its essential components, namely automobiles and portable cameras, are somewhat recent inventions. So too is the prevailing attitude that Africa's big game ought to be conserved and observed rather than hunted. Well before the photographic safari could be properly realized, game parks and reserves had to be delineated and any human residents from these spaces systematically removed. Not surprisingly, then, what we now recognize as "safari" is a relatively recent, Western invention, dating only as far back as Africa's colonial period.

As we learned previously, the earliest touristic safaris were hunting expeditions, first organized in the later decades of the nineteenth century and increasing in frequency during the initial decades of the twentieth century. Over time, the "camera safari" joined these hunting endeavors as a novel, alternative form of the endeavor, and steadily—certainly by the 1950s—the word "safari" came to exclusively describe the photographic variety, whereas hunting trips to Africa gradually dropped the term. Current marketing and promotional materials for these latter undertakings reflect this transition, generally referring to them as "hunting packages," "hunting trips," or at the very least, including "hunting" in the advertisement (e.g., "African hunting safari"). The ascendance of the camera safari and the corresponding decline of the hunting safari is reflected in the touristic geography of these respective pursuits: there is now significantly more space reserved on the continent for camera safaris than there is for big-game hunting.

This chapter examines the history of the camera safari, from its humble beginnings to its touristic preeminence. The more recent version of the safari constitutes the backbone of many African nations' tourism industries.

Consequently, skilled African organizers and staff carefully manage these undertakings. Every effort is made to expose tourists to what they have traveled to see, while keeping less agreeable aspects of these locales safely out of eyesight as foreign visitors engage on a quest to observe and photograph the continent's renowned wildlife and, in so doing, realize the "trip of a lifetime."

A Brief History of Safari and the Camera Safari

By considering the etymology of the word "safari," we are afforded interesting insights into its origins and evolution. According to the *Oxford English Dictionary*, the word initially meant "a party or caravan undertaking an extensive cross-country expedition on foot for hunting or scientific research, typically in an African country (originally in East Africa)." Divergently, contemporary usage indicates that the word means "a party travelling, usually in vehicles, into unspoiled or wild areas for tourism or game viewing,"[2] though we have already learned that we need to critically engage with the terms "unspoiled" and "wild," as game parks are carefully managed, artificial spaces. The word "safari" is borrowed from Kiswahili, a language of East Africa that itself borrows heavily from Arabic. The Swahili word appears to have entered the English language in 1890, and in its Swahili form referred to "a journey undertaken with a specific objective: expedition, pilgrimage, trek, or voyage." The word is associated with the term *msafara*, which derives from the Arabic word *safara*, meaning a journey or tour.[3] In practice, these *safara*, or "safaris" in the plural, were composed of caravans of porters carrying various faunal items, including "oils, skins, and rhinoceros horns out of the East African interior to be traded with the Swahili people of the coast and grew larger and more complex with the rise of the slave empire of Zanzibar [off the east coast of Tanzania] in the 19th century."[4]

Over time, European missionaries and explorers launched their own versions of these undertakings, seeking to penetrate Africa's mystifying interior. These trekking parties were typically heavily armed, prepared to subdue any hostile peoples they might encounter en route. In these configurations, Europeans were the heroes, boldly traversing "wild" Africa and "discovering" new lands, peoples, and animals as part of a triumphant Western narrative in which Africa was to be tamed. These endeavors "produced an imaginary idea of Africa as a land of the unknown, a place inhabited by exotic and hostile African tribes and dangerous wild animals."[5] Yet, even as these intrepid Westerners marched into the interior, African porters were already carrying commodities on these treks that we identify with contemporary safaris, such as wine and brandy.[6]

As Europeans overran the continent during the second half of the nineteenth century, they increasingly, and eventually exclusively, oversaw these excursions, with Africans serving as porters, trackers, gun bearers, cooks, and in various other capacities. Upon the formal establishment of the various colonial regimes in the concluding decades of the nineteenth century, the first accommodations for safari and other types of tourists were constructed. With Europeans now enjoying control over both the lands on which Africa's big game roamed, as well as the pools of local labor, safari experiences could commence in earnest.

In the initial decades of the twentieth century, the camera safari and associated touristic landscape was rapidly shifting. By the late 1920s, cruise ships docked along Kenya's Indian Ocean coast were facilitating "safaris" for passengers by rail to the capital city of Nairobi and back, enabling them to view and photograph game from the train windows as they traveled.[7] Meanwhile, advances in photography and the introduction of the automobile were dramatically accelerating the transition from safaris as hunting expeditions to photographic outings. The automobile, in particular, precipitated substantive change, not least because tourists used to approach game in cars before getting out to inch even closer to improve their photographs, a practice that was, thankfully, eventually forbidden. The safari also generally became shorter, as cars could cover much more territory within the same time period, thereby enabling visitors to "get around quickly and hurry away so as to boast of what they had done," though as one observer lamented, "You may scrape Africa's acquaintance by automobile, but you never touch the heart of her."[8]

The car also facilitated, or arguably prompted, the "champagne safari," on which luxury became a central part of the experience, "dripping with glamour" and foreshadowing the contemporary safari experience.[9] For example, a photographic safari participant during the 1920s commenting on the divergent costs of the various forms of this endeavor wrote that "a 'filter-and-water safari' was cheap but a 'champagne-and-ice safari' may run into the thousands of pounds monthly."[10] Overall improvements in the safari experience during this decade abounded, with one observer describing this endeavor in the 1920s as follows: "Called for the day at half-past four. . . . Under way at quarter of six in the morning—the sun rose at about quarter after. . . . Game-watch until mid-morning [coming to British East

Africa merely to look had become more acceptable by this time], lunch and sleep, go out again until dark. Then cocktails and the hot bath, dinner in pyjamas and mosquito boots, often in front of a blazing pile of logs because the night air was cold."[11] At the extreme, the decade also witnessed one of the most spectacular photographic safaris ever to "glamorize the Kenyan bush," which featured a private armored car, a mobile movie theater, motorcycle messengers, a generating plant, a medical lorry with X-ray unit, and a mobile drawing-room with a grand piano.[12] By the end of the decade, the British colonies of Kenya and Tanganyika (Tanzania), including the internationally renowned Serengeti and Ngorongoro regions in the latter, became the prime settings for camera safaris of all varieties—with or without pianos.

Photography was also making important strides during this period. Safari photography dates back to the 1860s, but advances in technology, namely reductions in the size and weight of camera equipment, rendered generating images of the celebrated fauna significantly easier. In particular, George Eastman, the wealthy founder of Eastman Kodak, made key contributions to this marriage of photography and safari during his 1926 excursion to East Africa at age seventy-two. This foray was especially notable because Eastman centered photography in the safari experience—not overly surprising given how he had generated his fortune. Although photographers had been traveling to Africa since the nineteenth century, the focus on photography instead of game hunting was still in its infancy. In fact, it was not until the 1920s that photography became a respectable safari activity, in good part "because of Eastman's Kodak products and the work of Martin and Osa Johnson [whom we encountered earlier in the book], whose lives became intertwined with his."[13]

The Great Depression naturally affected the fledgling camera safari industry just as it adversely affected hunting safaris, limiting the clientele who could afford this experience while driving out of business a great number of safari operators. The international aggression that characterized the mid-to-late 1930s, including Italy's 1935 invasion of Ethiopia, prolonged the moribund state of the safari industry, which would not rebound until after the conclusion of the Second World War.

As we learned earlier, mass air travel in the decade following the Second World War propelled the tourism industry in Africa to unprecedented heights. The 1950s also marked the unequivocal transition from hunting to photographic safaris. According to one estimate, before the global conflict,

"80% of safari tourists had come to Africa to hunt, 20% to take photographs; after the war, those percentages were reversed."[14] Another significant change was the predominance of Americans on camera safaris, in great part owing to the United States' postwar economic expansion. Automobile innovations, including the expansion of four-wheel drive, further facilitated shifts in the industry. Following the Second World War, surplus jeeps were used to traverse Africa's more challenging terrain, including in safari areas, followed by Land Rovers and, eventually, an array of four-wheel-drive vehicles.

With the independence of most African nations in the 1960s, camera safari tourism dipped temporarily, with prospective visitors waiting to determine how safe and secure these newly sovereign places would be. Departing, disgruntled setters added to this uncertainty, claiming that Africans would destroy the valuable fauna through mismanagement. Although the resultant reduction in safari tourism is understandable, what was less predictable was "the alacrity with which tourists responded once it appeared that the new nations were not only safe, but were also hospitable, rapidly expanding their tourism industries, with a democratizing emphasis on safari game viewing and photography."[15] In many ways, this heightened touristic activity reflected would-be visitors' shifting sentiments toward Africa, as well as the social and touristic objectives of newly installed African government officials. As Kenneth Cameron has compellingly argued,

> These governments encouraged changes that removed the most egregious symbols and memories of racialism. These changes were brought about by emphasizing game viewing rather than game-killing; by building lodges for numbers of visitors rather than safari-camping facilities for a few. The safari thus showed what in fact had always been true of it: it was not merely responsive to racial and political policy, but was a symbolic instrument of such policy.[16]

These efforts notwithstanding, hunting safaris persisted, as they do today in certain places. But by the 1960s, the prevailing trends were irreversible. The camera safari was ascendant, and it would only continue to grow in popularity over the ensuing decades. To further facilitate this expansion, many African governments banned hunting and aggressively designated acreage for game reserves and parks. Following the 1977 ban on hunting in Kenya, for example, a local newspaper's headline trumpeted this development as a "Farewell to Arms!"[17]

Safari in a Mythical, Imagined Africa

The setting has always been vital to the African camera safari experience. Fueled by the innumerable programs on television that offer glimpses of these famed animals in front of scenic backdrops, as well as a range of other reinforcing images delivered via various forms of popular culture, tourists desperately want to experience this "wild Africa" and, in particular, the continent's savannahs and the big game that reside there. Most tourists have imagined this Africa—*the* Africa—long before they ever reach the continent's borders. In this romanticized version, the continent is dangerous but simultaneously beautiful, far removed from the hustle and stress of the "more civilized," "more advanced" worlds in which they daily operate—an apparent journey back in time. This Africa is a "glorious Eden for wildlife" and an escape for visitors.[18]

The decades that followed political independence in Africa witnessed the emergence of various television programs that continued to feed earlier impressions of the continent as one giant savannah, seemingly lacking any human population while hosting an incredible range of wildlife. The 1970s marked the introduction of such programs as *Nova* (1974), joined in the 1980s by *Nature* (1982), both of which aired on PBS. Writing in 1992, Jonathan Adams and Thomas McShane contended that "more people probably got their first taste of Africa from public television than from any other source. 'Nature' alone has several million viewers every Saturday night. It is, thus, hardly surprising that in the popular mind, Africa consists entirely of wide grassy plains and wild animals."[19] With the expansion of cable television, additional channels, including Discovery (1985), Animal Planet (1996), and National Geographic (2001), joined the ranks of regular broadcasters of Africa's wildlife, further reinforcing reductive perceptions of the continent's topography while suggesting that animals reigned owing to the seeming absence of humans.[20]

The camera safari became the vehicle through which foreigners could access this enchanted land, observe in person the majestic game that they had previously only seen on television or in confined spaces, such as zoos, and witness the seemingly endless savannah, which served as the backdrop for this otherworldly experience. With the growth in disposable incomes, increased leisure time, and opportunities for long-haul travel, escalating numbers of foreign tourists realized this dream.[21] Confirming this increased volume of travelers, Curtis Keim has averred that "most upper-middle- and upper-class Americans know at least one person who has been on a photo safari in Africa" (fig. 5.2).[22]

FIGURE 5.2 An American child on safari in Eswatini, 2017. *Photo by author.*

Assessing the Photographic Safari: Good or Bad, and for Whom?

The world is, of course, much more complex than the "good-bad" binary that the title of this section suggests. But it is important to critically evaluate the camera safari while refashioning this query by asking: good or bad *for whom?*

The Foreign Tourist

We can start with the foreign tourist. I have yet to meet anyone who has failed to enjoy their safari experience in Africa—the animated comments from Jen Black from Idaho at the outset of this chapter are, in practice, quite standard. Safari participants are transported to the African wilderness that they had heretofore seen only on television or in film. Once there, they engage in a type of adventure, though the risks are acutely managed and minimized, even if the illusion of peril persists. Truly, only on walking safaris is there any real danger, and even then, the guides' knowledge, experience, and especially their high-powered rifles keep the clientele safe.

While traversing game parks and reserves, foreign tourists are invited to envision a time before humans became as numerous as they are now, or they might even imagine that they are traveling in a world without humans, or before humans, during some prehistoric era. Nature in this seemingly pristine form quickly becomes normalized, with the tourist only jolted out of this dreamscape upon an animal sighting or an encounter with another safari vehicle. With no Africans present in these carefully cultivated spaces, notions of Africa as a "primitive wilderness" or as "wild kingdom" remain unchallenged. Regarding the safari experience in its entirety, Keim compellingly argues that "if we take account of the larger structure of the experience—who can afford to go, how they get there, what they do, what they focus on, and what they think—we can see it as part of the whole Western pattern of experiencing the world. As such, it reconfirms what we already believe about Africa, as do zoos, natural history museums, animal amusement parks, nature television, and even *The Lion King*."[23] Naturally, safari participants would object to Keim analogizing their experience with a visit to a zoo, but his point is well-taken.

African Governments

Meanwhile, for African governments, the emergence of the photographic safari has generally been a positive development. Inheriting an array of game parks and reserves from their former colonial masters, the camera safari was a ready-made revenue generator. Moreover, aid agencies and international conservation organizations applauded the continent's governments for pursuing this form of sustainable, eco-friendly tourism. Still, an array of challenges remained. As we have learned previously, states were required to outlay capital for transport and touristic infrastructure, as well as improved security for the wildlife—the true stars of the safari. And in some cases where lands were newly designated for this purpose, such as in 1971 in Ghana's Mole National Park, residents had to be forcefully removed, reminiscent of the relocations of the colonial era. Governments also came under criticism for developing and protecting an industry that caters primarily to foreigners and, relatedly, for retaining fertile land for this type of luxury tourism rather than granting access to local farmers and hunters who could increase domestic food supplies.

Despite these challenges, the establishment of game parks and reserves has, overall, been good business for African governments. As the colonial period was at its apogee in the mid-1950s, just before its precipitous decline, only roughly 3.5 percent of sub-Saharan Africa was composed of national parks, game reserves, and other conservation areas in which wild animals were protected.[24] The majority of the spaces were situated in savannah zones in East and Southern Africa and, thus, primarily in former British colonial territory. By 1974, at a time when almost all of the continent had shed the colonial yoke, virtually every African country had at least one national park. With the explosion of tourists due to the developments outlined above, annual safari tourist numbers jumped from the thousands to the hundreds of thousands. If developmental economists had earlier cautioned that Africa's wildlife needed to "pay its way," it was unquestionably doing just that.

In turn, the rapid expansion of the camera safari industry rendered wildlife conservation an increasingly lucrative undertaking. In practice, only the most fertile land will outperform wildlife conservation and viewing in terms of revenue. In fact, wildlife is one of the most productive ways to utilize African lands, particularly semi-arid terrain. A study from 1992, for example, indicated that "mass wildlife tourism in Kenya produces $100 per hectare, with more exclusive safari tourism bringing in $50 per hectare . . . cattle ranching for beef on Zimbabwe's semi-arid pasture is actually a drain on the economy, *costing* $5 per hectare."[25] In terms of pure profits, these celebrated animals are simply hard to beat.

As we learned in the last chapter, these faunal revenues were not exclusively associated with elephants, lions, and rhinos. Before the launch of the Mountain Gorilla Project (MGP) in Rwanda in 1978, a tourist could visit the gorillas' habitat for a week after paying just a $5 entry fee, yet fewer than five hundred people per year were coming to Albert National Park. Following the commencement of the project, however, touristic entries to the park increased over 50 percent, visits to gorillas went up over 100 percent, and total park revenues increased 330 percent. For the first time ever, the number of foreign visitors exceeded that of residents.[26] By the early 1990s, annual tourist visits were surpassing seven thousand.

Over time, the revenues generated by "gorilla trekking," as it is known in the industry, encouraged the Rwandan government to pressure the MGP to increase the overall numbers of tourists who could access the gorilla habitats. Out of concern for the animals on display, the MGP limited visits to one hour in duration and dramatically increased the price of the experience. By 1992, for example, the price had risen to $200 per hour, while as of 2019, the cost had ballooned to $1,500 per person, still with a one-hour limit, though only eighty visitors per day were afforded this opportunity (slightly lower-cost gorilla viewing experiences are available in neighboring Uganda). Given the exorbitant costs, it is not surprising that this form of tourism is vital to the government's coffers, as gorilla gazers generate millions in revenue for the state while funding the ongoing maintenance of the industry, including, foremost, the well-being of the prized primates. In just over a decade, spanning 2008 to 2019, annual foreign exchange earnings from tourism in Rwanda roughly tripled, from $200 million to $600 million.[27]

Another more recent development, which had to wait for democratic rule in South Africa and the conclusion of conflicts in various settings in Southern Africa, has been the emergence of "trans-frontier safaris," which link game viewing settings across national borders, including South Africa, Botswana, Namibia, Zimbabwe, Malawi, Zambia, and Mozambique, thereby "erasing regional frontiers under a common brand of tourism."[28] This form of transnational cooperation enables animals to revert to migration patterns that had been interrupted by the imposition of colonial borders, which often featured fencing that cut through natural habitats. These touristic linkages have constituted high-profile examples of regional cooperation and meaningful partnerships for African governments, as they seek closer political and economic relations with other nations in their neighborhoods.

And Africans, Themselves

But what about the people whom these governments are supposed to serve? Has the emergence of the camera safari been good or bad for them? To answer that question, we need to divide Africa's population into a few different categories: individuals employed in the safari industry; members of communities residing adjacent or proximate to game parks and reserves; and Africans in the abstract, essentially everyone else. Irrespective of how one engages with or is affected by the camera safari industry, individual Africans have not equitably enjoyed the material benefits of an enterprise in their midst.

The industry obviously affects those Africans directly employed in it most profoundly. As we established previously, labor conditions for Africans during the colonial period were notoriously bad, with physical and mental abuse part and parcel of the employee-employer dynamic. On colonial-era safaris, Africans primarily participated as unskilled laborers, namely by carrying the necessary gear to support the clients and otherwise assisting them. Often, this meant providing service in the bush, where safari tourists slept or at least dined. As William Sutcliffe has contended, the "bush breakfasts" and "sundowner cocktails" that many contemporary safari operators offer "hanker back to an age when there were African servants to cater to one's whims. If you wanted your breakfast on top of a mountain, you could damn well have it, and someone would carry your breakfast things up there for you, right down to the last teapot, napkin and tablecloth."[29]

Exceptions to these types of menial positions included a small number of gun bearers, guides, and trackers, whom white safari leaders often deeply trusted and on whom they heavily relied for the safety of the clientele as well as themselves. These individuals also had significant utility on photographic safaris, as they knew the terrain, could help track and locate game for tourists to "shoot" with their cameras, and, if necessary, could help with the protection of guests. Following independence, some Africans—especially those who had worked in the industry during the colonial era—found work as park rangers, guides, and trackers servicing the hordes of foreign visitors who arrived on the continent to view its celebrated wildlife as part of the mass tourism that characterized this period. Africans also began to serve, even if only in relatively small numbers, as administrators, managers, officials, and in various government ministries that oversaw the network of parks and reserves in various countries.

Although most of these positions were held by African men owing to the experience they had gained during the colonial period and durable notions of the gendered divisions of labor, more recently women have been securing formal employment in the camera safari industry. Beginning in the mid-2000s, for example, women were hired as guides at Chobe Game Lodge, located in Chobe National Park, the nation's first, which opened in 1968. Although both men and women served in the capacity for a time, today the operation includes only female guides. Rather than a reflection of the country's reasonably progressive environment, the decision to exclusively employ female guides was largely financial. When the guide team "was coed, managers quickly noticed a pattern: vehicles driven by women used less gas, required fewer repairs, and lasted longer over time. Simply put, they were saving the company money."[30]

These female guides generally credit their former male colleagues for supporting them as they learned the trade. As Canah Moatshe, a Chobe guide, acknowledges, "I was the first and only lady among male guides. They never discriminated. That was the first time I drove a four by four, a Land Cruiser."[31] But some tourists weren't as supportive. These visitors were concerned about these women's ability to deliver viewings of the best animals, to handle any aggressive fauna, or even to change a safari truck tire. Yet these women haven't been deterred. As the (male) manager of the Lodge affirmed, "The ladies have developed quite a tough skin. They stand up for themselves. They give as good as they get out there."[32]

Positions for women in the industry aren't limited to guides or to Botswana. In Tanzania, for example, Angel Namshali is the manager of Dunia camp, a luxury safari lodge run by Asilia Africa, located in Serengeti National Park. Born on the slopes of Kilimanjaro, Namshali started as a housekeeper but quickly ascended to receptionist and eventually to her current managerial position. Commenting on the enterprise, Namshali explains, "I love how Asilia does things. I love the way they are supporting local communities, and especially how they focus on training their own staff, offering more opportunities for Tanzanians and giving them a position. In general, they value societies and wildlife, which is the perfect combination."[33]

Even if safari operators, like Asilia, do genuinely care about local communities, there are limited employment opportunities that these outfits can generate. Communities adjacent to safari areas have long experienced this lack of remunerative possibilities, even as a range of stakeholders, including government officials and tourism operators, have long targeted them for cooperation and attempted to sell them the financial benefits of conservation. Moreover, these communities often receive only nominal amounts of the revenue generated from the game viewing industry, despite promises to the contrary. For example, Chief Malama, who oversaw a large portion of a game management area in the Luangwa Valley in Zambia, at one point in the 1980s lamented, "Tourists come here to enjoy the lodges and to view wildlife. Safari companies come here to . . . make money. We are forgotten. Employment here is too low, the tourist lodge employs only about four people. . . . How can you ask us to cooperate with conservation when this is so?"[34]

This scenario for rural residents living adjacent to parks and reserves is typical across the continent. Research related to Chobe National Park, where nearby villagers experience few direct benefits from the lucrative camera safari industry, echoes the concerns raised by Chief Malama. In this scenario, the safari company hires "a few residents as camp staff or trackers, but for most people their contact with the visitors to Chobe is watching fancy 4-wheeled vehicles pass through their villages."[35] Even those trucks driven by Chobe Game Lodge's pioneering female guides offer little solace to these local residents, who derive few benefits from the industry.

Unfortunately, the resultant animosity toward these reserves persists, as contemporary African wildlife officials continue to exclude proximate communities from decisions regarding these spaces, nor do local populations typically benefit from the economic activity that these parks engender. Consequently, local communities often develop a lasting distrust of park authorities, "in part because of the glaring lack of attention those authorities, supported by conservationists, have traditionally paid to the link between park ecology, the survival of wildlife, and the livelihood of the displaced people."[36]

Another problematic dimension of this scenario is that because most African residents either do not have the disposable income to have a "proper" safari experience or simply aren't interested in doing so, African employees at parks and reserves are essentially servicing the Global North, reinforcing durable inequities. These power differentials also taint foreign visitors' impressions of Africans, deepening preconceived notions of them as "objects rather than as people."[37] The unequal manner of interaction further intensifies these impressions: Africans serve almost exclusively white clientele as drivers, trackers, cooks, servers, housekeeping staff, and in various other capacities. Moreover, indigenous cultural performances often fill the evening entertainment agendas for camera safari tourists, who spend these hours in full-service lodges. Indeed, what contact there is with local culture "occurs mostly through idealized re-creations of the African past in the form of dances, art, food, and 'ritual.'"[38]

More critically, a number of scholars have contended that the touristic gaze fails to differentiate between African landscapes, animals, and peoples. For example, scholars Barbara Kirschenblatt-Giblett and Edward Bruner argue that most tourist productions "play on the thematic image of Africa as an exotic wilderness in which wildlife, landscape, and native peoples form a single category and are rendered as timeless, unchanging, primitive entities."[39] Although camera safari tourists come to the continent primarily to view and photograph wildlife, this endeavor often reinforces their preconceived impressions of African peoples, even if only inadvertently.

Luxury in the Bush: The Evolution of Safari Infrastructure and Operators

Safari operators have a long history on the continent. As outlined previously, in the early decades of the twentieth century, white hunters led and organized safaris. Over time, though, they required more assistance, prompting the birth of commercial safari operations that could handle multiple clients at a time and make all of the necessary arrangements, including generating travel itineraries, outfitting arriving hunters, and providing local logistics and a safari crew, which included a white hunter (or hunters) and an array of African auxiliaries familiar with the local faunal and human landscapes.

In many ways, today's camera safari operator owes its existence to these pioneering enterprises, with both featuring business models that facilitate foreign tourists' ability to "shoot" Africa's big game. Yet, in most other respects, there is little that connects the two undertakings. Today's safari operators are no longer centered on small numbers of affluent hunters seeking to bag Africa's prized fauna; rather, modern outfits are intended to cater to large numbers of camera-laden tourists who are primarily driven around wildlife areas during the day and who sleep in comfortable, often luxurious, accommodations at night instead of in the bush.

Working in conjunction with travel agencies, governmental tourism entities, and other key partners, contemporary safari operators strive to promote a timeless Africa, the continent as it once was . . . sort of. We know, of course, that Africa's big game and human residents used to live much more proximately. Or at the very least, local populations weren't restricted from accessing lands that are now reserved for animals. These operators also insulate tourists from Africa's less agreeable aspects. Safari operators often collect arriving tourists directly from the airport and transport them on small buses to assigned hotels or lodges, some of which they also manage. The next morning, at or just before daybreak, the safari routine commences, with guests loaded into the awaiting vehicles and taken on "game drives," during which the objective is to view as many of the most celebrated animals, often referred to as "the Big 5" (lions, leopards, rhinos, Cape buffalo, and elephants), as possible. Ironically, it was big-game hunters who coined this term, as these five animals were the most dangerous to fell on foot. However, contemporary safari operators have unabashedly appropriated the label; any visit to a safari gift shop will inevitably feature an array of "Big 5" attire and paraphernalia, available to impress friends and family members upon returning home. Ultimately, upon the conclusion of the visit, the same buses return tourists to the airport.

In many cases, the safari operator also serves as a type of promoter and travel agency all in one, marketing the experience as a trip back in time, to an unsullied (and safe) place. For example, Taga Safaris, a South African–based operator, constructs a "contra-narrative to global tourism, based on the concept of locality as synonymous of: safety, personal and tailor-made arrangements, and local development combined with the protection of African Wildlife."[40] Further marketing material on Taga's website paints an alluring photographic safari experience for the tourist keen to travel to a time long since gone: "We feel that the ideal African safari should take you back in time to the Africa of old. Forget big lodges with crowds of people, or large game parks and reserves without privacy. They are not for travelers who want to capture the African heart and soul. All of the camps, lodges, and reserves that we visit cater to the discerning traveler and are small, private, and exclusive, which will give you an unforgettable experience of a lifetime."[41]

Among the assortment of contemporary, so-called nostalgia safari operators, Cottar's Camp, founded in Kenya in 1919, deserves special mention. Among Cottar's array of facilities is its "1920s Camp," an overtly sentimental 7,608-acre property situated proximate to both Kenya's Maasai Mara and Tanzania's Serengeti reserves. The furnishings in the 1920s Camp deliberately allude to the colonial period, when Karen Blixen and Denys Finch Hatton and their ilk enjoyed virtually everything Africa had to offer. Cottar's 1920s Safari Camp boasts that it "provides the romance of safari under cream canvas tents, the style of the bygone era of the twenties, while at the same time supplying the amenities required by today's modern world travelers, and professional guides whose qualifications are the highest in Africa."[42] Gramophones, typewriters, sepia-tinted photographs, mahogany furniture, a single-propeller airplane, and personal butlers donning "traditional" (i.e., colonial-era) attire for domestic servants are among the assortment of props that further authenticate this imagined trip back in time. It's easy to comprehend why this scenario would be appealing to prospective visitors, even though this exercise in "imperialist nostalgia" remains cost-prohibitive for many.[43] The prospect of viewing African wildlife while traveling back in time a century to live like a colonial-era aristocrat, enjoying the highest levels of luxury, is an easy sell for tourists already keen to visit the continent. Perhaps this experience would more appropriately be characterized as "fantasy tourism."

Increasingly wary that discerning travelers may also harbor concern for local populations, especially those communities that reside near game reserves, safari lodge and tour operators have also championed local enhancement programs. Given the pastoral location of most game reserves, many African governments have similarly embraced community-based programs as part of their rural development campaigns. But safari operators have more funds at their disposal and considerably smaller populations to service, or "develop," and are thus much more likely to self-consciously, and self-promotionally, engage in programs that benefit the nearby rural poor. For example, in touting its bona fides in this area, Extraordinary Journeys, founded in Kenya but now providing much more geographically extensive safari services, claims, "We send you to the small camps and lodges that support local communities and preserve natural environments, thereby assuring that every person we send to Africa makes a positive contribution to the well-being of the areas visited."[44] Similarly, Deeper Africa, which specializes in Eastern and Southern African photographic safaris, touts its ethical model as follows: "We invest in wildlife conservation projects that make a difference, invest in the people who enrich your safari, and invest in communities and individual entrepreneurs that are just outside the wild areas we visit. Your travel matters. Make choices that matter."[45] Unfortunately, it's unclear how these efforts matter to the local communities they profess to be benefiting.

Of course, many of these operators genuinely do care for neighboring communities and some even feature what are essentially local nongovernmental organizations (NGOs), operating under the same corporate umbrella as the core safari business. But it's hard not to be cynical when perusing their marketing materials. As some critics have persuasively argued, "These new, pro-poor practices sit uncomfortably in an industry steeped in the imagery of colonialism, on land formerly occupied by the rural poor and lost through colonial dispossession."[46] Consequently, these efforts and their associated promotional materials read much like the PR releases that multinational oil companies produce, which similarly showcase their "community development" efforts; meanwhile their drilling and piping activity simultaneously degrade the very environments in which these communities are located.

Far removed—at least figuratively—from these communities are the various types of accommodations in which safari tourists reside during their stays. Most guests stay in safari lodges, reasonably sized structures or compounds intended to house large numbers of people, while others stay in smaller, more exclusive and luxurious versions of the classic lodge or even in tented camps. Still others stay in tents within parks and reserves, seeking a more "authentic" experience. There are other options, including small hotels and even treetop structures, but the aforementioned types constitute the core of the array of safari accommodations.

The origins of the safari lodge can be identified in the original small, rustic camps composed of a series of rudimentary structures, situated in the midst of concentrated wildlife. The first "safari lodges," as they came to be called, were quite simple, and "travelers were encouraged to carry with them bedding, food, and cooking utensils."[47] One example of these early lodges is Sabi Sabi, which was established in 1930 on what is now a private game reserve (Sabi Sands) adjacent to Kruger National Park in South Africa. Sabi Sabi's history is typical of the genesis of the grand, colonial-era safari lodges that eventually emerged. Sabi Sabi opened in 1930 when Guy Chalkley bought Kingstown, "a farm named after a small Scottish border town, right on the banks of the Sabie River, which initially featured a thatched camp of six rondavels [Westernized version of African huts] and a long dining room and lounge. The camp still stands today, bracketed between a massive sausage tree and a huge jackalberry tree, only a few meters away from Sabi Sabi's River Lodge."[48] Not surprisingly, on the lodge's website, the operating enterprise markets its Selati Camp as a portal to an otherwise inaccessible past: "Indulgent and romantic, the historically themed Selati Camp is the Sabi Sabi of Yesterday. Conjuring up memories of when time drifted slowly and luxury embraced you in an effortless whisper."[49] Into the concluding decades of the colonial period, the establishment of lodges continued in this manner, with increasing attention paid to amenities and comfort.

Following independence, the range of lodges and "rustic" bush camps began undergoing significant renovations, most pronounced in the 1980s and 1990s, while "levels of luxury correspondingly grew."[50] These accommodations also began appearing in new areas on the continent, including in Zambia and Mozambique. The lodge itself had gradually become an extremely important component of the overall camera safari experience, in some respects as crucial as the wildlife. They are, after all, often the first place that tourists visit upon arrival, while their promoters boast of them as "the last bastion of civilization in the untouched wilderness."[51]

THERE IS scant resemblance between the original game-viewing safaris that traversed the East African hinterlands and the twenty-first-century version of these endeavors. Camera safari tourists are now invited to leave the modern world behind and transport back in time, ensconced in accommodations that harken back to the colonial period. These guests are implored to travel even further back in time once they arrive in the wildlife viewing areas, which are devoid of permanent residents (other than anti-poaching squads, whom the casual tourist never encounters), while featuring seemingly endless, "pristine" landscapes. As we know by now, this manner of marketing the continent is hardly novel. Africa as a timeless, "exotic" place is a well worn trope in the continent's tourism history.

Another type of tourism in Africa that invites a travel back in time, though for entirely different reasons, is "roots," or heritage, tourism. In this endeavor, peoples of African descent "return" to the continent to connect with their distant relatives, virtually all of whom were forcibly removed as part of the transatlantic slave trade. It is to this form of tourism that we turn in the next chapter.

CHAPTER SIX

Going Home

The Diasporic Quest for Belonging through "Roots" Tourism

> *Journey in our ancestors' footsteps as we visit the places they passed through on their enforced journey to the Americas. Cape Coast Castle, with its dungeons and door-of-no-return, and Elmina Castle of St. George both witnessed millions of our forefathers' footsteps on the very stone floors we will walk upon. In addition, we visit the many monuments and historical sites associated with Pan-African revolutionaries as you re-connect with your culture. An authentic journey experiencing traditional foods, crafts, drumming and dance whilst mixing with your African brothers and sisters during this homecoming tour.*
>
> —An Ashanti African Tours advertisement directed at African Americans, imploring them to visit Ghana as "roots," or heritage, tourists, 2019

> *Everyone has a homeland. People go, "Oh I'm from Ireland, I'm from Scotland." Being African American, I tell people I'm from New Orleans, like that's where I was born, you know? There's something healing about being here in Ghana, eating the food, meeting the people—it's the missing piece of the puzzle that connects you to who you really are.*
>
> —Tani Sanchez, an African American "roots" tourist in Ghana, 2019

TANI SANCHEZ is one of countless people of African descent who have "returned" to the continent as a "roots" or "heritage" tourist on a pilgrimage like the Ashanti African tour outlined above. This undertaking is emotionally powerful for these tourists from the African diaspora, who are seeking both a symbolic and tangible connection to the homeland of their ancestors. As these roots tourists visit the various sites on the heritage itinerary, they forge imagined bonds with the millions of Africans consumed by the tragic, centuries-long transatlantic commerce in slaves. These metaphoric connections can be made from afar, but standing in the dungeons of the castles where enslaved Africans were held before departing for the Americas and wading into streams and rivers where these captured individuals were often baptized before commencing the fateful journey provide palpable experiences that deepen, animate, and enhance these linkages. As Sanchez remarked, these endeavors also often fill a void in these tourists' lives, gaps in family history and identity that the slave trade brutally created. As historian James Campbell contends, "For white Americans, treading the old sod [their places of origin in Europe] was chiefly an exercise in nostalgia. For African Americans visiting Africa, the emotional palette was inevitably darker."[1] Ultimately, for heritage tourists, visiting Africa is often an act of self-realization, featuring affective, emotive experiences that are absent in other forms of tourism to the continent.

In 1976, Alex Haley's best-selling novel *Roots* was published, followed by a hugely popular television adaptation the following year. The story traces the ancestors of Haley, an African American, back to a village in Gambia. Arguably, the birth of this form of heritage tourism can be located in the aftermath of these book and television releases, which prompted many diasporan tourists to travel to this West African nation. Gambian officials initially scrambled to accommodate this unanticipated influx, but over time, it was another West African nation, Ghana, that emerged as the new epicenter for roots tourism. Today, the Ghana roots tourism industry dwarfs much more modest versions in Senegal, Sierra Leone, Gambia, and Angola. Although much larger numbers of enslaved Africans derived or departed from elsewhere on the continent, Ghana attracts the vast majority of these tourists. This phenomenon is attributable to a number of reasons, dating back to the independence of Ghana in 1957, the first sub-Saharan African nation to achieve its freedom from European colonial overrule, and the Pan-African outlook of its first prime minister and president, Kwame Nkrumah, who urged black peoples around the world to cohere for the benefit of the collective community.[2] Beyond his soaring rhetoric, Nkrumah invited peoples of African descent from the Americas to relocate to Ghana to contribute their resources, professional training, and technical expertise in order to help develop the fledgling country.[3] Many diasporans heeded his call and, although not tourists themselves, helped establish this inversed flow back to the continent.

Some decades later, in 1981, Flight Lieutenant Jerry Rawlings seized power in Ghana and was eventually elected to two presidential terms, leaving office in 2001. Rawlings echoed Nkrumah's call to the diaspora, appealing to peoples of African descent to return to Ghana, not permanently but rather as tourists. In conjunction with Rawlings's appeal, in the early 1990s Ghana began restoring the neglected, crumbling, European-built castles on its coast to serve as the centerpieces for the country's brand of roots tourism. Today, two of these structures, Elmina Castle and Cape Coast Castle, located some 8 miles from one another on Ghana's central coast, constitute the meccas of the heritage tourism industry. Designated UNESCO World Heritage Sites, the castles have been attracting upward of ten thousand African Americans annually since the 1990s (fig. 6.1). Ghana is also an inviting destination for heritage tourists owing to its peacefulness, its easy accessibility, and its robust transport and touristic infrastructures, including an array of Western-standard hotels.

This chapter examines the motivations, expectations, and experiences of these heritage tourists, including their interactions with local residents and the ways that African citizens, governments, and tour guides have shaped this industry. As with other types of tourism in Africa, interaction with members of local communities is typically limited to skilled guides, docents, performers, and merchants, all of whom strive to ensure that their guests have fulfilling experiences that meet or exceed their expectations. Despite their shared ancestry and skin complexion, heritage tourists are often surprised that locals consider them not as "brothers and sisters," as

FIGURE 6.1 Elmina Castle, Ghana. *Courtesy of Wikimedia Commons*

Ashanti African Tours suggests, but as foreigners and, moreover, as "white." As most roots tourists are actively seeking to deepen their personal connections to the continent and its peoples, Africans' insistence that these visitors are no different than other (i.e., white) tourists can be both unsettling and upsetting to these guests. This undifferentiated perception of foreign tourists helps explain why the residents who interact with these visitors strategically perform for them, fully aware that although these tourists are, in some sense, seeking the familiar in Africa, they also harbor perceptions of the continent as "exotic." In search of revenue, local residents respond accordingly.

The History of Ghana's Slave Castles

The physical foundation for Ghana's heritage tourism industry was laid centuries ago. The Portuguese were the first Europeans to arrive on West African shores, making land at points increasingly south over the first half of the fifteenth century. After negotiating permission with local rulers, the Portuguese erected Elmina Castle in 1482 to facilitate trade with local populations and, ultimately, to protect its commercial interests against encroachment by European rivals. Despite its efforts to monopolize this commerce, Portugal could not prevent competitors, including the British, French, Dutch, Danes, Swedes, and Germans, from trading with Africans along the coast and constructing their own fortifications. In Ghana alone, some eighty castles, forts, lodges, and other trade-related structures were built, more than on any other stretch of Africa's coast.[4] With only roughly 300 miles of coastline, this concentration of structures is exceptional.

Although European merchants in West Africa initially sought gold more than any other item, the trade in slaves gradually surpassed this earlier form of commerce. In turn, Europeans renovated the castles and other structures to house these human commodities, with spaces enlarged to hold upward of a thousand slaves. Defensive capabilities were also improved in order to protect this valuable cargo.[5] Yet this burgeoning commerce also precipitated the construction of myriad new trading posts, coinciding with the increased volume of the transatlantic slave trade in the seventeenth and eighteenth centuries. Rather than being modified to accommodate expanded numbers of slaves, these new structures were deliberately constructed for this exact purpose. These facilities also became increasingly secure, with prisons incorporated to ensure firmer control over the larger numbers of captives and to punish any who were uncooperative. A 1781 account from an Englishman, John Atkins, regarding the conditions in the holding cells of Cape Coast Castle illustrates the confinement experience: "In the Area of this Quadrangle, are large Vaults, with an iron Grate at the Surface to let in Light and Air on those poor Wretches, the Slaves, who are chained and confined there till a Demand comes. They are all marked with a burning Iron upon the right Breast, D.Y. [Duke of York]."[6] Ghanaian tour guides often repackage, without sanitizing, testimony of this nature, often triggering the emotions of roots visitors attempting to connect with their ancestors, the victims of this trade in human beings.

Roots Tourists' Motivations and Prearrival Experiences

As noted previously, there are a host of compelling reasons why heritage tourists journey to Africa. Many of these motivations are rooted in the often complicated relationship that many diasporans have with the continent. As with other types of tourists, powerful myths and misperceptions shape sentiments toward and understandings of Africa and Africans. In examining these misunderstandings, scholar Michelle Commander explains that "Afro-Atlantic communities perpetuate myths about slavery and their purported retentions from the original Africa—the imagined, pristine landscape from which their ancestors were stripped—despite temporal and geographic separations. . . . The folklore and myths that inform imaginaries about Africa are products of a complicated, transnational spectrum of longing."[7] It's not surprising that this longing, a desire to (re)engage and somehow (re)connect with the continent, is fueled by misunderstandings, as Africa's complex history is little known beyond the continent's borders and, arguably, even within them.

These sizeable gaps in comprehension are filled with an assortment of professed knowledge that is itself shaped both by the ways that Africa is presented abroad and by yearnings to connect with a seemingly lost past, which often prompts would-be tourists to romanticize the continent. As Saidiya V. Hartman, who has written extensively on this topic and has also been a heritage tourist herself, explains, "The journey back is as much motivated by the desire to return to the site of origin and the scene of the fall, as with the invisible landscape of slavery, the unmarked ports of entry in the United States, and the national imperative to forget slavery, render it as romance, or relegate it to some prehistory that has little to do with the present."[8] The motivational power of the original enslavement and eventual emancipation of Africans is undoubtedly strong as members of the diaspora contemplate visits to the continent. For example, Tani Sylvester, the daughter of Tani Sanchez, whom we encountered at the onset of this chapter, remarked just before her departure to Ghana, "We're the first people in our family who've ever gone back home to Africa. The last people that came from Africa, they came in chains. They were slaves, and we're going back as free people."[9]

In recent decades, DNA testing has also compelled many heritage tourists to engage with the continent, newly armed with genetic information related to their ancestry. Ironically, though, even if these data, still reasonably imprecise, point them to areas beyond Ghana's borders, they continue to converge on the country. This inclination suggests that the symbolic or representative nature of the experience is more salient than pinpointing one's actual place of origin. But it need not be an either-or proposition. For some African Americans interested in the geography of their ancestry, gathering information via DNA testing without necessarily traveling to the exact site, or even traveling to Africa at all, is perfectly reconcilable. Deatrice Rotimi is one such individual:

> The great promise of genetic ancestry tracing to me, as an African American, is not just to know that I am from Africa—this is rather clear to me. The difference is I want to know what part of Africa I am from. The question is—is it possible to reestablish the link, sense of who you are, where your family is from? Can we find our family, the family we have been separated from? We are looking for the magic bullet. . . . Can DNA testing do this? . . . I just want to know the immediate beginning of my family history. Slavery robs us of so much—our culture, our heritage. The question is, can genetics fill this void?[10]

The Roots Experience: On the Grounds of Our Ancestors

Diasporans' first encounter with Africa typically occurs at the international airport in Accra, Ghana's capital city. Upon arrival, passengers are herded into the immigration area, where long lines and extended wait times are the norm, and then proceed to the chaotic baggage claim area. A tour guide rounds up arriving passengers as they filter through the remaining halls and passages before emerging into a sea of people outside, where hawkers, taxi touts, baggage handlers, and a mélange of other Ghanaians crowd around to offer their services.

Heritage tourists may proceed directly to Cape Coast and Elmina castles or they may first spend some time in Accra or even travel to another area of the country. For example, Tani Sanchez used her time in Accra to forge relations with the roughly forty fellow roots tourists with whom she was traveling, while a tour guide taught them to sing a Ghanaian hymn and how to respond to a traditional call for attention in the local Akan language.[11] These endeavors help diminish, if only temporarily, some of the considerable differences that exist between diasporans and Africans, while giving tourists an opportunity to observe urban life on the continent, albeit from behind a bus window. A visit to the W. E. B. Du Bois Center in Accra may serve to further reduce this cultural gap, as the famed scholar's experiences in Ghana and his entombment (along with his wife, Shirley Graham Du Bois) within the center's grounds provide a tangible link between Africa and the diaspora.

Before reaching the slave castles, tourists may traverse a portion, or the entirety, of the so-called slave route itinerary. For example, BLASTours, an Accra-based agency, recommends a two-week trip that takes participants throughout the country and mixes sites significant to the country's history of slavery with lighter affairs, including visits to arts and crafts centers, while incorporating the exotic through visits to villages where foreign guests engage with traditional leaders.[12]

A popular undertaking on these itineraries is a visit to a river in which slaves were often bathed en route to the coast. Typically, the site for this undertaking is Assin Manso, a town some 40 kilometers north of Cape Coast along the Ndonko Nsuo, which means "slave river" or "slave water," and the site of a former slave market. This location was where slave handlers rested and bathed their captives, who had been seized and transported from much farther north, so as to fetch the highest price upon reaching the coast. Assin Manso also features the graves of two former slaves who were re-interred in the late 1990s as well as other touristic features and amenities, including a portrait gallery. In some respects, this primer for the ensuing tours of the slave castles can be just as powerful. An account of Tani Sylvester's immersion in the river illuminates the emotive dimension of this experience:

> The previous day, the group had visited a river farther inland where slaves were forced to bathe before imprisonment on the coast ahead of their journey to the Americas. . . . On the guide's invitation, Sylvester stepped into the creek, closed her eyes and

raised her hands in prayer. "I felt what my mom was saying about honoring the ancestors, like my ancestors would want me to get into that water and retrace their steps," she said. "And even just taking off my shoes and feeling the same ground that they walked on, getting into the water, I just feel like I came out of that water a different person." Afterward, Sylvester wrote with black marker on a pink memorial wall at the site, "Long journey home," and she and her mother signed their names: Tani S + Tani S.[13]

Each of these experiences is intended to prepare diasporic visitors for engagement with the slave castles. As discussed above, heritage tourists have long anticipated those moments prior to setting foot in the structures. Regardless, their physical presence is striking. As you travel along the coastal road, the castles are visible well before you are upon them.

Although both castles are physically imposing, the immediate approaches to them are extremely different. The town of Elmina is frenzied, the clogged streets forcing buses to proceed slowly and navigate around street vendors, pedestrians, fishmongers, and innumerable other fixed and mobile impediments. Even the walk from the bus to the castle entrance includes Ghanaians trying to make personal connections in the hopes of arranging the sale of a variety of wares to visitors. Conversely, Cape Coast is more subdued, the streets much less congested, and tourists largely ignored.

Of course, for some visitors, that is not the point. They desire interaction, no matter how jarring it may be, with the "real Africa"—the rawer the experience, the more "authentic" it is presumed to be. In this vein, many diasporans have accused the Ghanaian government of whitewashing their history by renovating the castles to improve their aesthetic appearance and, thus, the overall touristic experience. Should the castle walls be freshly painted, interior lighting expanded and amplified, walls restored, and glass windows installed? Many diasporic observers think not. For example, Imahküs Robinson, an outspoken scholar-activist and critic of these types of renovations, lamented in a 1994 contentious newspaper article: "Here I am today witnessing the 'White Wash' of African History. But I cannot sit in idleness and watch this happen without sounding an alarm. . . . Restore, preserve, renovate, maintain? Exactly what is being done?"[14] The tension between authenticity and renovation is not unique to the slave castles, yet it remains a highly polemical issue.

Upon entering the structures, guides typically provide heritage pilgrims with dedicated group tours, enabling them to have more private experiences and more freely express their emotions. Tours proceed gradually through the complexes, with extensive information imparted regarding the construction of the castles and the moments at which they changed hands from one European power to another, whether violently or peacefully. The routes taken through the structures vary, but the most charged moments occur in the male and female dungeons, where slaves were separated and detained while they awaited their transatlantic journeys. It is within these spaces that the victimization, the exploitation, and the inhumanity of the slave experience climax. And they are also where heritage tourists demonstrate their grief most robustly, often prompted by the guides reminding them that the floor beneath them is composed of "centuries of hard-packed feces, urine, blood, and flesh."[15]

Myriad visitors from the diaspora have generated accounts of the moments that they engaged with these traumatic spaces. Imahküs Robinson's reminiscence regarding her first visit to the dungeons, in 1987, remains among the most damning and most powerful. Intertwining fear, pain, sorrow, and, eventually, relief in her account of entering the women's dungeon at Elmina, she writes,

> I dropped to my knees, trembling and crying even harder. . . . As I rocked back and forth on the dirt floor, I could hear weeping and wailing . . . anguished screams coming from the distance. Suddenly the room was packed with women . . . some naked, some with babies, some sick and lying in the dirt, while others stood against the dungeon's walls, terror filling their faces. . . . Cold terror gripped my body, tears blinded me and the screams wouldn't stop. As I sat there violently weeping, I began to feel a sense of warmth, many hands were touching my body, caressing me, soothing me as a calmness began to cover over me. I began to feel almost safe as voices whispered in my ears assuring me that everything was all right. "Don't cry," they said, "You've come home. You've returned to your homeland." . . . After years of wandering and searching, I had finally found home. And one day, I wouldn't be leaving again.[16]

For other diasporan visitors, the experience prompts more conflicted responses. For example, Saidiya V. Hartman, writing candidly about her experience visiting the children's dungeon at the Maison des Esclaves (House of Slaves), a structure similar to, though much more modest than, the Ghanaian slave castles on Gorée Island off the coast of Dakar, Senegal, confesses,

> The tour through the slave house is extremely fast paced in order to get large groups in and out in twenty to thirty minutes. Besides the odd collection of detail and anecdote, scant historical information is provided on the tour. Prompting black visitors to shed tears seems to be its principle aim. The tour starts out at the children's dungeon. Upon entering, some of the women begin to cry. I am surprised since I have been unable to shed a single tear; moreover, this shoddy and sensationalist tour incites my anger, which seems the only emotion I can express with any ease.[17]

These divergent reactions to heritage experiences underscore the complicated, often fraught, relationship between grieving, history, memory, and tourism. Of course, each tour can't be tailored to individual visitors, who will, in any event, react in a variety of ways. But Hartman's emotions should not be dismissed as anomalous or simply idiosyncratic.

Meanwhile, for those tourists without African ancestry, the slave castle experience often provokes feelings of empathy, guilt, and remorse. For Europeans and Americans of European descent, for example, some of their ancestors were the "consumers" of African slaves. In the presence of heritage tourists who are actively and imaginatively diminishing the temporal gap between the era of the slave trade and the moment of their visit, it's hard to avoid doing the same as a white visitor to the castle, even if one is certain that his or her ancestors were not slave owners. Peter Nelson, an American of Norwegian descent, illustrates these complex feelings in an article in which he reflects upon his experience at Elmina castle, participating on a tour with a group of Ghanaian schoolchildren:

> As we follow the guide down into the dungeons where the male slaves were held, my discomfort grows. I half expect the guide to turn to me and say, "As the only white man here, perhaps

you can explain to the children how your ancestors could en-slave and murder our people?" I expect the schoolchildren to at least glance suspiciously at me, or edge nervously away from me, but nothing of the kind occurs. I have no Portuguese, Dutch, or British [the various proprietors of the castle] blood in me, but I have been raised to understand that it was my people, white people, who did this thing. I've never heard of any Norwegian immigrants owning plantations or slaves, no cruel squareheaded masters forcing African captives to pick lefse or toil in the lu-tefisk mines, but I feel guilty. Or maybe I feel like I ought to feel guilty, some stray politically correct impulse to enlarge my consciousness and share the pain.[18]

As a historian of Africa, I often discuss the transatlantic slave trade with students in my classes in a somewhat detached, factual manner, while never downplaying the tragedy that permeated absolutely every aspect of it. On tour in these dungeons, however, it has been impossible for me not to swell with empathy, the inhumanity seemingly palpable. Of course, this experience is not intended for me to locate my roots or to pay testament to my heritage, but the emotions I have experienced, especially the first few times I visited the castles, are undeniably powerful. Moreover, these emotions run much more deeply when I am in the presence of roots tourists, whose passionate, often demonstrative reactions heighten these feelings.

The Door of No Return, or the Door of Return?

Following visits to the various dungeons, guides lead tourists to the so-called doors of no return, the actual embarkation points at which Africans left the continent, most often permanently. To reach these departure thresholds, slaves were forced down dark, narrow passages that brought them to doors that led outside the castle walls and onto small platforms. From there, they were rowed out to the sea-going slave ships that would transport them to the Americas. Guides inform tourists that the passages and doors were narrowed with the onset of the slave trade to restrict movement and limit the possibilities for escape while these captives were being relocated. Tourists walk in the footsteps of the slaves, hunched over and in single file, transitioning from the dark, dank dungeons to the glaring sun, fresh air, and ocean breezes. For African captives, however, an additional segment of their journey quickly followed, as they were thrust into their new hells in the hulls of slave ships and prepared to embark on the horrific "Middle Passage."

For most heritage tourists, their engagement with the "door of no return" prompts expressions of profound grief. Tour guides often try to uplift these visitors' spirits by ensuring them that the label, "door of no return," is misleading because, after all, "Now, you are back!"[19] These docents are not alone in emphasizing the triumphant narrative of diasporans "returning" to the continent, somehow rendering the infamous door a two-way portal. A notable case includes the 2019 visit of US Speaker of the House of Representatives Nancy Pelosi and thirteen members of the Congressional Black Caucus to Cape Coast Castle, where they refashioned the portal the "Door of Return."[20] Given that Somali-born representative Ilhan Omar was part of this delegation, the gesture was especially poignant. And timely: the government of Ghana declared 2019 "The Year of Return," and in November of that year formally granted Ghanaian citizenship to 126 African Americans and Afro-Caribbeans who were already living in the country under Ghana's "Right of Abode" law.[21] This emphasis on return is important for many diasporans, as it often constituted the impetus for their travels to Africa in the first place.

For some visitors, though, the touristic performance of this reinterpretation and the celebratory insistence on return is highly disagreeable. As Saidiya Hartman has written, "Ironically, the declaration, 'You are back!' undermines the very violence that these memorials assiduously work to present by claiming that the tourist's excursion is the ancestor's return. . . . The most disturbing aspect . . . is the suggestion that the rupture of the Middle Passage is neither irreparable nor irrevocable but bridged by the tourist who acts as the vessel for the ancestor. In short, the captive finds his redemption in the tourist."[22]

In practice, the arrival of the tourist does nothing to undo or temper African slaves' dreadful experiences, nor is it clear that these returns are meaningful for contemporary Ghanaians, the presumed "receivers" of these returns. For many observers, the return of a diasporan to the continent should not be embedded in this narrative of return, lest it eclipse the tragedy of slavery or become patently self congratulatory. As Hartman contends, "the celebration of return threatens to undermine the work of mourning by simulating a condition of intactness, rather than attending to the ruin and wreckage of slavery and by declaring that those deported have in fact returned through their descendants."[23]

Afterward

As visitors leave the castles, they are often encouraged to sign guest books. This seemingly simple act is, however, anything but. Tourists often struggle to reconcile the somberness of the experience with a desire not to offend their hosts. Thus, many foreign visitors may be thankful that there is only minimal space provided in which to craft comments. In the citizenship column, some Americans simply jot down "U.S.A." or "America," while others offer "African-American." Regarding this experience, Peter Nelson, the Norwegian American tourist we encountered earlier, observed, "Visitors from Europe all write something like, 'Very romantic. Quite beautiful.' Visitors from Ghana write, 'Very educational.' 'Quite interesting.' Or, 'Very historical.' Visitors who sign in as either 'African-American' or 'U.S.A.' write things like, 'Horrible,' or, 'This must never happen again,' or, 'Profoundly moving—never forget.'"[24] Even succinct comments such as these provide considerable insight into the varied experiences that people have at the slave castles predicated on history, identity, and ancestry.

Having experienced these sites, heritage tourists eventually make their way back to Accra before heading home, heads filled with conflicting sentiments and cameras filled with emotive images. This return journey is a time of significant contemplation, as it often is for all types of first-time visitors to the continent. As they struggle to determine what to convey about their trips to friends and relatives, they also often struggle to reconcile narratives of pain and suffering with images of themselves posing and smiling at the various sites they visited. Heritage pilgrims often portray the continent as idyllic, a place where they connected with their ancestors, their true homes. It was this tendency that prompted an expatriate friend of Saidiya Hartman's in Ghana to implore her to provide friends and relatives with an unvarnished account of her experiences on the continent: "Don't lie when you go back home. Everyone goes home and lies. . . . The naiveté that allows folks to believe they are returning home or entering paradise when they come here has to be destroyed."[25] Perhaps this penchant to misinform, whitewash, or otherwise obscure is inadvertent, a reaction to the social contexts into which heritage tourists return, many of which feature racial tension and discrimination. Theater and performance scholar Sandra Richards explains this inclination to generate distortive narratives of heritage experiences that stress unwavering advancement:

Heritage tourism assumes a continuity between past and present, with progress understood as an inevitable, natural process. . . . Even those who cast themselves as serious-minded pilgrims, rather than fun-seeking tourists, are likely to produce concomitant narratives of resilience, justice, or transcendent purpose, thereby reassuring themselves that their ancestors' lives and their own have some meaning other than degradation. Indeed, these are the memories that African Americans produce in travel accounts, poems, or videos. Further, the memory of oppression raises issues of the responsibility, complicity, and guilt of the original perpetrators, accomplices, and possibly of their descendants—questions that do not offer an escape from reality, but confront visitors with ethnic or racial tensions analogous to what they may experience at home.[26]

Ghanaians, Heritage Tourism, and Interaction with Roots Tourists

Although the emphasis on this chapter has largely been on roots tourists, it's also important to consider their hosts, the local residents with whom these visitors interact and rely upon for their touristic needs. Of course, Africans do not need to be directly involved in this industry to have opinions regarding how tourism should be managed in their respective countries. Some local residents comprehend the sector as a revenue generator that, if managed correctly, should deliver to national citizenries improved standards of living, for example via the development of enhanced transportation and healthcare infrastructure. For them, tourism is essentially an engine for economic development.

For others, especially those who live near or work at sites where heritage tourism is popular, the diasporic visitors force, by their mere presence, local residents to re-engage with the history of slavery and the roles that their ancestors may have played in this inhumane commerce. Although Africans and diasporans share a common ancestry, their historical experiences have been, and continue to be, divergent. As each diasporic group arrives to engage with painful moments in their ancestral past, "Ghanaians must remember a history they learned to forget" in order to continue to attract these very tourists.[27] Indeed, slavery and the slave trade are topics that Ghanaians rarely discuss. Consequently, for these locals, opinions about the roots tourism industry are typically more charged and there is often an uneasy tension between them and their foreign guests. For example, in various interviews and focus groups, many Ghanaians noted that "African Americans become very emotional during visits to the castles and dungeons; from a Ghanaian perspective, they become almost 'too emotional.'"[28]

These experiential differences, undergirded by divergent lived histories, are what prompt Ghanaians to commonly refer to African Americans as *obruni*, an Akan word meaning stranger, foreigner, and, by extension, a white person.[29] Many African Americans, while on tours of their imagined homelands and keen to connect with Africans as part of the roots endeavor, object to being clumped in with white Americans and Europeans. Whereas these Africans Americans see themselves as "black and at home, the term 'obruni' labels them as both white and foreign."[30] Yemi, a dreadlocked attorney from Atlanta, confirmed these local impressions of her and others like her, commenting on her roots experience following a 2009 visit to the country: "Probably the thing that surprised me most is that there were a lot of Ghanaians that perceived me as more like a European, a regular tourist. I didn't necessarily expect them to embrace me as if I were family, per se, at least not all of them, but I was surprised that they would go so far as to view me the same as a European or Caucasian American despite the fact that before I opened my mouth, I looked like any other African or Rastafarian walking the streets."[31]

Not only do Ghanaians typically try to maintain distance between themselves and heritage tourists, these visitors can be the primary target of residents' grievances. In the account of his travels in the country, Nelson shared experiences of this nature, writing, "Some people in the tourism industry in Ghana will tell you, in a whisper, glancing about to make sure they aren't overheard, that the African-American tourists, some of them, are the new ugly Americans there, that they're rude to the wait staff, or look down on the average Ghanaians. 'I could write a book,' one hotel owner told me."[32]

These fraught relations are, however, not unidirectional. As Ghanaians generally perceive heritage tourists to be foreign and wealthy, these visitors often complain about their African hosts, sensing a "strange mix of envy and contempt that they feel locals are displaying towards them."[33] Others feel that they receive inferior treatment compared to tourists of European descent. Many of these diasporan tourists "observe how whites are given better service than blacks in hotels, restaurants, and government offices, reproducing a colonial racial order."[34]

Regardless of the sentiments of particular Ghanaian residents, many local grievances concerning tourists are not exclusively directed at heritage visitors. Complaints from more conservative Africans abound regarding Western tourists wearing minimal clothing, while others bemoan tourists photographing locals without their permission. This disrespectful act is, of course, not confined to areas in which heritage tourism flourishes, but given that these locations are high-volume tourist sites, the likelihood is certainly greater. As one sexagenarian Ghanaian woman complained, "They [tourists] take pictures without the consent of the people. Some intentionally take pictures of naked and badly dressed people. These pictures give a bad impression about us when they are sent abroad."[35]

Promoting a Forgotten Past: African Governments' Embrace of Roots Tourism

African governments play important mediating roles in these roots tourism encounters. State officials must first foster favorable conditions for tourism, striving to make what can be very uncomfortable experiences for heritage visitors occur in the most comfortable environments possible. Governments also need to physically maintain the particular heritage sites that feature on tours. This endeavor is laden with competing agendas and interests, requiring that officials upkeep, for example, the slave castles in Ghana, while eschewing potential "whitewashing" renovations that threaten to conceal these structures' tragic pasts. Finally, state-appointed guides are charged with delivering narratives tailored to specific audiences.

Governmental Promotion of Roots Tourism: Uncomfortable Visits in Comfortable Conditions

Although heritage visitors can be intrepid types, like most other tourists they want to enjoy the best, most comfortable travel and visitation conditions possible. To this end, African governments seeking to attract roots tourists must also invest in a broad range of touristic infrastructure and, in general, cultivate domestic political and social environments that will attract, rather than repel, both roots and other visitors alike. In the case of Ghana, political instability hindered the development of the tourist industry following independence in 1957 and the coup d'état that removed Kwame Nkrumah from power in 1966. Reflecting this domestic tumult, "between 1966 and 1973 there were more than eight changes in the name, status, and mandate of Ghana's National Tourism Organization."[36] Even while navigating these turbulent touristic waters, Ghanaian officials knew that their country held a competitive advantage over other West African nations due to the significant number of extant forts and castles along its Atlantic coast.

By the 1980s, the political turmoil in the country was safely in the rearview mirror, which offered a more promising environment in which to develop the industry. Ghanaian officials immediately began highlighting the nation's touristic assets, including "miles and miles of sun-dappled beaches," but also a rich cultural heritage, including arts and crafts, such as kente cloth weaving and decorative adinkra symbols.[37] And by the middle of the decade, Ghana's government had begun earnestly "developing and promoting tourism as a major contributor to the expansion of the nation's economy."[38] Various international funding bodies, including the United Nations Development Programme (UNDP), the World Tourism Organization, and USAID, as well as the private sector, assisted the country in its efforts to develop the sector, culminating in the elevation of the industry to ministerial level in 1993. Consequently, by the middle of the 1990s, Ghana was attracting over two hundred thousand tourists annually, while the industry had surged to become the third-most important, behind gold and cocoa, contributing over 5 percent of the nation's GDP and injecting roughly $370 million into the economy.[39]

A growing portion of these arrivals was composed of roots tourists. In response, the Ministry of Tourism was refashioned the Ministry of Tourism and Diaspora Relations in an attempt to proactively attract additional tourists of African descent. Studies have shown that heritage travelers, in general, "stay in hotels more frequently and for longer periods of time, visit more destinations, and generally spend more money than their 'non culturally-oriented, traveling counterparts.'"[40] Thus, the monuments to which these apparently enthusiastic spenders would visit needed to be properly prepared for their arrival.

Castles or Dungeons? Touristic Infrastructure Debates

The preservation, restoration, and presentation of any historical site is an undertaking inherently fraught with contention. These sites may have served different purposes during different eras and, more importantly, often mean profoundly different things to different groups of people, or even to individuals within these groups. These concerns fuel debates over how these sites should be presented to visitors. An objective to tell multiple stories, capture multiple voices, and reflect multiple perspectives is laudable but also acutely difficult to realize. The slave castles of West Africa constitute a perfect example of this complex challenge.

Once Ghana launched its tourism campaign in earnest, it was clear that the showpiece castles needed to be restored. But restored to what? The strongholds were constructed centuries ago and were not originally intended to house or facilitate the sale of African slaves; rather, they were the sites of transactions in gold and ivory, while the internal spaces that became dungeons initially served as storage rooms for these and other commodities. Moreover, following the conclusion of the slave trade, these structures were converted into offices or utilized for other purposes. At a fundamental level, many of the Ghanaians in charge of these facilities simply want to "stabilize" them against the elements, including the salt air, the sun, and of course, time. One such individual charged with this undertaking explained that "the weather here is brutal on castles, with the sun and the heat and the wetness. . . . The castle's eaves were built by Europeans who failed to appreciate that in the tropics, the rain often comes in on the horizontal. We have fierce driving rains here. The short eaves cannot possibly protect the masonry."[41]

Another challenge involves the figurative ownership of the castles. In many respects, diasporans posit historical claims on these structures given that their ancestors emerged from them as part of the hellish process that stretched across the Atlantic. Some diasporans are uncomfortable with any type of restoration, or certainly with renovation, of the castles. Rather, they want them frozen in the time of slavery. The dungeon walls should not be repainted, nor should electricity be installed in the narrow passages between the men's and women's dungeons that lead to the "door of no return." They allege that these types of material upgrades undermine the roots experience by inaccurately presenting the conditions in which their ancestors were held. Worse, some diasporans feel that these solemn structures will be turned into theme parks, commoditizing the atrocity and placing revenue above all else.[42]

In contrast, many Ghanaians feel strongly that the castles are theirs alone. Local residents often campaign to use the spaces to display their own history, of which slavery constitutes only a part, though these efforts have not been particularly effective. Meanwhile, individuals employed at the castles, including guides and administrators, often complain about African American intrusions into their patrimonial affairs. Sedu Goodman, both a guide and an architect involved in the restoration of the castles, offers comments that capture this discontent: "These places were trading posts before slavery, and offices after slavery, and they were prisons and police and government headquarters—so, much of what we are doing is undoing what the government did when the castle was being used for offices. But, the African Americans think we are whitewashing their history. They think we're trying to make it look better than it was. We have to save the castle for everybody, not just for them."[43]

This debate, which further complicates relations between diasporans and Africans, arguably peaked in 1993, revolving around the opening of a bar and restaurant above the male dungeon in Cape Coast Castle. Museum officials reasoned that the restaurant "would encourage visitors to stay longer and possibly learn more," while enhancing tourists' comfort levels and generating revenue.[44] Others were less enthusiastic about this development. Some African Americans felt that this decision was "analogous to opening a restaurant at a cemetery," claiming it served to "whitewash" the tragedy associated with the structure.[45] Tensions on all sides flared. For example, African American Kohain Halevi opined that "the average Ghanaian does not understand what we're so upset about. They think we're being overemotional troublemakers. So, they've tried to leave us out of the process. It's more convenient that way. . . . These people talk about how we need to contribute financially if we want more of a voice in this project. My response is that the ancestors of African Americans paid the highest price already."[46] Francis Duah, the regional director of Ghana's Museum and Monuments Board at this time, dismissed Halevi's emotional plea, offering biting criticism of Africans Americans instead: "What I hate is the hypocrisy. They come in here and they cry and throw themselves on the ground, but they don't want to contribute anything to what we're doing. Then they want to have a big say in what we do."[47] Professor Kwame Arhin, based at the University of Ghana's Institute for African Studies, was more diplomatic: "No one is trying to whitewash history. We want to make sure that when people come to these monuments they say, 'We cannot allow this evil to happen again.'"[48] Ultimately, officials closed the restaurant and bar in response to the protestations, but not before further damage to relations between diasporans and Ghanaians had been done. As Richards reminds us, African Americans continue to serve as "fictive kin to a nation [Ghana] whose borders, languages, and customs largely exclude them."[49]

Although the various sites on the heritage tourism itinerary powerfully deliver the tragic history of the slave trade without any human mediation necessary, the guides who steward tourists through these spaces play an extremely important role in this introspective process. Their descriptive words animate various sites, most pronouncedly in the slave dungeons, and drive many guests to tears, as these visitors mentally reconstruct the tragic experiences of the captives who once occupied them. As mentioned earlier, guides regularly adjust their delivery according to the visiting party, as they are both aware of and sensitive to their varied audiences.[50] Tours performed for groups of diasporans typically differ from those intended for mixed audiences. In fact, guides often utilize a "matter-of-fact tone and historical framing for mostly white audiences, while they employ a more graphic, emotional, and deliberately spoken narrative for diasporan tourists."[51]

These constant recalibrations suggest that these government employees possess considerable nimbleness as they deliver local history to the various groups of tourists. Although there are aspects of this past that are consistently covered, the guide's performance and narrative differ with each tour. Guides will also alter the narrative according to visitors' articulated queries, not just their perceived interests. Anthropologist Edward Bruner confirms that the guides "cater to groups' varied interests by shifting the emphasis of the tour. If a group expresses a special concern with the architecture of the castle, for example, the guides will emphasize that aspect."[52] The slave experience always remains at the center of the narrative, but there are certainly opportunities to delve more deeply into other dimensions of local history; the guides' depth and breadth of knowledge is undeniably impressive.

The importance of the tour guide to heritage tourism is not particular to Ghana. In other settings, these "deliverers of the past" play equally pivotal roles and have demonstrated the same adroitness as their Ghanaian counterparts. Saidiya Hartman's experience on Gorée Island in Senegal highlights these presentation and performance skills:

> At La Maison de Esclaves on Gorée Island, I join a group of African-American tourists from Miami comprised mostly of retired teachers and nurses. The curator of the slave house, Mr. Boubacar N'Diaye, attuned to the longings of African-American tourists, spins a history of slavery designed to remedy its injuries

and confirm African-American exceptionality. In narrating the history of the slave trade, N'Diaye describes those captured and taken to the Americas as the most beautiful people in Africa, and, as proof of this, he points to the superior physique of the African-American athlete. For us, he makes a production of joining the group, as if he has just decided to join us because of the auspiciousness of our return, and promises that it will be a special tour because we have returned home. . . . The special pitch geared for African Americans endows every remark with undue gravity, enshrines each object, requires additional aides to escort those crying out of the children's dungeon and to the Door of No Return, and ultimately casts himself not only as the guardian of memory, but as the original slave.[53]

It is clear from Hartman's account that the diasporic visitors' engagement with and experience at the site would have been dramatically divergent if Mr. N'Diaye had delivered an alternative narrative. Not all guides specifically invoke African Americans, but his attentiveness to the particular audience and his articulation of the indelible connections, no matter how distant, of Africans and African Americans clearly resonated with these heritage visitors.

ALTHOUGH ROOTS tourism features similarities with other perceptions, dynamics, and praxes of tourism in Africa, there remain important differences. Whereas most touristic activity is pursued for the purpose of leisure, heritage itineraries bring visitors to sites that often prompt pain, anguish, and loss—feelings not typically associated with a relaxing vacation. But these endeavors are also intended to bridge past and present and to be corrective, unifying, healing undertakings. Thus, they feature a responsibility, or arguably a burden, that is not present when, for example, an American of Irish descent travels to an ancestral village in the "homeland." As anthropologist Jennifer Hasty has argued, "Heritage tourism is intended to reestablish an essential solidarity among Africans on the continent and in the diaspora, overcoming the betrayal and holocaust of the slave trade as well as several hundred years of separate historical experience."[54]

In many respects, heritage tourism is still in its infancy compared to other forms of tourism in Africa and, therefore, may undergo significant experiential changes going forward. For example, new roots destinations may emerge, such as in Angola, where a fledging industry has begun to gain some traction; the slave castles may become less central to the overall experience; and narratives of the past may well evolve as new historical research amends prior knowledge or tourism officials decide to emphasize different aspects of regional histories. The next chapter examines an assortment of other, more recent forms of tourism, many of which may come to dominate the industry on the continent going forward.

CHAPTER SEVEN

Controversial New(er) Forms of Tourism in Africa

Last spring, my pastor asked me to go with him and a team to Africa. I prayed about it and I felt like God wanted me to go—so I started preparing and praying for my trip. I prayed for several specific things: that God would be glorified in everything we did, that I would see the people of Africa as God sees them, and that God would "break my heart" for these people. . . . Those ten days of travel changed my life. God has shown me how blessed I am and how much work still needs to be done. . . . I hope to return soon . . . to visit with my new friends and to help continue God's work in Africa.

> —Kelley Lewis, a member of Thomasville Road Baptist Church in Tallahassee, Florida, blogging about her church's mission trip to Senegal, 2016

Tourism has destroyed our youngsters. . . . Today, they want easy and fast cash; they want the tourists' lifestyles. . . . As long as tourism is in our midst and tourists are intermingling with our youths, then we are in a big mess, insurmountable trouble.

> —"Ed," a veteran fisherman from Malindi, Kenya, complaining about the sex tourism industry in his resort town, 2012

THE COMMENTS made by the churchgoer from Florida and the fisherman from Kenya both capture sentiments, albeit opposing, regarding some of the more recent forms of tourism in Africa. As the twenty-first century unfolds, most of the types of tourism outlined in the preceding chapters persist, yet a number of new varieties have more recently materialized, including ecotourism, cultural tourism, "poverty" tourism, so-called voluntourism, sex tourism, and trophy hunting. Although many of these more recent modes of tourism are ethically controversial, each generates revenues sufficient to encourage stakeholders, including African governments and private tour operators, to either promote them or at least not obstruct or prohibit them. Owing to these explicit and implicit endorsements, coupled with the continent's powerful touristic allure, these more contemporary forms of tourism annually attract millions of foreign visitors to the continent.

Although many of these types of tourism are, indeed, newfangled, at the most basic level, these newly arriving foreigners—seeking exposure to divergent cultures, animal trophies, or even sexual interaction—are perpetuating durable consumption patterns of the continent's peoples, wildlife, and landscapes. In practice, even if these forms of touristic "consumption" are relatively new, these visitors are attracted to Africa for many of the same reasons that outsiders have always been. Moreover, with virtually all of these newer varieties of tourism, long-standing power dynamics situate foreign guests in a superior position vis-à-vis their African hosts, enabling these visitors to engage with the continent from a position of considerable privilege. In these asymmetrical scenarios, Africans typically operate as marginalized actors, often forced to sacrifice, at various times, their dignity, their self-respect, or even their bodies. However, in many other ways, Africans have been able to exert significant agency and derive material advantages from these more recent forms of touristic activity. This chapter engages with these oft-controversial newer forms of tourism, while remaining mindful of the underlying power dynamics and their continuities with more traditional forms of tourism.

Ecotourism

At first glance, there is not much to dislike about ecotourism. No less an authority than The International Ecotourism Society (TIES) defines this endeavor as "responsible travel to natural areas that conserves the environment, sustains the well-being of the local people, and involves interpretation and education."[1] Given the problems associated with many traditional forms of tourism, this approach seems comparatively thoughtful and respectful. Yet it too has its critics. For example, Garth Allen and Frank Brennan argue that "this model . . . is equally culpable in the simplification and reduction of vast complexities into easy currency, while claiming the high ground of an apolitical development that resolves all of the dilemmas of tourist development and its social and environmental impacts."[2] In other words, it problematically simplifies the myriad complexities that tourism inherently generates. More forcefully, tourism scholar Brian Wheeller contends that "the costs and benefits of tourism can never be evenly distributed, and that the literature on ecotourism is merely a distraction and offers at best a short-lived micro-solution to the problems caused everywhere by mass tourism."[3] For many observers, ecotourism constitutes a middle-class preoccupation that offers no real alternative to mass tourism; in fact, it often serves as the vanguard for mass tourism.[4] For proof of its pretentious origins and appeal to status, a 1994 article in the *Observer* declared, "Eco-tourism . . . It's not in any dictionary yet, but if you want to impress at your next dinner party, it's a dead cert."[5]

Putting aside both advocates and naysayers of ecotourism for a moment, it is easy to see why it would be appealing to individuals who are interested in traveling to Africa, engaging with its natural features and human populations in a minimally impactful manner. Even so, in many ways, these more conscientious visitors harbor the same sentiments about Africa's "pristine" landscapes and "untarnished" peoples "not yet completely destroyed by the evils of Western modernity" as their touristic predecessors did. From the ecotourist's perspective, Africa's supposedly unchanging physical and human landscapes can be safely observed and experienced, but only if done so in a way that is both environmentally and culturally sensitive. Meanwhile, it is also perfectly understandable why some African officials would want to protect their touristic assets while promoting more sensible, sustainable engagement, which includes meaningful participation by local communities.

These noble intentions notwithstanding, although there is seemingly a collective "will" to pursue and promote ecotourism, the "way" is not always as straightforward. Advocates consistently cite the importance of empowering local (often rural) communities, but how to get these communities on the tourist map in the first place is a very real, very formidable challenge. It is, for example, difficult to sufficiently promote "small-scale, community-led tourism initiatives among the predominantly white, upmarket tourist industries on the continent."[6] Indeed, despite ecotourists' avowed intention to generate minimal social and environmental disruption, they still demand quality amenities that small communities in "off-the-beaten-track" locations may not be able to provide. After all, although ecotourists proclaim to value sustainability and mindfulness, suggesting a type of respectful intrepidness, they all hail from privileged classes, confirmed by their ability to fly to distant parts of the world and spend ample time "exploring." In short, although these visitors often fashion themselves "travelers," in reality they're still "tourists."

Another problematic aspect of ecotourism is the fanciful notion that these visitors are traveling back in time to a "pristine" Africa. As we have repeatedly established, this is a foundational block in the edifice of African touristic promotion, which also suggests that the continent's landscapes, peoples, and wildlife are "unchanged," "untamed," and "exotic." As human settlements specialist Ian Munt contends, "For the individual representatives of this new tourist middle-class, it is their desire to confirm and legitimate their cultural and environmental sensibilities that is inherent in their concern with ecology and Third and Fourth World 'otherness.'"[7] Encounter Overland, a now defunct ecotourism outfit, promoted the alleged exceptionality of the eco-adventure traveler by claiming they are "today's custodian of the ancient relationship between traveler and the native, which throughout the world has been the historic basis for peaceful contact."[8] Upon reflection, it's quite difficult to determine why this new brand of tourist should be entrusted with overseeing all interactions between tourists and locals or how they would go about forging peace between these disparate communities.

In practice, ecotourism is also neocolonial in nature, reinforcing long-standing, unequal power dynamics between Africans and foreigners on the continent. An emphasis on the "discovery" of foreign lands and penetration of a foreboding wilderness harken to the precolonial and colonial periods, when Europeans "bravely" ventured into "hostile" African lands. As Munt argues, "This is romanticism for both the wildness and travel modes of the colonial period, in which racism and class subordination are recreated in more invidious forms. . . . And it has invoked a nostalgic longing for untouched, primitive, and native peoples."[9] In a similar vein, consider how one ecotourism provider, Exceptional Travel, presents its African destinations: "The historic heart of adventurous exploration, Africa has been the focus of many a celebrated tale, conjuring up delicious images of the wild unknown."[10]

Another example of a type of mythical time travel to an unsullied wilderness comes from a piece written by novelist Janice McIlvaine McClary and a subsequent retort by Edward Bruner and Barbara Kirshenblatt-Gimblett. Following a gorilla viewing session, itself a form of ecotourism, in Zaire

(Congo) in 1985, McClary wrote the following for the Sunday *New York Times* about her experience: "It was an unforgettable moment. Somehow, the gorillas symbolized what is left of the wilderness, of a world belonging to the animals, free and unbridled by men and materialism. To see the greatest of the great apes at close range was to see a glimpse of Eden, of the world as it once was, without computers or condominiums, schedules and the draining sense of time."[11] Writing some years later, Bruner and Kirshenblatt-Gimblett pulled back the self-congratulatory curtain on this encounter between Western tourists and African wildlife that featured in McClary's "glimpse of Eden," averring,

> What McClary actually saw through the leaves was an ape, and what she read into the experience was all the Western intellectual baggage about a return to origins, primitiveness, and what we once were—unspoiled, unpolluted, uncomplicated. The imagery suggests that we have exhausted the metaphoric potentiality of primitive man and must recede even further to the irreducible ape. The glimpse of Eden, of course, was not there in the Zairean forest, but in McClary's head. Her account tells us more about the subject, McClary, than about the object, the gorillas.[12]

If Bruner and Kirshenblatt-Gimblett's contentions are accurate, ecotourism as a more recent form of tourism actually has rather old foundations. Casting it as a more ethical, responsible approach to tourism conceals foreigners' underlying motivations to "discover" Africa and the durable ways that they perceive the continent and its peoples. Ecotourism, as a more conscientious touristic way to engage Africa, should undoubtedly be welcomed and further encouraged, but the continuities with the colonial past and its neocolonial nature still render it a problematic "solution" to the continent's myriad touristic challenges.

Cultural Tourism

Cultural tourism constitutes another more recent type of engagement with Africa. In 2017, the World Tourism Organization defined this undertaking as follows: "Cultural tourism is a type of tourism activity in which the visitor's essential motivation is to learn, discover, experience and consume the tangible and intangible cultural attractions/products in a tourism destination."[13] Although cultural tourism on the continent dates back to the early twentieth century, it has experienced a more recent renaissance, driven by entrepreneurial Africans, and its current iteration diverges significantly from its earliest varieties. In recent decades, cultural tourism in Africa has largely entailed foreigners visiting sites in which a particular community showcases various aspects of its (seemingly static) culture. Think Colonial Williamsburg in rural Africa. During these tours, performers ordinarily engage in a drumming or dancing routine, while an individual in "traditional" attire narrates seemingly timeless customs, foodways, and so forth for the visitors. As some observers have argued regarding cultural tourism in Africa, "The tourist steps into the imagined archaeological tracks of 'early explorers' and 'white pioneers' in a well-rehearsed colonial encounter."[14]

As with ecotourism, advocates of cultural tourism argue that this manner of engaging with Africa supposedly constitutes a more mindful, respectful way of consuming the continent. After all, foreign visitors are ostensibly interested in learning more about an African culture and wish to interact with members of local communities, albeit in highly artificial settings and circumstances. But, of course, what is most appealing are the various dimensions of these cultures that seemingly contrast so sharply with the tourist's own. For example, visitors don't want to know that the Africans with whom they are interacting likely utilized either public or private vehicles to reach the cultural tourism site and spent much of the time before their shifts began on their cell phones. An extreme example of this phenomenon comes from a Kenyan operator who ran tours among the semi-nomadic Samburu peoples. According to the guide, "The tourists were always disappointed by the t-shirts and jeans that the locals wore, so the nomads had taken to changing into traditional clothing exclusively for the tourists. It got to the point where I was calling them on their mobile phones to say, 'Take off your shorts and t-shirts because I'm bringing tourists by.'"[15] Foreign visitors want to imagine an alien people, wholly unlike themselves, from some distant past that is, unfathomably, somehow also part of the present. Other observers have contended that cultural tourism "gives tribalism and colonialism a second life by bringing them back as representations of themselves and circulating them within an economy of performance."[16] Again, colonial-era dynamics color these contemporary touristic interactions.

The main challenges for cultural tourism organizers include generating the capital necessary to construct and staff the locations and, more importantly, attracting tourists to them. Some of these sites hold UNESCO World Heritage status, which enhances their touristic allure. Moreover, many of them feature on much longer itineraries as part of packaged tours, which is how most tourists experience the continent given their lack of knowledge, expertise, time, or inclination to make their own travel arrangements.[17] For cultural heritage sites to succeed, it is helpful if they are located in countries that already attract large numbers of visitors and are proximate to the major tourist attractions or destinations within these countries.

Once the guests arrive, the touristic presentations and performances must be delivered in appealing ways. That means performances should be reasonably short, comprehensible, and offer excellent photographic opportunities so that guests can share these images with friends and family members back home, accompanied by their own interpretive narrative. More importantly, the site should be "safe, accessible, comfortable, and clean, and the performance must be regularly scheduled and reliably performed so that groups can book space and plan itineraries well in advance."[18] And, of course, there must be ample opportunities for tourists to purchase "authentic" souvenirs and, in any way imaginable, spend money beyond the cost of admission. Thus, culture is literally for sale, and cultural tourism sites across the continent zealously adhere to this commercial formula.

Cultural Tourism among the Dogon in Mali: Safeguarding Revenues and Cultural Integrity

One example of cultural tourism in which Africans have creatively reconciled the dual aims of generating revenue and maintaining the integrity of local culture comes from the Dogon people of Mali, a former French colony. Since the 1980s, the Dogon have been a major touristic attraction owing to their renowned mask dances, which are associated with funerals. By offering public dances for tourists while retaining their own ritual dances, or *dama*, for themselves, the Dogon communities have devised a way to both commodify their culture and preserve it. Even the masks utilized for the highly choreographed tourist performances are produced solely for those commercialized occasions; ritual masks are exclusively utilized for the actual funeral ceremonies. By modeling the theatrical performances on one portion of the *dama*, they add to their seeming authenticity. However, there are many important differences between the two versions of the performance, including the permissible timing and location, as well as the ages of the performers.

Observers of these dynamics report that tourists are typically satisfied with their experiences, convinced that they have witnessed an "authentic" cultural performance that reflects the "deep history and intricate cosmology" of the Dogon.[19] Anthropologist Walter van Beek suggests that these performances "offer the Dogon a stage to 'play themselves' for an appreciative audience."[20] In fact, some foreign visitors reportedly feel that, due to an array of modern pressures, including, ironically, the presence of tourists, they might be among the last visitors to witness the Dogon in this seemingly "natural state." External influences on local cultures across the continent are certainly formidable, but the strategic separation of theatrical and ritual performances grants Dogon culture a resiliency that tourists aren't really intended to perceive.

Cultural Tourism in the "New" South Africa

In South Africa, the end of apartheid in the mid-1990s roughly coincided with the emergence of cultural tourism industries elsewhere on the continent. In many respects, the country is ideal for this brand of tourism, as it already attracts large numbers of foreign visitors. During apartheid, African cultures were typically not showcased for foreign visitors, as black South Africans were forced to reside in racially segregated areas and thus were not readily encounterable anyway. As the apartheid regime considered "white culture" to be superior, there was no impetus to feature "African cultures" for visitors.

There did exist, however, periodic "tribal" displays of black African, or "Bantu," cultures during the apartheid era, even if these black South Africans generally objected to "being put on display like cattle for inquisitive tourists."[21] C. V. Bothma, the apartheid government's chief ethnologist, condoned these types of performances provided they occur within the homelands (areas specifically designated for black South Africans), and so long as different ethnic groups performed only their own culturally specific dances. In some respects, this stance is not surprising given that the apartheid regime incessantly sought to reinforce not only racial differences, but also divisions between various ethnic groups as part of its "divide and rule" approach to governance. The persistence (and proliferation) of these ethnically delineated cultural performances well past the end of the apartheid era is, however, much more surprising. As one scholar commented regarding this durability, "The irony in many instances is that the cultural distinctiveness of indigenous groups, as the apartheid regime divide and rule policies defined it, is being reproduced in an era that is supposed to have superseded it."[22] In this respect, employing the lens of tourism does much to blur the otherwise monumental divide between apartheid South Africa and what has ensued since its dismantlement.

If cultural tourism precedents can be identified during the apartheid era, the proliferation and expansion of the industry is what differentiates the "new" (i.e., postapartheid) South Africa. Following the end of apartheid, entrepreneurial Africans have created whole "cultural villages" to introduce tourists to "authentic, tribal" communities. These sites are typically situated near major tourist routes and holiday resorts and are "distinct from their environment in their neat and idealized layouts. The contrast to reality is most marked. Carefully sanitized and removed from the way of life of the vast majority of the population, they represent fictional and idealized recreations of 'tribal' lifestyles and activities."[23] Given the apartheid regime's insistence on discrete "tribal" communities, which disregarded any ethnic complexity or hybridization, in many ways the foundations for cultural villages were already laid by the dawn of the "new" South Africa.[24]

Despite disavowing apartheid-era practices and policies, cultural villages promote a notion of ethnic purity that essentializes these communities. Thus, most cultural villages showcase a particular ethnic group. For example, at the DumaZulu cultural village in Zululand, in eastern South Africa, guests are invited to "experience the traditions and language of the Zulu people, learn and interact with a living culture, one of our planet's most indigenous cultures. A visit to our Cultural Village is an experience of a lifetime. Discover the Zulu way of life and watch the pulsating traditional dancing with the taste of Zulu beer on your lips and the drumbeat of the Zulus echoing in your ears."[25] Yet not all cultural villages feature only a single ethnic group. For example, the organizers of Lesedi Cultural Village, located near Johannesburg, offer visitors a chance to "encounter people of Zulu, Xhosa, Pedi, Ndebele and Basotho origin. You'll meet real people (not actors in fancy dress), enter their homes and listen to stories about their individual cultures and rituals of daily life."[26] Regardless, in both settings, ethnicities are presented as distinct and homogenized, perhaps to resonate with foreigners' stereotypical understandings of certain personality or behavioral characteristics uniformly associated with individuals from particular nations (e.g., Germans are punctual and lack a sense of humor). And, of course, both types of sites offer a taste of "real Africa," with its constituent exoticism and timelessness.

Slum/Poverty Tourism

Another recent touristic development in Africa has been the emergence of the guided slum tour, derisively known as "poverty porn," in which local guides lead visitors through impoverished urban or peri-urban neighborhoods, often on foot. This exoticization of poverty takes visitors into places they would not likely otherwise traverse and brings them into contact with Africans with whom they might not otherwise interact.

Although this form of tourism is relatively new in Africa, emerging in the 1990s in South Africa, the current epicenter of the industry, and spreading in Kenya during the ensuing decade, it derives from a much older practice. Curiosity about slums "is at least as old as the slum itself. When 'slum' evolved in Standard English, the word 'slumming' also found its way into upper crust London's 'West-Side-Lingo.' The term described the burgeoning leisure time activity of upper class Londoners who were setting off for the 'undiscovered land of the poor' in the East End in the middle of the 19th century."[27] This diversion subsequently featured in Harlem and Chicago and in an array of cities in continental Europe.[28] Fast forward to twenty-first-century Africa, and privileged outsiders are once again venturing into spaces in which the impoverished "other" resides. Although slum tourism diverges in some respects from the other types of tourism we have considered previously, the touristic motivations and objectives are remarkably consistent.

The black townships that encircled urban centers and continue to serve as the addresses for the black urban poor are the settings for slum tours in contemporary South Africa. These tours claim to offer glimpses into the vibrant daily life of the township, which often includes an array of colorful characters who play it up for tourists, but also plenty of other residents who stare uncomfortably at the gazing visitors. These tours, which claim to promote South Africa's "living culture, political resistance, and modern life," annually attract up to five hundred thousand tourists, eager to enter spaces previously off-limits to whites, including white South Africans.[29] The (primarily) black townships of Johannesburg and Cape Town are the main sites for these touristic endeavors, but Durban also has a smaller industry. These areas would generally be considered too dangerous for unaccompanied tourists to navigate, thereby fueling the sense that these visitors are engaged in a dangerous discovery of the unknown.

Proponents of slum tourism invariably cite the human development opportunities it provides for locals. In the ideal scenario, the African guide of the slum tour, who acts as the liaison between the community and the tourists, distributes the revenue generated from paying customers among those locals who participate in the tour and, perhaps, more broadly, to all residents of the areas visited. Local residents can invite the tour groups into their homes to demonstrate how they live, impart information about the community, sell curios or other souvenirs, or, though less commonly, host the visitors for a meal or even overnight. The more significant the engagement, the greater the income that residents can potentially earn.

Visitors on these tours typically express an interest in contributing to the development of the host community by paying a fee to participate in the endeavor and, often, by purchasing various types of souvenirs. Obligingly, most tour operators will provide "narrative and experiential frames that enable tourists to think of themselves as agents of change in the slums."[30] These tourists also want, like so many foreign visitors to the continent, to experience the "real Africa." Influenced by powerful stereotypes, outsiders often reason that no place is more "real" than a slum. Visitors often romanticize these sites, conceiving of them as places that feature genuine "community and locality" and "poor but happy" residents, aspects of society that may be absent in foreigners' often impersonal existences.[31]

Although there exist myriad critics of this controversial form of tourism, studies have shown that, in general, tourists' perceptions about slums and slum dwellers positively change as a result of the tour.[32] Similarly, local residents often note that this form of tourism "helps challenge negative stereotypes, breaks their isolation, and instills a sense of pride that foreign tourists are interested in their locality and the overall development of the neighborhood."[33] Ironically, the most successful slum tour destinations eventually become part of mainstream tourism, as the undertaking becomes a "must-do" for visitors to the destination.[34] What was once a fringe activity becomes a touristic imperative.

As slum tourism grows in popularity, the industry has both expanded and formalized. In some settings, large tour and travel companies, unable to resist the profits available, have moved in and muscled aside local operators as part of a process that experts call "displacement." In South Africa, the more sizeable operators usually feature white ownership and are not, themselves, located in the townships where the tours take place. As part of this touristic evolution, the tours are increasingly professionalized. In more mature destinations, for example, a wide range of small and large businesses with "varying degrees of professionalism are involved in tour operation, guiding, crafts, performance, visitor attraction, accommodation, and catering, e.g., 'authentic' restaurants, bars and *shebeens* (unlicensed, informal bars popular with black South Africans), with some of these establishments serving African 'traditional fare.'"[35]

As you might imagine, the innumerable detractors of this form of touristic activity claim that it exoticizes, objectifies, and commercializes poverty by rendering substandard living conditions a "must-see." Dignity is an important factor in these criticisms, as many tourists snap off photographs of human suffering and impoverishment, often without permission, simply to share with their friends and family members upon returning home. Critics also contend that slum dwellers serve as a backdrop for these images, "remaining like mute actors, performing in a play without a say or control . . . which can, in the long run, lead to feelings of disempowerment."[36] The harshest rebukes, though, relate to the alleged enjoyment that these voyeuristic tourists derive from this endeavor at the expense of local residents. As scholars Kyle Powys Whyte, Evan Selinger, and Kevin Outterson have reproved, "These tourists seek to be entertained by others' most unfortunate of circumstances, often without their consent. . . . It is hard to make the case for the permissibility of entertainment that comes at the expense of peoples' misfortunes, especially when it is accompanied by degradation, disrespect, and perpetuation of social subordination."[37] Finally, critics note that the residents subjected to the tourist gaze rarely profit from these tours owing to the increased control of the industry by deep-pocketed companies. For all the advocates and purported benefits of slum tourism, there is no shortage of naysayers, but until the visitors stop coming, this industry will not only persist into the foreseeable future but will most likely continue to expand.

Voluntourism

For foreigners who desire more than a brief touristic encounter with Africa, volunteering in some capacity related to social welfare and development has become an increasingly popular way to arrange an extended engagement on the continent. The prospect of combining a prolonged, immersive vacation with volunteering is particularly appealing for many prospective visitors. However, because these volunteers pay for these opportunities, typically accomplish very little that endures, and usually can't or simply don't spend a particularly long time in Africa, this endeavor has been derisively labeled as "voluntourism." Moreover, owing to the asymmetrical power dynamics inherent in these arrangements, this touristic enterprise is "emerging as a key site of encounters between privilege and poverty."[38] As with slum tourism, the debates revolve around who benefits, issues of human dignity, and the inequalities manifest in these interactions.

Although voluntourism is a rather recent phenomenon, there's a long history of foreigners volunteering in Africa. For example, during the early decades of the colonial period, many Europeans volunteered to serve as part of missionary societies, which established schools and medical clinics, staffing these facilities throughout this era. Following independence, certain governments on the continent, including Mozambique, Tanzania, Zambia, and Angola, invited foreigners to volunteer their expertise to help their fledgling nations develop, while many African leaders encouraged volunteerism among their citizenries to the same end. These foreigners were commonly motivated "by a desire to build a fairer and better world, to alleviate poverty, and bring development, as well as a desire for adventure."[39] Going forward, international volunteers continued to participate in various development projects on the continent, primarily facilitated by NGOs, including the long-standing Operation Crossroads Africa, founded in 1958, as well as by a vast array of religious groups, though governmental programs such as the US Peace Corps also fit in this category. But the more recent "pay to volunteer" form of engagement with Africa is substantively and experientially divergent from its predecessors.

Voluntourists are compelled to participate for a variety of reasons, some of which overlap. In general, volunteering "is usually considered to be an unmitigated public good," and as scholars Ruth Prince and Hannah Brown remind us, "It's capable of mobilizing individuals and groups and of marking out the possibilities of acting in the service of a greater good by addressing social inequalities or perceived deprivation. It can be framed as a means to act upon suffering, and used to promote a vision of a better integrated society or a more equal world."[40] For many voluntourists, these reasons are exactly what motivates them to spend time on the continent. For others, this form of engagement is based on "Christian ethics of compassion and pity producing charitable action and 'doing good.'"[41] Religiously motivated voluntourists participate by going on "mission trips," like the one outlined at the onset of this chapter that Floridian Kelley Lewis experienced. Generally, these trips constitute short excursions to the continent during which time unskilled foreigners engage in tasks that could otherwise have been performed by locals. For example, visitors often provide supplies (e.g., medical or building materials) and a dash of labor. Other voluntourists want to gain an advantage in the labor market by showcasing experiences that differentiate them from others or that make them appear worldly, engaged, and concerned. It is, of course, conceivable that these volunteers earnestly want to improve the plight of the Africans that they are attempting to assist, but the thousands of dollars they pay to secure this opportunity could undoubtedly be better spent if the objective is genuinely to improve the well-being of the continent's citizens.[42] Ultimately, this affective experience is primarily about the foreign voluntourist, rather than the African "voluntouree."

It is precisely this reality that has prompted growing criticism of this form of touristic engagement with Africans. Volunteering as an "altruistic, noble act" provides perfect cover for a scenario in which global inequalities underpin the daily interactions between wealthy foreigners and locals. In turn, this dynamic reinforces colonial-era racial hierarchies while highlighting Africans' "otherness" as culturally distinct from the volunteers' home countries in the Global North. The very existence of this industry also inherently suggests that Africans want or even *need* this type of assistance, while it's not clear that they do.

Moreover, when voluntourists do not have the appropriate skills for their assigned placements, they can be more of a burden than a resource. At times, this scenario can turn deadly, as was the case with Renee Bach, an American who established a malnutrition clinic and posed as a "white doctor" in the city of Jinja, Uganda, a hub of American voluntourism to which "American teens raised in mostly evangelical churches were streaming in to volunteer."[43] During Bach's oversight of the clinic, from 2010 through 2015, 105 children died.[44] Commenting on this tragedy, Lawrence Gostin, who directs the Center on National and Global Health Law at Georgetown University, declared, "Just think of the arrogance. Who are you to assume that you can do better than they can? It's not your judgment call to make. . . . The American cultural narrative is that these countries are basket cases, so Americans assume that whatever their qualifications, they're sure to be of help. People think that they're doing good. And they have no idea how much harm they can cause. People in the U.S. are often complicit because when these volunteers write blogs or post videos to share their exploits, they're celebrated."[45]

Although Bach's case is, thankfully, exceptional, less severe developments featuring similar power dynamics continue to plague receiving societies in Africa, in great part because for-profit companies run the industry. These enterprises gladly accept the considerable fees that participants pay for this opportunity, which obliges these companies to assign their customers to a particular entity or project, regardless of skill level or appropriateness. As one critic has observed, "It is the great flexibility, choice and support offered to volunteers that characterizes the newer volunteering organizations, rather than their ability to match volunteer skills with the needs of the recipient communities."[46] These organizations play a central role not only in facilitating these assignments but also in ensuring that the supply of voluntourists does not wane. To that end, they aggressively advertise these opportunities, assuring participants that they can, in fact, help Africans without "destroying" their culture.

These organizations are also quick to differentiate the experiences they offer from purely touristic endeavors. As anthropologist Eileadh Swan explains, "Tourism is used frequently throughout the websites of volunteering organizations in a negative sense to reassure potential volunteers that even if what volunteerism *is* is left slightly unclear, it is definitely *not* tourism. Potential volunteers are told that their experience of life in a 'different culture' will be something that a tourist could never experience."[47] This disparagement of tourism as a short-term undertaking is somewhat ironic, as most voluntourism experiences typically don't last for longer than two weeks. Regardless, it's a common refrain.

Although voluntourists are adamant that they are *not* tourists, in many respects, that is exactly what they are. They differentiate their trips by insisting that their experiences are not just longer, but also more "authentic" and "deeper." The words of a voluntourist who was placed in Ho, in eastern Ghana, underscore this sentiment: "Volunteering is completely different from being a tourist because we live and work for an extended time in another culture. You are not just an observer passing through, so you understand and learn more."[48] Yet research has demonstrated that local Africans don't distinguish between (white) tourists, volunteers, NGO workers, and missionaries, as all of them have the time, freedom, and money to travel to the continent.[49]

These voluntourists also often establish internal hierarchies within their groups predicated on how long they have been "in the field," or are planning to be.[50] Those who stay longer typically try to adopt particular customs or habits that allegedly demonstrate their comprehension and espousal of local culture, which is allegedly only possible with the passage of time. Of course, when the difference between a "short stay" of, say, two weeks, and a "long stay" of perhaps six weeks is only a handful of weeks, this claim of cultural integration is dubious. It should be noted that this attempt to prove one's "authentic" immersion into local culture based on the duration of exposure to it is not unique to voluntourists. Tourists, themselves, often measure the quality of their trips vis-à-vis others based on how long they are. Similarly, foreign aid workers and expatriates living in Africa often compare their experiences on the continent against others based on duration and, quite absurdly, if and how many times they might have contracted malaria, apparently a rite of passage in order to have an "authentic" experience.[51]

Perhaps most problematic about the voluntourism industry is the negligible impact that these otherwise well-meaning individuals have, which is readily recognized by both self-aware volunteers and members of local communities. Testimony from a disgruntled voluntourist placed in Ghana offers significant insight: "If other companies are like this one, then any impact volunteering can make is small. I would never recommend this one to someone who wanted to do serious volunteering work. This is basically to help volunteers understand the place they visit so they can impress their family and friends because they have survived the 'wilds' of Africa. Their family will never know the luxury they really experienced."[52] Given the transactional nature of the industry, in which the voluntourist pays for the opportunity, when the facilitating company doesn't deliver the envisioned experience—no matter how unrealistic it may have been—the paying client naturally becomes embittered.

Locals also feel resentful when what they were promised is not delivered. In particular, African schools often accept voluntourists, assuming that these foreigners will have had at least some pedagogical training. When local educators learn that is not the case, comments such as the following rhetorical question posed by a Ghanaian teacher flow freely: "Would you let a Ghanaian or even a British person who had not been to teacher training come and teach in your schools? I do not believe you would."[53] Even more troubling, these arrangements reinforce colonial and neocolonial race and power relations, in which whiteness is inherently perceived as superior, even in the form of an unqualified, untrained "teacher." Lamenting this scenario and casting blame in every direction, another Ghanaian educator decried, "We say we are independent, but we are still favoring useless whites over trained blacks to teach our children. When will we ever learn? All this talk of cross-cultural learning or whatever is nonsense; every time an untrained volunteer comes to teach, our children are still seeing that white is best. It is just neo-colonialism."[54] Presumably, these heartfelt words will never feature in a voluntourism agency's promotional material.

Sex Tourism

Another more recent form of tourism in Africa entails Western women traveling to the continent to engage in "sex tourism" with young African men. These women typically would not pursue this type of interaction in their home countries, but their behavioral norms and expectations differ in these purportedly "hedonistic" tropical locales. As with other seemingly novel types of tourism, this endeavor also has reasonably deep roots, with some scholars suggesting that women began traveling to Rome, Italy, as early as the mid-1800s seeking these types of experiences.[55] In Africa, the practice probably dates to the 1960s, in Gambia, where local men who engage in this practice are known as "bumsters," and subsequently, in other places in West Africa as well. And, of course, Western men have been traveling around the globe, including to Africa, for some time engaging in sex with local women in an array of arrangements. In Africa, however, although male tourists may well engage with a female (or male) prostitute while on vacation, the primary actors in this touristic scenario are single, middle-aged (or older) Western women of some means and African men, typically in their 20s, in a series of coastal cities around the continent, including Banjul, Gambia; Cape Town, South Africa; and Malindi, Kenya.

Although sex constitutes a major motivation for these sojourns, these women often want local companionship as well and, thereby, insights into a society to which they would not otherwise enjoy access. Consequently, scholars also refer to this engagement as "romance tourism," in part to distinguish it from prostitution, but also because there are occasions when these relations extend beyond the duration of the vacation (unlike with prostitution), though the wholesomeness that the word "romance" connotes may exaggerate the depth or genuineness of the relationship. Indeed, sociologist Jacqueline Sanchez-Taylor has argued that "the tendency to de-sexualize female sex tourism by labelling it as 'romance' hides the complexities involved in the social interaction between affluent, western women and poor black men from the host destinations."[56]

Regarding the power dynamics in this form of tourism, gender roles are reversed: it is the women who have the "power, freedom, and money to engage in these liaisons."[57] In return, they receive not only sexual gratification but also experiences that take them away from the well-beaten tourist path, into local society.[58] Yet very few of these visitors acknowledge the problematic nature of these exchanges, nor would many of them describe themselves as sex tourists or their African partners as sex workers. The exemplary account of "Jarngerd," a middle-aged Norwegian woman on a beach holiday in Kenya, underscores these attitudes and reveals the standard methods for initiating and cultivating these relationships:

> It all started at the beach. This guy sold me a souvenir then proposed a "cheap" safari to Tsavo West National Park. . . . Since then, we have become [sex] partners. . . . Definitely, this cannot be called sex tourism. We are simply helping one another. He helps me to "see" and "discover" Kenya, while I help him with some pocket money as a sign of appreciation. Having sex with him is just a side thing . . . to keep ourselves busy at night. Of course, I enjoy it. I am a normal woman . . . with normal sexual feelings. But, I am not a sex tourist. I am against sex tourism. It degrades the local people. It is disrespectful to local cultures.[59]

The local men who engage in sex tourism are called by various nicknames across the continent, including "beachboys," "bumsters," "playboys," and "hustlers," each of which stresses their sexuality and its utility as a financial asset. These enterprising men become involved in this industry for a variety of reasons, including to maintain a more comfortable lifestyle than their educational status would otherwise dictate; to avoid what they might consider more menial, monotonous livelihoods; to attempt to parlay these sexual relationships into permanent residence in Europe or North America; and for some, to pursue genuine friendships or to experience a type of pride in hosting and introducing foreigners to local life and customs.

If the Western women who engage with these African men are often reluctant to characterize their actions as sex tourism, these "hustlers" are typically much more unreserved about their intentions, objectives, and experiences in this industry. These men are normally much more open about these interactions and candid in their comments. For example, in discussing the differences between various European sex tourists, "Jones," a male sex worker in Kenya, indicated in an interview with a scholar conducting research on the subject that

> it is much easier to get a German partner. . . . Germans are very good, understanding, accommodating, out-going and friendlier than other *wazungu* [Kiswahili word for white people]. They do not care whether you speak German. . . . But, you have to be a performer. . . . They are sexually starved. . . . However, British

women are the worst . . . they are bullies. Even if you speak English like Shakespeare, you will end up nowhere with them. Their relationships with us male sex workers are like "hit-and-run" sex affairs. You sleep with one, but when you meet with her the following day, she pretends that she has never seen you. They are too mechanical.[60]

For Jones and others, their involvement in this endeavor is inherently temporary, as they rather quickly age out of this livelihood, replaced by younger, more sexually attractive men. Consequently, they need to hustle, often aggressively. They usually approach visitors in heavily touristed areas, offering local tours that will take the visitor beyond the "tourist bubble," help them barter with curio merchants (though some of them also sell their own souvenirs), or assist them with carrying items. These initial encounters can then lead to sustained accompaniment, companionship, and, ultimately, sex. Once the process commences, these men "often play on sexual and racial myths about the exotic African Other by offering tourists unlimited virility and other such sexual experiences."[61] The costs associated for this array of services tend to be "more open-ended and loosely specified, with prices and limits not always negotiated in advance," the way that they are between prostitutes and their clients.[62]

If both tourist and "bumster" are content with these transactional relationships, local community members largely disdain them. In particular, more senior members of African societies are especially critical of these young men (and often, of tourism itself), accusing them of immoral, disrespectful, lazy, and menacing behavior, all with the goal of personal enrichment or, more cynically, trying to "get rich quick." Certainly, these bumsters' eschewal of traditional forms of work irks many of these older men and women. In Muslim settings, such as Malindi, Kenya, these young men are contravening innumerable local gender, sexual, and behavioral codes of conduct by openly cavorting with much older female tourists; conservative elements within local society consider these women "morally depraved and sexually deprived."[63] Young African women who seek to engage male tourists as clientele are also often on the receiving end of local criticism, though they are further stigmatized as "whores," who tarnish the reputation of the community.[64] Indeed, many Africans believe that sex tourism of any variety stains their communities and, more broadly, their respective countries.

Trophy Hunting as Tourism

We learned earlier in the book that foreigners have been traveling to Africa to fell its renowned wildlife for centuries. In that sense, there is nothing novel about visitors to the continent seeking a faunal trophy as part of what constitutes, for many, the ultimate hunting experience. But the exorbitant costs, governmental restrictions, reduced hunting spaces, and global controversy surrounding the contemporary trophy hunting industry are all new. The hunt itself has also radically changed. Although these tourists fancy themselves modern-day Roosevelts, their experiences are entirely illusory: animals are conveniently confined within private reserves, and any perils associated with the hunting of yesteryear have been eliminated. This form of tourism generates limited employment opportunities for local residents but considerable revenue for tour operators and the governments of the two dozen African countries in which it is permitted. This touristic undertaking can also—as occurred following the illicit shooting in 2015 of Zimbabwe's beloved "Cecil the Lion" by a Minnesota dentist—generate unwanted attention and, in that particular case, criminal charges.

The most controversial version of the twenty-first-century hunting "safari" is the so-called canned hunt, which is arranged within private, fenced game reserves and typically includes animals bred in captivity solely for that purpose.[65] As the animals, often lions, have virtually no chance to avoid their lethal fate, the hunt is critically referred to as "canned." Although upward of fifteen thousand foreign hunters arrive in Africa each year to engage in various types of trophy hunting, Southern Africa and, in particular, South Africa, is the capital of canned hunting. The country features an estimated ten thousand game ranches, which cover roughly 50 million acres of land, approximately 17 percent of South African territory, and are collectively part of an extensive, vertically integrated captive-breeding/canned-hunting industry.[66] Much of this land is owned by white South African farmers and was previously used for livestock or agriculture, but the economic appeal of this form of tourism simply became too much to resist.

What is most striking about this industry is the amount of money involved. A South African governmental report from 2013, for example, indicated that direct revenue from foreign tourist hunters amounted to almost $100 million, while "related expenditures, including travel, food, permits, taxidermy, shipping, and side trips, contributed an additional $40–45 million to the country's economy."[67] That year, roughly seven thousand foreign hunters, some 55 percent of whom came from the United States and another 40 percent from Europe, engaged in 7,638 hunts in South Africa, taking home some forty-four thousand trophies.[68] And they paid dearly for them: lion hunts on game ranches in the country range from $20,000 to $40,000, though in other settings, including Tanzania, they can exceed $75,000. Clearly, only individuals with very deep pockets can even entertain this touristic undertaking.

Underscoring the financial importance of this industry, in the roughly two dozen African countries in which trophy hunting is permitted, governments have reserved more land for hunting than for national parks. Although photographic safaris produce greater overall revenues than does trophy hunting, the latter has significant appeal for African administrations for a number of reasons. First, trophy hunting generates much more revenue per tourist than does the camera safari industry. This equates to a reduced environmental impact per visitor while still maintaining high levels of touristic income. Second, trophy hunting does not preclude other forms of resource use. In contrast to most national parks, "many hunting zones permit regulated natural resource extraction by local communities in the form of grazing, firewood collection, and in some cases controlled subsistence hunting."[69] Third, the industry can generate revenues under a wider range of scenarios than can the camera safari industry.[70] In areas that lack robust "infrastructure, attractive scenery, or high densities of viewable wildlife," for example, trophy hunting can still be financially viable.[71] It is even sustainable in countries experiencing political instability, where other forms of tourism shrink significantly. Finally, more of the revenue generated from hunting safaris stays within the host country than do profits from camera safaris. Whereas camera safari packages are often booked through agents located overseas, hunting safari operators are typically located on the continent, which means that African governments retain, in the form of taxes and fees, more revenue and thereby minimize any loss of profits, or "leakage," as it's known in the industry.

To rebut the trenchant criticism that the trophy hunting industry relentlessly faces, proponents claim that there would not be sufficient funds to establish or maintain Africa's vast national parks network without the revenue that the trophy hunting industry generates. Tourism associated with national parks, even in countries with high tourism volumes such as South Africa, does not produce enough revenue to cover the considerable operating costs of these animal sanctuaries. Thus, from roughly the 1980s on, industry representatives and government officials, especially in Southern Africa, began to collaborate on conservation initiatives, while garnering support from international donor and conservation agencies. The industry also boasts that it can play a central role in the preservation, or even revival, of endangered species, "even when excessive hunting was the original cause of the conservation problem."[72] According to ecological experts Peter Lindsey, Pierre Roulet, and Stephanie Romañach,

> Initially, when species are critically endangered, a complete cessation of all human-caused mortality is necessary. Subsequently, however, revenues from tightly regulated trophy hunting can provide important incentives for careful management, protection, and reintroductions. On private land in South Africa, for example, trophy hunting has facilitated the recovery of certain species by providing financial incentives for reintroductions. Similarly, the recovery of southern white rhinoceros populations was accelerated by incentives from trophy hunting, which encouraged reintroductions onto game ranches.[73]

There is also ample evidence to suggest that local communities are more willing to participate in conservation programs when they benefit materially from trophy hunting. As outlined above, hunting lands often feature sustainable access and user rights for adjacent communities. This dispensation, combined with revenues that these communities earn directly from trophy hunters, create a powerful incentive for local residents to support conservation objectives, even when they're imposed by the state or other entities with whom these communities might have more contentious relations. Research has shown that wildlife populations have consequently increased, while some African communities have even requested to have a portion of their lands included in wildlife management projects.[74]

Of course, not everyone is convinced that the trophy industry is an indisputable force for good in the world. Critics include animal rights activists, who challenge the conservation claims that the industry relentlessly makes, suggesting that "harvesting animal trophies and sound environmental management" are irreconcilable.[75] This highly charged debate between advocates and opponents often degenerates into personal attacks, which advance neither side's agenda. Critics of the industry regularly point to the unethical practices that feature on some game ranches, including "shooting from vehicles, shooting female animals or young animals; luring animals from [national] parks; using baits [as was the case with 'Cecil'] and spotlights; hunting leopards with dogs; put-and-take hunting (the practice of releasing trophies immediately prior to the onset of a hunt); and 'canned hunting.'"[76] In fact, animal welfarists and trophy hunters have both "condemned the worst excesses of the canned hunting industry," though their sentiments otherwise only very rarely align.[77]

Animal rights groups have pressured African governments to restrict trophy hunting and, in particular, canned hunting, while pursuing a global campaign aimed at both the industry and its clientele. The most notable and effective has been the South Africa–based Campaign Against Canned Hunting (CACH). This activist group has organized protests, including the "Global March for Lions" in 2014, which was held in over sixty cities and two dozen countries, and actively lobbies governments to restrict this type of hunting, citing the animals' defenselessness and the general cruelty of the affair. CACH has also pointed out that the relative ease of these hunts means that they can be "marketed to clients who lack the requisite skill and experience to kill animals without undue pain and suffering under more challenging hunting conditions."[78] For example, some hunters are so inexpert that they might need a dozen or more shots to fell a lion, causing the animal to experience a slow death.

CACH has also lobbied foreign governments from which tourist-hunters derive to ban the importation of lion trophies. The idea is that if foreign hunters are unable to return home with these faunal prizes, fewer of them will want to engage in this activity in the first place. These efforts have met with mixed results: the US Fish and Wildlife Service initially balked, though it did institute some protective measures going forward, while the European Union applied the ban only to lion trophies from West Africa, where overall lion numbers are quite small. Only Australia completely banned all lion imports. However, a somewhat unexpected push by airlines to ban lion trophies as cargo has given CACH cause for optimism. Led by South African Airways, the movement quickly gained momentum. After Cecil's highly publicized death in 2015, Delta Airlines, which operates one of the only direct flights between Africa and the United States, joined the embargo, followed quickly by American Airlines and United Airlines. Celebrations regarding these corporate decisions were short-lived, though, as the Trump administration began rolling back US trophy importation restrictions that had been instituted under President Obama. It is unclear whether this issue will continue to ebb and flow based on the political stripes of the US president, but it is clear that CACH and other animal activists will not desist in their efforts.

This chapter has examined a number of forms of tourism that have recently emerged on the continent. Although considered separately, there are numerous intersections among these various touristic endeavors. For example, many Western tourists "volunteer" on lion farms, at which the animals are raised for the trophy hunting industry, and just like "voluntourists," these individuals pay thousands of dollars for these opportunities.[79] And, of course, a visitor to the continent may engage in many different types of tourism on a single trip (e.g., go on safari one day and on a "slum tour" the next). Going forward, there will undoubtedly be even more intersectional permutations, especially with the emergence of additional, as of yet undeveloped, forms of tourism.

AS WE have seen over the course of the book, the tourism sector in Africa is plagued by various forms of labor exploitation, while revenues continue to flow disproportionately to proprietors of tourist facilities and tour organizers (often foreigners), significantly enriching them. Yet most foreign visitors to the continent are largely unaware of these realities for Africans involved in the sector. Although these local employees daily service these guests, they remain largely invisible in the touristic gaze. In practice, Western visitors have obscured these Africans for centuries, relying upon their vital assistance but barely mentioning them in accounts and memoirs of their experiences. This lack of visibility notwithstanding, Africans have both formally and informally carved out livelihoods in this steadily expanding industry for centuries. From safari porters to sex tourism workers, Africans have creatively engaged with the industry, often in entrepreneurial and enterprising ways, especially following the conclusion of the colonial period. Today, they are poised to make even more significant contributions to the continued growth of the sector across the continent, as expanded access to education and training enables their ascension into more prominent positions in the industry and increased access to capital renders them more likely to launch their own touristic businesses.

And what about the foreign visitors they will service? As we have seen, outsiders have long been attracted to the continent and its peoples. Over time, foreigners cultivated notions of Africa as an unparalleled place to escape the relentless expansion of technology, descending upon the continent to seemingly travel back in time to a simpler, less frenetic place. As we have seen, these would-be visitors have been able to reconcile these powerful, romanticized images of tourist Africa with the prevailing notions of "non-tourist" Africa as a place of poverty, disease, and war. Touristic experiences on the continent generally feed this dualistic understanding, as Africans in the industry carefully manage visitors' engagement with the peoples and places—and even the wildlife—they encounter during their travels. Thus, Africans have played a central role in the perpetuation of the continent's appeal, though they have historically been abetted in this process by a host of other actors with economic interests in the industry.

As we ponder the future of tourism in Africa, the most significant long-term challenge for the industry is, ironically, its ongoing growth. As tourism both contributes to development and is, itself, a form of development, it is rapidly eroding two of the continent's greatest touristic assets: the remnants of supposedly "timeless" and thereby "authentic" African communities and the spaces within which the wildlife that tourists pay so dearly to observe in person reside. Although Africans employed in the sector will continue to service and perform for foreign visitors, continued development steadily renders the continent's peoples, sights, and sounds (seemingly) less exotic and thus makes even these obviously contrived touristic displays less "traditional." Ultimately, the greatest threat to Africa's tourism industry—itself dependent upon enduring illusions originally cultivated centuries ago—may well be its own success.

As you've surely realized by now, you're more than just part of the audience for this book; you, as a prospective or even a veteran tourist to the continent, are an integral part of this unfolding story. At the onset of this book, I asked if you have ever dreamed of visiting Africa as a tourist. Now that you have finished reading the book and can, ideally, make a more informed decision as a result, I hope that you still do and will, ultimately, realize this aspiration.

STUDY GUIDE AND SELECTED READINGS

THIS SECTION is intended for readers and instructors who wish to delve more deeply into the book's contents via further discussion and reading. For each chapter, questions are posed that are intended to generate conversation about the various topics and themes examined in the book, followed in each case by a list of relevant source materials.

Introduction: Touristic Illusions and Realities

This chapter introduces readers to the history of tourism in Africa, with a focus on the durable allure of the continent for outsiders. It frames the narrative and engages with core themes that are considered in the ensuing chapters.

Discussion Questions

1. Have you ever wanted to visit Africa as a tourist? Why or why not? Has reading the book influenced or altered your decision?

2. Are your overall notions of Africa different from your impressions of the continent as a tourist destination? Why or why not?

3. Why is Africa often perceived by outsiders as "exotic"? How have these notions contributed to its touristic appeal over time?

Selected Readings

Hickey, Dennis, and Kenneth C. Wylie. *An Enchanting Darkness: The American Vision of Africa in the Twentieth Century.* East Lansing: Michigan State University, 1993.

Keim, Curtis. *Mistaking Africa: Curiosities and Inventions of the American Mind*, 3rd ed. Boulder: Westview Press, 2014.

Magee, Carol. *Africa in the American Imagination: Popular Culture, Racialized Identities, and African Visual Culture.* Jackson: University of Mississippi Press, 2012.

Zuelow, Eric G. E. *A History of Modern Tourism.* London: Palgrave, 2016.

Chapter 1: Initial Touristic Incursions to Africa

Chapter 1 examines the initial ventures by outsiders to the continent over the course of the nineteenth century and highlights their dependency on

Africans' logistical support. These visitors' rac(ial)ism and limited under-standings of what and whom they encountered generated legion misper-ceptions and further exoticized the continent.

Discussion Questions

1. Why were these early visitors to Africa attracted to the continent? In what ways did their experiences encourage other foreigners to visit Africa?

2. What roles did Africans play in these early touristic forays to the continent?

3. What long-term implications did these initial visits to Africa have for the continent and its peoples?

Selected Readings

Anderson, Martin. "The Development of British Tourism in Egypt, 1815 to 1850." *Journal of Tourism History* 4, no. 3 (2012): 259–79.

Hunter, F. Robert. "Tourism and Empire: The Thomas Cook & Son Enterprise on the Nile, 1868–1914." *Middle Eastern Studies* 50, no. 5 (September 2004): 28–54.

Manley, Deborah, ed. *Women Travelers on the Nile: An Anthology of Travel Writing through the Centuries.* Cairo and New York: American University in Cairo Press, 2016.

Chapter 2: Hunting in Africa: Invisible Guides, Big Game, and Bigger Egos

Chapter 2 considers the history of foreigners' hunting expeditions, or "sa-faris," in sub-Saharan Africa from the nineteenth century through the end of the colonial period on the continent. None of these undertakings would have been possible without vital assistance from the large numbers of Afri-can scouts, guides, guards, cooks, and porters, upon whom visiting hunters relied to facilitate these excursions.

Discussion Questions

1. How did hunting safaris reinforce external impressions of Africa? Of Africans?

2. How were Africans impacted by the development of the hunting safari, especially following the onset of European colonialism?

3. How did the hunting safari change over the period of time that the chapter considers? Why?

Selected Readings

Bull, Bartle. *Safari: A Chronicle of Adventure.* London: Penguin Books, 1988.

Cameron, Kenneth M. *Into Africa: The Story of the East African Safari*. London: Constable, 1990.

Steinhart, Edward. *Black Poachers, White Hunters: A Social History of Hunting in Colonial Kenya*. London: James Currey, 2006.

Chapter 3: Profits and Propaganda: Tourism in Colonial Africa

Chapter 3 explores the range of investments that European colonial regimes made in tourism in order to generate much-needed income. Colonial governments used both the revenues and the political and propagandistic value that tourism produced to perpetuate their presence on the continent, while many Africans took advantage of the employment opportunities that the expansion of the industry generated to carve out livelihoods in these demanding contexts.

Discussion Questions

1. How did the promotion of tourism in Africa help colonizing nations maintain or even deepen imperial control over their territories on the continent? How were these colonies marketed to prospective visitors?

2. How did Africans respond to the expansion of tourism industries during the colonial period? Why was the sector appealing for some African workers? What aspects of the industry were disagreeable for African employees?

3. How did South Africa promote its expanding industry? How was the country able to continue to attract foreign tourists even after the implementation of apartheid?

Selected Readings

Grundlingh, Albert. "Revisiting the 'Old' South Africa: Excursions into South Africa's Tourist History under Apartheid, 1948–1990." *South African Historical Journal*, no. 56 (2006): 103–22.

McGregor, JoAnn. "The Victoria Falls 1900–1940: Landscape, Tourism and the Geographical Imagination." *Journal of Southern African Studies* 29, no. 3 (September 2003): 717–37.

Wrigley, Andrew. "Against the Wind: The Role of Belgian Colonial Tourism Marketing in Resisting Pressure to Decolonise from Africa." *Journal of Tourism History* 7, no. 3 (2015): 193–209.

Chapter 4: Paradoxes of Independence: Modernizing by Promoting Primitivism

Chapter 4 examines the decisions that newly independent African states made to generate tourist appeal and revenue in support of national development, often perpetuating the agendas that their colonial predecessors had initiated. In practice, these governments' investments in fulfilling foreigners' touristic fantasies were prompted by the continuing need to generate revenue and the associated desire to create employment opportunities for their respective citizenries.

Discussion Questions

1. What factors influenced newly sovereign African states' deliberations regarding the development of tourism industries? What were some of their touristic options once they decided to proceed?

2. What challenges did those countries that wanted to establish or expand their tourism industries face? How did they attempt to surmount them?

3. How did the expansion of tourism on the continent impact Africans? How did African residents shape their engagement with both the industry and the foreign visitors it delivered?

Selected Readings

Akama, John. "The Role of Governance in the Development of Tourism in Kenya." *International Journal of Tourism Research* 4, no. 1 (2002): 1–13.
Deike, P. U. C. "Tourism in Sub-Saharan Africa: Development Issues and Possibilities." In *Tourism: The State of the Art*, edited by A. V. Seaton, 53–64. New York: John Wiley & Sons, 1994.
Shivji, I. G., ed. *Tourism and Socialist Development*. Dar es Salaam: Tanzania Publishing House, 1973.

Chapter 5: The Touristic Invention of the African Camera Safari

Chapter 5 traces the history of the renowned African camera safari, a thoroughly Western invention. Safaris grew out of the adventures of the original explorers and matured as hunting expeditions before the First World War, but are now almost exclusively intended for foreign tourists seeking to photograph—rather than slaughter—Africa's celebrated wildlife.

Discussion Questions

1. How and why did the African camera safari rise to touristic preeminence on the continent?

2. In what ways does the photographic safari extend, or even deepen, prevailing notions of Africa?

3. How did the steady growth of the camera safari impact Africans? How have Africans shaped their engagement with this touristic endeavor and the industry it has spawned?

Selected Readings

Adams, Jonathan S., and Thomas O. McShane. *The Myth of Wild Africa: Conservation without Illusion*. New York: W. W. Norton, 1992.

Cejas, Mónica. "Tourism 'Back in Time': Performing 'the Essence of Safari' in Africa." *Intercultural Communication Studies* 16, no. 3 (2007): 121–34.

Little, Kenneth. "On Safari: The Visual Politics of a Tourist Representation," in *The Varieties of Sensory Experience: A Sourcebook in the Anthropology of the Senses*, edited by David Howes, 148–63. Toronto: University of Toronto Press, 1991.

Chapter 6: Going Home: The Diasporic Quest for Belonging through "Roots" Tourism

Chapter 6 explores "roots" tourism, in which peoples of African descent "return" to the continent of their ancestors to discover and, thus, attempt to better understand their heritage. These visitors often powerfully experience this symbolic homecoming, facilitated by African guides, docents, performers, and merchants who skillfully perform for these tourists, striving to fulfill these visitors' expectations of a relatable, yet no less exotic, Africa.

Discussion Questions

1. In what ways are heritage tourists to Africa different from nonroots tourists? How are they similar?

2. Why has Ghana become the epicenter for this form of tourism? How should the country's government present the various castles that constitute the core physical infrastructure of this industry?

3. In what ways do Africans mediate and influence the roots tourism experience?

Selected Readings

Essah, Patience. "Slavery, Heritage, and Tourism in Ghana." *International Journal of Hospitality & Tourism Administration* 2, no. 3/4 (2001): 31–49.

Hartman, Saidiya V. "The Time of Slavery." *South Atlantic Quarterly* 101, no. 4 (2002): 757–77.

Richards, Sandra L. "What Is to Be Remembered? Tourism to Ghana's Slave Castle-Dungeons." *Theatre Journal* 57, no. 4 (December 2005): 617–37.

Chapter 7: Controversial New(er) Forms of Tourism in Africa

Chapter 7 examines more recent forms of tourism on the continent, including ecotourism, cultural tourism, "poverty" tourism, so-called voluntourism, sex tourism, and trophy hunting. African states and tour operators readily promote these various types of visits owing to the revenues they generate, even if some are exploitative or otherwise ethically controversial.

Discussion Questions

1. In what ways are those more recent forms of tourism grounded in and motivated by long-standing (mis)perceptions of the continent?

2. In what ways are these more recent forms of tourism exploitative or denigrating for Africans? Conversely, in what ways are they encouraging, empowering, or even enriching for the continent's residents?

3. How have Africans exerted their agency to shape the various forms of tourism considered in this chapter?

Selected Readings

Bruner, Edward M., and Barbara Kirshenblatt-Gimblett. "Maasai on the Lawn: Tourist Realism in East Africa." *Cultural Anthropology* 9, no. 4 (November 1994): 435–70.

Frenzel, Fabian, Ko Koens, Malte Steinbrink, and Christian M. Rogerson, "Slum Tourism: State of the Art." *Tourism Review International*, no. 18 (2015): 237–52.

Prince, Ruth, and Hannah Brown, eds. *Volunteer Economies: The Politics and Ethics of Voluntary Labor in Africa.* Woodbridge: James Currey, 2016.

Schroeder, Richard A. "Moving Targets: The 'Canned' Hunting of Captive-Bred Lions in South Africa." *African Studies Review* 61, no. 1 (April 2018): 8–32.

Van Beek, Walter, and Annette Schmidt, eds. *African Hosts and Their Guests: Cultural Dynamics of Tourism.* Suffolk: Boydell and Brewer, 2012.

NOTES

Introduction: Touristic Illusions and Realities

1. Given the various foci laid out in this paragraph, domestic tourism by African residents, including the growing numbers of middle-class Africans, as well as so-called VFR (visiting friends and relatives) remain outside the scope of this volume.

2. Even then, the word had a technical meaning: the "agricultural tourist" took note of the size and composition of fields. See Bennetta Jules-Rosette, *The Messages of Tourist Art: An African Semiotic System in Comparative Perspective* (New York and London: Plenum, 1984), 2.

3. Eric G. E. Zuelow, *A History of Modern Tourism* (London: Palgrave, 2016), 9.

4. Zuelow, *A History of Modern Tourism*, 7. Zuelow even reports that there was very old graffiti carved into even older walls.

5. Alexis Gregory, *The Golden Age of Travel, 1880–1939* (New York: Rizzoli, 1999), 10.

6. Eric J. Leed, *The Mind of the Traveler: From Gilgamesh to Global Tourism* (New York: Basic Books, 1991), 139.

7. Leed, *Mind of the Traveler*, 5.

8. John Towner, "Tourism History: Past, Present and Future," in *Tourism: The State of the Art*, ed. A. V. Seaton (New York: John Wiley & Sons, 1994), 722–23.

9. Peter John Massyn and Eddie Koch, "African Game Lodges and Rural Benefit in Two Southern African Countries," in *Tourism and Development Issues in Contemporary South Africa*, ed. Christian M. Rogerson and Gustav Visser (Pretoria: Africa Institute of South Africa, 2004), 102.

10. Jonathan S. Adams and Thomas O. McShane, *The Myth of Wild Africa: Conservation without Illusion* (New York: W. W. Norton, 1992), 12

11. Kevin C. Dunn, "Fear of a Black Planet: Anarchy Anxieties and Postcolonial Travel to Africa," *Third World Quarterly* 25, no. 3 (2004): 486.

12. Dennis Hickey and Kenneth C. Wylie, *An Enchanting Darkness: The American Vision of Africa in the Twentieth Century* (East Lansing: Michigan State University Press, 1993), 159.

13. Adams and McShane, *The Myth of Wild Africa*, 12.

14. Christian Saglio, "Tourism for Discovery: A Project in Lower Casamance, Senegal," in *Tourism—Passport to Development? Perspectives on the Social and Cultural Effects of Tourism in Developing Countries*, ed. Emanuel de Kadt (New York: Oxford University Press, 1979), 321.

15. Curtis Keim, *Mistaking Africa: Curiosities and Inventions of the American Mind*, 3rd ed. (Boulder, CO: Westview Press, 2014), 73.

16. Carol Magee, *Africa in the American Imagination: Popular Culture, Racialized Identities, and African Visual Culture* (Jackson: University of Mississippi Press, 2012), 81.

17. Leed, *The Mind of the Traveler*, 137.

18. Leed, *The Mind of the Traveler*, 136.

19. David Harrison, ed., *Tourism and the Less Developed Countries* (London: Belhaven, 1992), 14.

20. Linda K. Richter, "Political Instability and Tourism in the Third World," in Harrison, *Tourism and the Less Developed Countries*, 43.

21. Richter, "Political Instability and Tourism in the Third World," 35.

22. I. G. Shivji, ed., *Tourism and Socialist Development* (Dar es Salaam: Tanzania Publishing House, 1973), xi.

23. Garth Allen and Frank Brennan, *Tourism in the New South Africa: Social Responsibility and the Tourist Experience* (London: I. B. Tauris, 2004), 3.

Chapter One. Initial Touristic Incursions to Africa

1. Adams and McShane, *The Myth of Wild Africa*, 7.

2. Adams and McShane, *The Myth of Wild Africa*, 10. Emphasis mine.

3. Adams and McShane, *The Myth of Wild Africa*, vii.

4. Adams and McShane, *The Myth of Wild Africa*, 9.

5. Louise Henderson, "Publishing Livingstone's *Missionary Travels*," in *Livingstone Online*, ed. Adrian S. Wisnicki and Megan Ward, University of Maryland Libraries, last modified 2015, http://livingstoneonline.org/uuid/node/2dcod511-087c-40dc-ab6b-4fe769ddo3f7.

6. Adams and McShane, *The Myth of Wild Africa*, 11.

7. Adams and McShane, *The Myth of Wild Africa*, 13.

8. Adams and McShane, *The Myth of Wild Africa*, 14.

9. Adam Hochschild, *King Leopold's Ghost: A Story of Greed, Terror, and Heroism in Colonial Africa* (New York: Mariner Books, 1999), 29.

10. Kenneth M. Cameron, *Into Africa: The Story of the East African Safari* (London: Constable, 1990), 21.

11. Zuelow, *A History of Modern Tourism*, 100.

12. Martin Anderson, "The Development of British Tourism in Egypt, 1815 to 1850," *Journal of Tourism History* 4, no. 3 (2012): 267.

13. Zuelow, *A History of Modern Tourism*, 100.

14. Anderson, "The Development of British Tourism in Egypt," 259.

15. Anderson, "The Development of British Tourism in Egypt," 262.

16. Anderson, "The Development of British Tourism in Egypt," 277.

17. Anderson, "The Development of British Tourism in Egypt," 278.

18. F. Robert Hunter, "Tourism and Empire: The Thomas Cook & Son Enterprise on the Nile, 1868–1914," *Middle Eastern Studies* 50, no. 5 (September 2004), 31.

19. Hunter, "Tourism and Empire," 31.

20. Hunter, "Tourism and Empire," 34.

21. Hunter, "Tourism and Empire," 35.

22. Hunter, "Tourism and Empire," 38.

23. Hunter, "Tourism and Empire," 43.

24. Hunter, "Tourism and Empire," 43.

25. Gregory, *The Golden Age of Travel*, 160.

26. Hunter, "Tourism and Empire," 43.

27. Karl Baedeker, *Egypt: Handbook for Travellers*, 5th ed. (Leipzig: Karl Baedeker Publisher, 1902), 212.

28. Hunter, "Tourism and Empire," 44.

29. Hunter, "Tourism and Empire," 44.

30. Deborah Manley, ed., *Women Travelers on the Nile: An Anthology of Travel Writing through the Centuries* (Cairo and New York: American University in Cairo Press, 2016), 55.

31. Manley, *Women Travelers on the Nile*, 121–22.

32. Manley, *Women Travelers on the Nile*, 61.

33. Manley, *Women Travelers on the Nile*, 65–66.

34. Hunter, "Tourism and Empire," 48.

Chapter Two. Hunting in Africa: Invisible Guides, Big Game, and Bigger Egos

1. Adams and McShane, *The Myth of Wild Africa*, 30.

2. Adams and McShane, *The Myth of Wild Africa*, 30.

3. Bartle Bull, *Safari: A Chronicle of Adventure* (London: Penguin, 1988), 28.

4. Bull, *Safari*, 14.

5. Bull, *Safari*, 42.

6. Bull, *Safari*, 43.

7. Bull, *Safari*, 43.

8. Bull, *Safari*, 46.

9. Bull, *Safari*, 49.

10. Bull, *Safari*, 52.

11. Bull, *Safari*, 53.

12. Bull, *Safari*, 62.

13. Bull, *Safari*, 62.

14. Clifton C. Crais and Pamela Scully, *Sara Baartman and the Hottentot Venus: A Ghost Story and a Biography* (Princeton: Princeton University Press, 2009), 80.

15. Bull, *Safari*, 64.

16. Bull, *Safari*, 91.

17. Bull, *Safari*, 91.

18. Bull, *Safari*, 91.

19. Cameron, *Into Africa*, 171.

20. Hilaire Belloc, *The Modern Traveller* (London: Edward Arnold, 1898), n.p.

21. Bull, *Safari*, 123.

22. Bull, *Safari*, 127.

23. Bull, *Safari*, 127.

24. Bull, *Safari*, 127.

25. Bull, *Safari*, 110.

26. Bull, *Safari*, 114.

27. Bull, *Safari*, 114.

28. Bull, *Safari*, 114.

29. Bull, *Safari*, 119.

30. Theodore Roosevelt, *African Game Trails* (New York: St. Martin's Press, 1988), ix. The book was named "Book of the Year" by New York's *Herald Tribune*.

31. Keim, *Mistaking Africa*, 132.

32. Bull, *Safari*, 179.

33. Keim, *Mistaking America*, 133.

34. Cameron, *Into Africa*, 56.

35. Adams and McShane, *The Myth of Wild Africa*, 29.

36. Cameron, *Into Africa*, 79.

37. Lord Cranworth, *Kenya Chronicles* (London: Macmillan, 1939), 208.

38. Bull, *Safari*, 223.

39. Keim, *Mistaking Africa*, 133.

40. Bull, *Safari*, 203.

41. Cameron, *Into Africa*, 81.

42. Bull, *Safari*, 256.

43. Percival would again lead Hemingway on safari upon his return to East Africa in the early 1950s.

44. Cameron, *Into Africa*, 93.

45. Bull, *Safari*, 276.

46. Cameron, *Into Africa*, 93.

47. Cameron, *Into Africa*, 93.

48. Bull, *Safari*, 225.

49. Bull, *Safari*, 228.

50. Bull, *Safari*, 238.

51. Cameron, *Into Africa*, 173.

52. Cameron, *Into Africa*, 183.

53. Cameron, *Into Africa*, 183.

54. Cameron, *Into Africa*, 83.

55. Robert Boardman, *International Organization and the Conservation of Nature* (London: Macmillan, 1981), 34; Edward Steinhart, *Black Poachers, White Hunters: A Social History of Hunting in Colonial Kenya* (London: James Currey, 2006), 180.

56. Sanette L. A. Ferreira, "Sustainable Tourism in Post-Colonial Southern Africa," in *Tourism and Development Issues in Contemporary South Africa*, ed. Christian M. Rogerson and Gustav Visser (Pretoria: Africa Institute of South Africa, 2004), 293.

57. Ferreira, "Sustainable Tourism in Post-Colonial Southern Africa," 293.

58. Keim, *Misunderstanding Africa*, 134.

59. Keim, *Misunderstanding Africa*, 134.

60. Donald Sinden, *A Touch of the Memoirs* (London: Hodder and Stoughton 1982), 174–75, 185.

Chapter Three. Profits and Propaganda: Tourism in Colonial Africa

1. Philipp Bachmann, *Tourism in Kenya: A Basic Need for Whom?* (New York: Peter Land, 1988), 49.

2. JoAnn McGregor, "The Victoria Falls 1900–1940: Landscape, Tourism and the Geographical Imagination," *Journal of Southern African Studies* 29, no. 3 (September 2003): 728.

3. Andrea Arrington, *Power, Culture, and Colonial Development around Victoria Falls, 1880–1910* (PhD diss., Emory University, 2007), 17.

4. McGregor, "The Victoria Falls," 729.

5. McGregor, "The Victoria Falls," 732.

6. McGregor, "The Victoria Falls," 732.

7. McGregor, "The Victoria Falls," 727.

8. McGregor, "The Victoria Falls," 727.

9. McGregor, "The Victoria Falls," 732.

10. F. Robert Hunter, "Manufacturing Exotica: Edith Wharton and Tourism in French Morocco, 1917–20," *Middle Eastern Studies* 46, no. 1 (January 2010): 59.

11. Hunter, "Manufacturing Exotica," 59.

12. Hunter, "Manufacturing Exotica," 71.

13. Hunter, "Manufacturing Exotica," 70.

14. Andrew Wrigley, "Against the Wind: The Role of Belgian Colonial Tourism Marketing in Resisting Pressure to Decolonise from Africa," *Journal of Tourism History* 7, no. 3 (2015): 208.

15. Andrew Wrigley, *Marketing Cold War Tourism in the Belgian Congo: A Study in Colonial Propaganda, 1945–1960* (MA thesis, University of Stellenbosch, 2014), 74.

16. Wrigley, *Marketing Cold War Tourism in the Belgian Congo,* 59.

17. PIDE is an acronym for the Polícia Internacional e de Defesa do Estado.

18. The expression "winds of change" relates to the address given by Great Britain's prime minister, Harold Macmillan, to the South African Parliament in February 1960, cautioning the apartheid regime that political independence for African territories was inevitable.

19. Joseph P. B. M. Ouma, *Evolution of Tourism in East Africa (1900–2000)* (Nairobi: East African Literature Bureau, 1970), 87.

20. Wrigley, *Marketing Cold War Tourism in the Belgian Congo,* 71.

21. Ouma, *Evolution of Tourism in East Africa,* 83.

22. Franco Ferrario, *An Evaluation of the Tourist Resources of South Africa* (Cape Town: Department of Geography, University of Cape Town, 1978), 48.

23. Ferrario, *An Evaluation of the Tourist Resources of South Africa,* 48.

24. Ferrario, *An Evaluation of the Tourist Resources of South Africa,* 49.

25. Ferrario, *An Evaluation of the Tourist Resources of South Africa,* 49.

26. Albert Grundlingh, "Revisiting the 'Old' South Africa: Excursions into South Africa's Tourist History under Apartheid, 1948–1990," *South African Historical Journal*, no. 56 (2006): 111.

27. Ferrario, *An Evaluation of the Tourist Resources of South Africa*, 49.

28. Shirley Brooks, "Images of 'Wild Africa': Nature Tourism and the (Re) creation of Hluhluwe Game Reserve, 1930–1945," *Journal of Historical Geography*, no. 31 (2005): 220.

29. David Bunn, "Comparative Barbarism: Game Reserves, Sugar Plantations, and the Modernization of South African Landscape," in *Text, Theory, Space: Land, Literature and History in South Africa and Australia*, ed. Kate Darian-Smith, Liz Gunner, and Sarah Nuttall (London: Routledge, 1996): 39.

30. Carel Birkby, *Zulu Journey* (London: Lawrence G. Green, 1937), 9.

31. Brooks, "Images of 'Wild Africa,'" 222.

32. Ferrario, *An Evaluation of the Tourist Resources of South Africa*, 52.

33. Grundlingh, "Revisiting the 'Old' South Africa," 106.

34. Grundlingh, "Revisiting the 'Old' South Africa," 112.

35. These casino resorts were established more to feed the domestic touristic demand than any international demand.

36. Fernando Cunhica, interview with the author, Maputo, Mozambique, June 28, 2017. "Preto" is a pejorative term in Portuguese for Africans.

37. Arrington, *Power, Culture, and Colonial Development*, 163.

38. Arrington, *Power, Culture, and Colonial Development*, 163.

39. Pedro Manhiça, interview with the author, Maputo, Mozambique, July 5, 2017.

40. Arrington, *Power, Culture, and Colonial Development*, 18.

41. Vasco Manhiça, interview with the author, Maputo, Mozambique, June 29, 2017.

42. Luís Macáucau, interview with the author, Maputo, Mozambique, June 20, 2017.

43. José Manhique, interview with the author, Maputo, Mozambique, July 4, 2017.

44. Birkby, *Zulu Journey*, 142.

45. Brooks, "Images of 'Wild Africa,'" 229.

46. Brooks, "Images of 'Wild Africa,'" 229.

Chapter Four. Paradoxes of Independence: Modernizing by Promoting Primitivism

1. Reginald Green, "Toward Planning Tourism in African Countries," in de Kadt, *Tourism—Passport to Development?*, 81–82.

2. Richter, "Political Instability and Tourism in the Third World," 36.

3. O. B. Kopoka, "Bridges or Hotels," letter from August 10, 1970, in Shivji, *Tourism and Socialist Development*, 67.

4. Christian M. Rogerson and Gustav Visser, "Tourism and Development in Post-Apartheid South Africa: A Ten-Year Review," in *Tourism and Development Issues in Contemporary South Africa*, ed. Christian M. Rogerson and Gustav Visser (Pretoria: Africa Institute of South Africa, 2004), 2.

5. Bachmann, *Tourism in Kenya*, 68.

6. U. Bennett, "Financing for Tourism Projects in Developing Countries," in *Tourism: The State of the Art*, ed. A. V. Seaton (New York: John Wiley & Sons, 1994), 31.

7. John Akama, "The Role of Governance in the Development of Tourism in Kenya," *International Journal of Tourism Research* 4, no. 1 (2002): 3.

8. Akama, "The Role of Governance," 3.

9. Bennett, "Financing for Tourism Projects in Developing Countries," 31.

10. Akama, "The Role of Governance," 3.

11. Akama, "The Role of Governance," 3.

12. *Republic of Kenya Development Plan, 1966–1970* (Nairobi: 1965), 204.

13. *Republic of Kenya Development Plan*, 430.

14. Rodger Yeager and Norman N. Miller, *Wildlife, Wild Death: Land Use and Survival in Eastern Africa* (Albany: SUNY Press, 1986), 32.

15. Yeager and Miller, *Wildlife, Wild Death*, 32.

16. Yeager and Miller, *Wildlife, Wild Death*, 32. Measured in bed nights, the figures were 242,000 in 1979 and 292,000 in 1980.

17. Neocolonialism can be defined as the use of economic, political, cultural, or other pressures to control or influence other countries, especially former dependencies.

18. "Comment," *The Standard*, May 25, 1970, 1.

19. "Socialist," *The Standard*, June 22, 1970, 38.

20. P. U. C. Deike, "Tourism in Sub-Saharan Africa: Development Issues and Possibilities," in Seaton, *Tourism: The State of the Art*, 59.

21. Deike, "Tourism in Sub-Saharan Africa," 59.

22. Deike, "Tourism in Sub-Saharan Africa," 59.

23. David Harrison, "Tradition, Modernity and Tourism in Swaziland," in Harrison, *Tourism and the Less Developed Countries*, 152.

24. Harrison, "Tradition, Modernity and Tourism in Swaziland," 154.

25. Harrison, "Tradition, Modernity and Tourism in Swaziland," 161.

26. Waleed Hazbun, *Beaches, Ruins, Resorts: The Politics of Tourism in the Arab World* (Minneapolis: University of Minnesota, 2008), 6.

27. Robert A. Poirier and Stephen Wright, "The Political Economy of Tourism in Tunisia," *Journal of Modern African Studies* 31, no. 1 (March 1993): 162.

28. Poirier and Wright, "The Political Economy of Tourism in Tunisia," 162.

29. Hazbun, *Beaches, Ruins, Resorts*, 46.

30. Yeager and Miller, *Wildlife, Wild Death*, 21.

31. Yeager and Miller, *Wildlife, Wild Death*, 32.

32. The UDI, or Unilateral Declaration of Independence, government was led by Ian Smith and was supported by the small white settler population, which comprised only about 5 percent of the colony's population. No country recognized the UDI.

33. Rosaleen Duffy, *Killing for Conservation: Wildlife Policy in Zimbabwe* (Oxford: James Currey, 2000), 73.

34. Duffy, *Killing for Conservation*, 73.

35. Adams and McShane, *The Myth of Wild Africa*, 195.

36. Adams and McShane, *The Myth of Wild Africa*, 197.

37. It was at this time that Fossey was brutally murdered. It is believed that Fossey was killed by a poacher at Karisoke camp, which she had founded in 1967, though no suspect has ever been identified or arrested.

38. Adams and McShane, *The Myth of Wild Africa*, 199.

39. William M. Adams and Mark Infield, "Who Is on the Gorilla's Payroll? Claims on Tourist Revenue from a Ugandan National Park," *World Development* 31, no. 1 (2003): 179.

40. Yeager and Miller, *Wildlife, Wild Death*, 121.

41. Bachmann, *Tourism in Kenya*, 195.

42. Adams and McShane, *The Myth of Wild Africa*, 201.

43. Adams and McShane, *The Myth of Wild Africa*, 203.

44. David Wilson, "The Early Effects of Tourism in the Seychelles," in de Kadt, *Tourism—Passport to Development?*, 212.

45. Wilson, "The Early Effects of Tourism in the Seychelles," 234.

46. Wilson, "The Early Effects of Tourism in the Seychelles," 233.

47. David Wilson, "Unique by a Thousand Miles: Seychelles Tourism Revisited," *Annals of Tourism Research*, no. 21 (1994): 29.

48. Wilson, "Unique by a Thousand Miles," 30.

49. Ulla Wagner, *Catching the Tourist: Women Handicraft Traders in the Gambia* (Stockholm: Stockholm Studies in Social Anthropology, 1982), 28.

50. Wagner, *Catching the Tourist*, 8.

51. Wagner, *Catching the Tourist*, 29.

52. Harrison, "Tradition, Modernity and Tourism in Swaziland," 149.

53. Harrison, "Tradition, Modernity and Tourism in Swaziland," 155.

54. Bachmann, *Tourism in Kenya*, 191.

55. Wilson, "Unique by a Thousand Miles," 25.

56. Wilson, "Unique by a Thousand Miles," 25.

57. S. A. Kibona, "Tourism and Socialism Are Compatible," in Shivji, *Tourism and Socialist Development*, 74.

58. Harrison, "Tradition, Modernity and Tourism in Swaziland," 160.

59. Bachmann, *Tourism in Kenya*, 194.

60. Bachmann, *Tourism in Kenya*, 58. In fact, the three leading destinations—Egypt, Morocco, and Tunisia—accounted for 59 percent of arrivals.

61. Victor B. Teye, "Coup d'État and African Tourism: A Study of Ghana," *Annals of Tourism Research* 15, no. 3 (1988): 331.

62. Harrison, "Tradition, Modernity and Tourism in Swaziland," 158.

63. Freda Rajotte, "The Tourist Industry in East Africa," *Centre des Hautes Etudes Touristiques* (February 1981): 41.

Chapter Five. The Touristic Invention of the African Camera Safari

1. Ferreira, "Sustainable Tourism in Post-Colonial Southern Africa," 292.

2. Patricia T. O'Conner and Stewart Kellerman, "We're on Safari," *Grammarphobia* (blog), January 29, 2013, https://www.grammarphobia.com/blog/2013/01/safari.html.

3. Mónica Cejas, "Tourism 'Back in Time': Performing 'the Essence of Safari' in Africa," *Intercultural Communication Studies* 16, no. 3 (2007): 121.

4. Cejas, "Tourism 'Back in Time,'" 121.

5. See J. Akama, "The Evolution of Tourism in Kenya," *Journal of Sustainable Tourism* 7, no. 1 (1999): 6–25; and Cejas, "Tourism 'Back in Time,'" 122.

6. Cejas, "Tourism 'Back in Time,'" 122.

7. Cameron, *Into Africa*, 81.

8. Cameron, *Into Africa*, 84.

9. Cameron, *Into Africa*, 82.

10. Cameron, *Into Africa*, 86.

11. Cameron, *Into Africa*, 87.

12. J. A. Hunter, *Hunter* (New York: Harper, 1952), 88.

13. Cameron, *Into Africa*, 88.

14. John Gunther, *Inside Africa* (New York: Harper, 1955), 108.

15. Cameron, *Into Africa*, 107.

16. Cameron, *Into Africa*, 108.

17. Cameron, *Into Africa*, 110.

18. Massyn and Koch, "African Game Lodges and Rural Benefit," 104.

19. Adams and McShane, *The Myth of Wild Africa*, 13.

20. Massyn and Koch, "African Game Lodges and Rural Benefit," 105.

21. Massyn and Koch, "African Game Lodges and Rural Benefit," 105.

22. Keim, *Mistaking Africa*, 136.

23. Keim, *Mistaking Africa*, 139.

24. N. C. Pollock, *Animals, Environment and Man in Africa* (Lexington: Lexington Books, 1974), 94.

25. Adams and McShane, *The Myth of Wild Africa*, 172. Emphasis mine.

26. Adams and McShane, *The Myth of Wild Africa*, 197.

27. Hannah Nielsen and Anna Spenceley, "The Success of Tourism in Rwanda: Gorillas and More," Background paper for the African Success Stories study; Background paper for the World Development Report (Washington, DC: World Bank, 2010), 234.

28. Cejas, "Tourism 'Back in Time,'" 127.

29. William Sutcliffe, "Kenyan Safari: Beast, Blanket, Babylon," *The Independent*, October 22, 2005.

30. Hillary Richard, "The Wonder Women of Botswana Safari," *New York Times*, August 22, 2017, https://www.nytimes.com/2017/08/22/travel/botswana-safari-women-chobe.html.

31. Richard, "The Wonder Women of Botswana Safari."

32. Richard, "The Wonder Women of Botswana Safari."

33. "Interviews with Female Guides in East Africa," Yellow Zebra Safaris, October 23, 2018, https://yellowzebrasafaris.com/us/inspiration/blog/guide-clinic/the-female-safari-guides-of-east-africa/.

34. Adams and McShane, *The Myth of Wild Africa*, 164.

35. Adams and McShane, *The Myth of Wild Africa*, 164.

36. Adams and McShane, *The Myth of Wild Africa*, xv.

37. Keim, *Mistaking Africa*, 140.

38. Keim, *Mistaking Africa*, 140.

39. Kenneth Little, "On Safari: The Visual Politics of a Tourist Representation," in *The Varieties of Sensory Experience: A Sourcebook in the Anthropology of the Senses*, ed. David Howes (Toronto: University of Toronto Press, 1991), 150.

40. Cejas, "Tourism 'Back in Time,'" 127.

41. Cejas, "Tourism 'Back in Time,'" 128.

42. "Your Stay: 1920s Camp," Cottar's Safaris, accessed June 25, 2020, https://cottars.com/1920s-camp/.

43. Renato Rosaldo, *Culture and Truth: The Remaking of Social Analysis* (Boston: Beacon Press, 1989), 68.

44. "Why Us: A Passion for People & Planet," Extraordinary Journeys, accessed June 25, 2020, https://www.extraordinaryjourneys.com/why-us/.

45. "Ethical Tourism," Deeper Africa, last modified 2016, http://www.deeper-africa.com/ethical-tourism/.

46. Massyn and Koch, "African Game Lodges," 106.

47. Cameron, *Into Africa*, 114.

48. Massyn and Koch, "African Game Lodges," 103.

49. "Selati Camp," Sabi Sabi, accessed 2020, https://www.sabisabi.com/.

50. Massyn and Koch, "African Game Lodges," 105.

51. Little, "On Safari: The Visual Politics of a Tourist Representation," 153.

Chapter Six. Going Home: The Diasporic Quest for Belonging through "Roots" Tourism

1. James Campbell, *Middle Passages: African American Journeys to Africa, 1787–2005* (New York: Penguin Press, 2006), 371.

2. In sub-Saharan Africa, Ethiopia, Liberia, South Africa, and Zimbabwe were, at this time, not under colonial control for various reasons. Thus, Ghana is putatively considered the first country in sub-Saharan Africa to gain its independence.

3. Adia Benton and Kwame Zulu Shabazz, "'Find Their Level': African American Roots Tourism in Sierra Leone and Ghana," *Cahiers d'Études Africaines* 49, no. 193/194 (2009): 486.

4. Patience Essah, "Slavery, Heritage, and Tourism in Ghana," *International Journal of Hospitality & Tourism Administration* 2, no. 3/4 (2001): 31.

5. Essah, "Slavery, Heritage, and Tourism in Ghana," 35.

6. Essah, "Slavery, Heritage, and Tourism in Ghana," 38.

7. Michelle D. Commander, *Afro-Atlantic Flight: Speculative Returns and the Black Fantastic* (Durham, NC: Duke University Press, 2017), 5.

8. Saidiya V. Hartman, "The Time of Slavery," *South Atlantic Quarterly* 101, no. 4 (Fall 2002): 774.

9. Alessandra Prentice, "An African American Mother and Daughter Journey to Their Family's Past in Ghana," Reuters, August 22, 2019, https://www.reuters.com/article/us-africa-slavery-usa/an-african-american-mother-and-daughter-journey-to-their-familys-past-in-ghana-idUSKCN1VC16H.

10. Charles M. Rotimi, "Genetic Ancestry Tracing and the African Identity: A Double-Edged Sword?," *Developing World Bioethics* 3, no. 2 (2003): 151–58.

11. Prentice, "An African American Mother and Daughter," n.p.

12. "Slave Route Tour," BLASTours, last modified 2013, https://blastours.com/ghana-tours/ghana-slave-route-tour.

13. Prentice, "An African American Mother and Daughter," n.p.

14. Edward M. Bruner, "Tourism in Ghana: The Representation of Slavery and the Return of the Black Diaspora," *American Anthropologist* 98, no. 2 (1996): 294. Imahküs Robinson now goes by the name Imahküs Njinga Okofu Ababio.

15. Prentice, "An African American Mother and Daughter," n.p.

16. Commander, *Afro-Atlantic Flight*, 87.

17. Hartman, "The Time of Slavery," 769.

18. Peter Nelson, "The Castle of St. George at Elmina and the Problem with Heritage," *Iowa Review* 28, no. 2 (1998): 55.

19. Hartman, "The Time of Slavery," 766.

20. Denise Oliver Velez, "Nancy Pelosi and Ilhan Omar Walk Together through the 'Door of Return' in Ghana," *Daily Kos*, August 1, 2019, https://www.dailykos.com/stories/2019/8/1/1876045/-Nancy-Pelosi-and-Ilhan-Omar-walk-together-through-the-Door-of-Return-in-Ghana.

21. While August 2019 marks four hundred years since enslaved Africans arrived in the United States, "The Year of Return, Ghana 2019," celebrates the cumulative resilience of all the victims of the transatlantic slave trade who were scattered and displaced throughout the world. See https://www.yearofreturn.com. Passed in 2001, the Right of Abode law grants anyone of African descent the right to stay in Ghana indefinitely.

22. Hartman, "The Time of Slavery," 767–68.

23. Hartman, "The Time of Slavery," 768.

24. Nelson, "The Castle of St. George at Elmina," 64. Somewhat cynically, he continues, "The Europeans, of course, grew up with castles all around them, and see the Castle of St. George at Elmina as a continuation of their romantic past, a breezy and exotic outpost on the edge of darkest Africa, built at a time when Europe was the dominant world power, and domination was considered a good thing."

25. Michelle D. Commander, "Ghana at Fifty: Moving toward Kwame Nkrumah's Pan-African Dream," *American Quarterly* 59, no. 2 (June 2007): 436.

26. Sandra L. Richards, "What Is to Be Remembered?: Tourism to Ghana's Slave Castle-Dungeons," *Theatre Journal* 57, no. 4 (December 2005): 632.

27. Richards, "What Is to Be Remembered?," 626.

28. Bruner, "Tourism in Ghana," 292.

29. Commander, *Afro-Atlantic Flight*, 89.

30. Bruner, "Tourism in Ghana," 295.

31. Benton and Shabazz, "Find Their Level," 490.

32. Nelson, "The Castle of St. George at Elmina," 66.

33. Jennifer Hasty, "Rites of Passage, Routes of Redemption: Emancipation Tourism and the Wealth of Culture," *Africa Today* 49, no. 3 (2002): 63.

34. Hasty, "Rites of Passage," 64.

35. Bruner, "Tourism in Ghana," 299.

36. Teye, "Coup d'État and African Tourism," 343.

37. Richards, "What Is to Be Remembered?," 621.

38. Essah, "Slavery, Heritage, and Tourism in Ghana," 45.

39. Essah, "Slavery, Heritage, and Tourism in Ghana," 40.

40. Richards, "What Is to Be Remembered?," 619.

41. Nelson, "The Castle of St. George at Elmina," 48.

42. Hartman, "The Time of Slavery," 760.

43. Nelson, "The Castle of St. George at Elmina," 64.

44. Richards, "What Is to Be Remembered?," 630.

45. Richards, "What Is to Be Remembered?," 630.

46. Stephen Buckley, "U.S., African Blacks Differ on Turning Slave Dungeons into Tourist Attractions, *Washington Post*, April 17, 1995, A10.

47. Richards, "What Is to Be Remembered?," 631.

48. Buckley, "U.S., African Blacks Differ," A10.

49. Richards, "What Is to Be Remembered?," 631.

50. Bruner, "Tourism in Ghana," 294.

51. Commander, *Afro-Atlantic Flight*, 78.

52. Bruner, "Tourism in Ghana," 294.

53. Hartman, "The Time of Slavery," 768.

54. Hasty, "Rites of Passage," 57.

Chapter Seven. Controversial New(er) Forms of Tourism in Africa

1. "What Is Ecotourism?," International Ecotourism Society, last modified 2019, https://ecotourism.org/what-is-ecotourism/.

2. Allen and Brennan, *Tourism in the New South Africa*, 3.

3. Allen and Brennan, *Tourism in the New South Africa*, 4.

4. Allen and Brennan, *Tourism in the New South Africa*, 4.

5. Katie Wood, "Belize Cleans up in Eco-tourism Stakes," *The Observer*, October 6, 1991, 65.

6. Allen and Brennan, *Tourism in the New South Africa*, 5.

7. Ian Munt, "Eco-tourism or Ego-tourism?," *Race and Class*, no. 36 (1994): 53.

8. Munt, "Eco-tourism or Ego-tourism?," 53.

9. Munt, "Eco-tourism or Ego-tourism?," 54.

10. "Africa," Exceptional Travel, accessed June 25, 2020, https://exceptional-travel.com/.

11. Janice McIlvaine McClary, "A Glimpse of Eden on Safari in Zaire," *New York Times*, August 11, 1985.

12. Edward M. Bruner and Barbara Kirshenblatt-Gimblett, "Maasai on the Lawn: Tourist Realism in East Africa," *Cultural Anthropology* 9, no. 4 (November 1994): 438.

13. "Tourism and Culture," World Tourism Organization, last modified 2017, http://ethics.unwto.org/content/tourism-and-culture.

14. Leslie Witz, Ciraj Rassool, and Gary Minkley, "Repackaging the Past for South African Tourism," *Daedalus* 130, no. 1 (2001): 278.

15. Keim, *Mistaking Africa*, 158.

16. Bruner and Kirshenblatt-Gimblett, "Maasai on the Lawn," 438.

17. Bruner and Kirshenblatt-Gimblett, "Maasai on the Lawn," 448.

18. Bruner and Kirshenblatt-Gimblett, "Maasai on the Lawn," 459.

19. Walter van Beek, "To Dance or Not to Dance? Dogon Masks as a Tourist Arena," in *African Hosts and Their Guests: Cultural Dynamics of Tourism*, ed. Walter van Beek and Annette Schmidt (Suffolk: Boydell and Brewer, 2012): 54.

20. Van Beek, "To Dance or Not to Dance?," 56.

21. Grundlingh, "Revisiting the 'Old' South Africa," 120.

22. Grundlingh, "Revisiting the 'Old' South Africa," 120.

23. Gerhard Schutte, "Tourists and Tribes in the 'New' South Africa," *Ethnohistory* 50, no. 3 (2003): 473.

24. These sites also attract large numbers of domestic tourists, in this case white South Africans, who were largely forbidden during apartheid to engage in these types of interactions with black residents. Thus, these ethnically essentialized black South Africans can be just as "exotic" to white South Africans as they are to foreign tourists.

25. "DumaZulu Traditional Village," SA-Venues, accessed June 25, 2020, https://www.sa-venues.com/things-to-do/kwazulunatal/dumazulu-traditional-village/.

26. "Lesedi Cultural Village," Guateng, accessed June 25, 2020, https://www.gauteng.net/attractions/lesedi_cultural_village.

27. Fabian Frenzel et al., "Slum Tourism: State of the Art," *Tourism Review International*, no. 18 (2015): 240.

28. Ko Koens, "Slum Tourism: Developments in a Young Field of Interdisciplinary Tourism Research," *Tourism Geographies* 14, no. 2 (February 2012): 4.

29. Witz, Rassool, and Minkley, "Repackaging the Past for South African Tourism," 283.

30. Frenzel et al., "Slum Tourism: State of the Art," 242.

31. Frenzel et al., "Slum Tourism: State of the Art," 241.

32. Frenzel et al., "Slum Tourism: State of the Art," 245–46.

33. Frenzel et al., "Slum Tourism: State of the Art," 245–46.

34. Frenzel et al., "Slum Tourism: State of the Art," 241.

35. Frenzel et al., "Slum Tourism: State of the Art," 242.

36. Frenzel et al., "Slum Tourism: State of the Art," 247.

37. Kyle Powys Whyte, Evan Selinger, and Kevin Outterson, "Poverty Tourism and the Problem of Consent," *Journal of Global Ethics* 7, no. 3 (2011): 340.

38. Ruth Prince and Hannah Brown, "Introduction—The Politics & Ethics of Voluntary Labour in Africa," in *Volunteer Economies: The Politics and Ethics of Voluntary Labor in Africa*, ed. Ruth Prince and Hannah Brown (Woodbridge, Suffolk: James Currey, 2016), 3.

39. Prince and Brown, "Introduction—The Politics & Ethics of Voluntary Labour in Africa," 20.

40. Prince and Brown, "Introduction—The Politics & Ethics of Voluntary Labour in Africa," 3–4.

41. Prince and Brown, "Introduction—The Politics & Ethics of Voluntary Labour in Africa," 11.

42. For example, Family Legacy, a company that places voluntourists on month-long mission trips in Zambia, is, as of 2020, charging $4,500, though it is unclear if that figure includes international airfare. See www.familylegacy.com.

43. Nurith Aizenman and Malaka Gharib, "American with No Medical Training Ran Center for Malnourished Ugandan Kids. 105 Died," *All Things Considered*, NPR, August 9, 2019. Bach herself had been a voluntourist in 2007, working at a missionary-run orphanage for nine months.

44. Aizenman and Gharib, "American with No Medical Training."

45. Aizenman and Gharib, "American with No Medical Training."

46. Eileadh Swan, "'I'm Not a Tourist. I'm a Volunteer': Tourism, Development and International Volunteerism in Ghana," in van Beek and Schmidt, *African Hosts and Their Guests*, 240.

47. Swan, "I'm Not a Tourist," 241.

48. Swan, "I'm Not a Tourist," 243.

49. Swan, "I'm Not a Tourist," 248.

50. Swan, "I'm Not a Tourist," 244.

51. I have been party to countless conversations of this nature. As someone who has contracted malaria, I can assure you that there is absolutely nothing positive about this draining, potentially lethal experience.

52. Swan, "I'm Not a Tourist," 246.

53. Swan, "I'm Not a Tourist," 248.

54. Swan, "I'm Not a Tourist," 252.

55. Fred Katerere, "Cape Town on World Sex-Tourism Map," Independent Online, January 28, 2007, https://www.iol.co.za/news/south-africa/cape-town-on-world-sex-tourism-map-312732.

56. Jacqueline Sanchez-Taylor, "Sex Tourism and Child Prostitution," in *Tourism and Sex: Culture, Commerce, and Coercion*, ed. Stephen Clift and Simon Carter (London and New York: Pinter, 1999), 38.

57. Lucy McCombs, "Host-Guest Encounters in a Gambian 'Love' Bubble," in van Beek and Schmidt, *African Hosts and Their Guests*, 301.

58. McCombs, "Host-Guest Encounters," 301.

59. Wanjohi Kibicho, "Sex Trade and Tourism in Kenya: Close Encounters between the Hosts and the Hosted," in van Beek and Schmidt, *African Hosts and Their Guests*, 281.

60. Kibicho, "Sex Trade and Tourism in Kenya," 284.

61. McCombs, "Host-Guest Encounters," 304.

62. McCombs, "Host-Guest Encounters," 293.

63. Kibicho, "Sex Trade and Tourism in Kenya," 284.

64. Kibicho, "Sex Trade and Tourism in Kenya," 280.

65. Richard A. Schroeder, "Moving Targets: The 'Canned' Hunting of Captive-Bred Lions in South Africa," *African Studies Review* 61, no. 1 (April 2018): 8.

66. Schroeder, "Moving Targets," 9–10. South Africa's private hunting grounds host an estimated seven thousand foreign hunters and some two hundred thousand domestic hunters annually.

67. Schroeder, "Moving Targets," 11.

68. Schroeder, "Moving Targets," 11.

69. Peter A. Lindsey, Pierre A. Roulet, and Stephanie S. Romañach, "Economic and Conservation Significance of the Trophy Hunting Industry in Sub-Saharan Africa," *Biological Conservation* 134, no. 4 (February 2007): 464.

70. Lindsey, Roulet, and Romañach, "Economic and Conservation Significance," 464.

71. Lindsey, Roulet, and Romañach, "Economic and Conservation Significance," 464.

72. Lindsey, Roulet, and Romañach, "Economic and Conservation Significance," 461.

73. Lindsey, Roulet, and Romañach, "Economic and Conservation Significance," 461.

74. Lindsey, Roulet, and Romañach, "Economic and Conservation Significance," 463.

75. Schroeder, "Moving Targets," 15.

76. Lindsey, Roulet, and Romañach, "Economic and Conservation Significance," 465.

77. Schroeder, "Moving Targets," 15.

78. Schroeder, "Moving Targets," 14.

79. Schroeder, "Moving Targets," 14.

INDEX